UNEMPLOYMENT AND GOVERNMENT
Genealogies of the Social

While joblessness is by no means a phenomenon specific to this century, the concept of 'unemployment' is. This book follows the invention and transformation of unemployment, understood as a historically specific site of regulation. Taking key aspects of the history of unemployment in Britain as its focus, it argues that the ways in which authorities have defined and sought to manage the jobless have been remarkably varied. In tracing some of the different constructions of unemployment over the last 100 years – as the problem of 'character', as a social 'risk', or today, as a problem of 'skills' – the study highlights the discursive dimension of social and economic policy problems. But the technical aspect of governing is also emphasized. The book examines such institutionalized practices as the labour bureau, unemployment insurance, and the present 'New Deal' as 'technologies' of power. The result is a challenge to our thinking about welfare states.

WILLIAM WALTERS is an Assistant Professor in the Department of Political Science at Carleton University, Canada. His previous work has been published in such journals as *Economy and Society*, *Politics and Society*, and *Policy and Politics*.

CAMBRIDGE STUDIES IN LAW AND SOCIETY

The broad area of law and society has become a remarkably rich and dynamic
field of study. At the same time, the social sciences have increasingly engaged
with questions of law. In this process, the borders between legal scholarship and
the social, political and cultural sciences have been transcended, and the result
is a time of fundamental rethinking both within and about law. In this vital
period, Cambridge Studies in Law and Society provides a significant new book
series with an international focus and a concern with the global transformation
of the legal arena. The series aims to publish the best scholarly work on legal
discourse and practice in social context, combining theoretical insights and
empirical research.

UNEMPLOYMENT AND GOVERNMENT

Genealogies of the Social

William Walters
Carleton University

CAMBRIDGE
UNIVERSITY PRESS

PUBLISHED BY THE PRESS SYNDICATE OF THE UNIVERSITY OF CAMBRIDGE
The Pitt Building, Trumpington Street, Cambridge, United Kingdom

CAMBRIDGE UNIVERSITY PRESS
The Edinburgh Building, Cambridge CB2 2RU, UK   http://www.cup.cam.ac.uk
40 West 20th Street, New York, NY 10011–4211, USA   http://www.cup.org
10 Stamford Road, Oakleigh, Melbourne 3166, Australia   http://www.cup.edu.au
Ruiz de Alarcón 13, 28014, Madrid, Spain

First published 2000

Printed in Singapore by Craft Print Pte Ltd

Typeface New Baskerville 10/12 pt. *System* QuarkXPress® [BC]

A catalogue record for this book is available from the British Library

National Library of Australia Cataloguing in Publication data
Walters, William H. C.
Unemployment and government: genealogies of the social.
Bibliography.
Includes index.
ISBN 0 521 64333 3 (hbk.).
1. Unemployment – Great Britain – History – 20th century.
2. Employment (Economic theory). 3. Great Britain –
Economic conditions – 20th century. I. Title. (Series:
Cambridge studies in law and society).
331.1379410904

ISBN 0 521 64333 3 hardback

CONTENTS

ACKNOWLEDGEMENTS

Countless people and institutions made the completion of this project possible, and I want to acknowledge as many as I can here. My sincere apologies for any omissions. This book began as a doctoral dissertation which I undertook at York University, Toronto. I reworked it whilst a lecturer in Political Science at the University of Dundee, and then in Sociology at Goldsmiths College, London. I finished it in Political Science at Carleton University, Ottawa. First of all, thanks are due to the 'co-supervisors' of my dissertation, Leo Panitch and Mariana Valverde. It was Mariana who got me interested in historical sociology and suggested doing a genealogy of unemployment at a time when I was flitting nervously between dissertation topics. Among the many valuable things I have learnt from her is that one can think theoretically without adopting the role of Theorist. Leo did not always agree with the theoretical premises of my project, but his periodic critical interventions nevertheless contributed to any merits it might have. I appreciate his respect for my intellectual 'space'. Nikolas Rose generously offered 'unofficial' supervision during a term I spent at Goldsmiths College. I am extremely grateful for the support he has given me as a graduate student, and later as a colleague. Greg Albo, Isa Bakker, Colin Leys, and Lorna Weir all did a sterling job as Ph.D. examiners, pointing out ways I could strengthen my argument.

Transforming the dissertation into a book manuscript was not easy, but would have been much harder without the encouragement and insights of a whole host of people. Pat O'Malley had me send my manuscript to this Law and Society series and in return got to read more drafts of it than he probably anticipated. He deserves special thanks for being such a careful and patient series editor. But I also thank other series editors – Sally Merry, Susan Silbey, and Martin Chanock – for their comments on an earlier draft. Phillipa McGuinness and Sharon Mullins governed the book at a considerable distance, and with great skill and diplomacy.

Whether for reading drafts, or just exchanging ideas, I would like to thank: Les Back, Geoff Bunn, Steve Cross, Mitchell Dean, Samir

Gandesha, Vered Hopkins, Alan Hunt, Michael Keith, Gavin Kendall, Lucy Luccisano, Rianne Mahon, Paula Maurutto, Peter Miller, Martin Morris, Clifford Shearing, Nick Thoburn, Jim Tomlinson, Fran Tonkiss, Lorna Weir, and Gary Wickham. I also benefited from attending numerous History of the Present meetings in London and Toronto. None of the above bear any responsibility for the book's shortcomings or mistakes.

Spending a considerable amount of time in archives and libraries I came to appreciate the work of some of the people who run them, often under difficult circumstances. I am grateful for the work of archivists, librarians, security guards, and cleaners in the British Library, the British Library of Political and Economic Science, the Public Record Office at Kew, and Robarts Library, Toronto.

Material support for this project came in several forms. As a graduate student I received financial help in the shape of an Ontario Graduate Scholarship, and two small grants for the study of things English from the St George's Society of Toronto. A number of travel grants from York University facilitated research trips to the UK. The Carnegie Trust for the Universities of Scotland kindly provided a small grant which helped underwrite some of the research for later chapters. The Department of Political Science at Dundee University kindly gave me a reduced teaching load in my first year. The Centre for Criminology at University of Toronto provided me with office space, resources, and a welcoming intellectual environment for two successive summers.

Parts of Chapters 1 and 2 first appeared as 'The Discovery of "Unemployment": New Forms for the Government of Poverty' *Economy and Society* 23(3), 1994, 265–90.

For their love and support I thank my mother, Sally, and step-father, Gene. For her love, and for being behind this project in more ways than anyone else, I thank Christina Gabriel. I wish my father could have seen this book. Finally I am indebted to Bryan Hanson for years of friendship and support. He took citizenship seriously. I wish he also could have read this book.

INTRODUCTION

'"Unemployment" is perhaps the most illusive term which confronts the student of modern industrial society.'[1] These are the words of John Hobson in one of the first tracts to give theoretical content to the word. One hundred years later one would hardly describe the subject as illusive. On the contrary, when one considers just how extensively it has been studied by economists, econometricians, political scientists, sociologists, psychologists, social policy scholars, and of course historians, by academics and journalists alike, it seems fair to say that unemployment has been the subject of a greater variety of social-scientific investigations and theories than most social questions.

The net effect of this impressive feat of inquiry has been a considerable enhancement of our understanding of the making of unemployment policy, the social and personal experience of the unemployed, and the economic and institutional factors which are assumed to explain its incidence, its variation between places, and many other things besides. Yet at the same time, a side-effect of this relentless interrogation of unemployment and its unfortunate subjects has been that we have come to take it for granted. Unemployment has become obvious, mundane, self-evident; the eternal opposite of 'work', the poor relative of 'leisure', a familiar feature of the social and economic landscape. Unlike Hobson, no one today feels the need to place it within speech marks.

One motivation for the present study is a desire to bring a greater degree of analytical reflexivity to the study of unemployment, to disrupt this self-evidence, to make the phenomenon of unemployment somehow less familiar, less obvious. This is a challenge which has been taken up in recent years by a number of social historians, working mostly

1

in France.[2] Concentrating mostly on the period at the beginning of this century, these scholars have examined the social, political, and industrial conditions under which an administrative and theoretical category of unemployment first emerged. Moreover, they have shown how it unsettles and ultimately transforms the conceptual universe within which the nineteenth century thought the problem of the poor, and how 'unemployment' became central to modern modes of poverty administration.

In terms of its attention to questions surrounding the historical formation of theoretical and administrative categories, its concern to situate these in terms of changing modes of social regulation, and its desire to foreground the 'constructedness' of unemployment, the present study has much in common with this literature. However, it differs in at least two important respects. First, a difference of scope. While this volume is based solely on the experience of the UK and is therefore not comparative, in covering a hundred-year period it does have the advantage of being able to compare different problem-atizations of unemployment. This is crucial for the purposes of the second theme of the book, which I shall elaborate below, namely its use of unemployment as a focus for investigating wider questions about the way in which we are governed, and govern ourselves.

The second way in which this book departs from most existing historical sociologies of unemployment is in terms of its methodological and theoretical framework. This study examines the question of unem-ployment through the lens of a burgeoning interdisciplinary literature to which, for the sake of simplicity, I shall refer as 'governmentality'. What is governmentality, and what might it bring to the study of the regulation of the unemployed?

GOVERNMENTALITY AND UNEMPLOYMENT

The past ten years or so have seen the flourishing of work on the theme of governmentality. Its intellectual point of departure is Michel Foucault's unfinished reflections on the emergence in Europe, some-time between the sixteenth and eighteenth centuries, of an art of government, and the subsequent transformations of this art.[3]

Foucault's scattered remarks and lectures on government provide an intellectual counterpoint to his earlier, and better known, work on disci-pline, his 'microphysics' of power. Whereas his analyses of discipline addressed the exercise of power in terms of its deployment of the body in specific institutional sites like the school, the prison, and the hospital, with his reflections on government Foucault considers the totalizing aspect of power, how it comes to target the population, the social body.[4]

Nikolas Rose and Peter Miller, who have been at the forefront of attempts to generate a research agenda around the governmentality theme, nicely capture what is at issue here. With his remarks on governmentality Foucault 'sought to draw attention to a certain way of thinking and acting embodied in all those attempts to know and govern the wealth, health and happiness of populations'.[5]

There are at least three clusters of analytical themes one finds within the governmentality literature, and which serve to establish its ambitions. A summary of these should help to frame the objectives and scope of the present study. The first is a concern with *mentalities of rule*. Governmentality is interested in the language of government: it investigates the manner in which the exercise of power is always discursively mediated. It does not attribute fixed, hidden, or underlying motives to the statements of political authorities and experts, as would a perspective of ideology. Instead, it takes the statements of ruling bodies at their word, so to speak. From such statements – be these speeches, treatises, diaries, committee minutes, or whatever – governmentality scholars seek to reconstruct the various ways in which questions concerning, say, the wealth of the nation, the health of the population, or the living conditions of the poor come to be posed as problems for officialdom. In other words, it aims to give an account of the forms of political reasoning that are embedded in governmental discourse, the forms of expert discourse, and the ethical concerns in terms of which social and political problems are rendered as meaningful and salient phenomena.

What does it mean to situate unemployment in terms of governing mentalities then? What this study aims to do is to understand *how* unemployment has been rendered as a problem for government: what sort of problem it is imagined to be, and how this changes. It will stress that there is never a general or prediscursive representation of unemployment (or any other problem); there are only problematizations in terms of particular (dominant) forms of political reason and embedded cultural assumptions. Let us take an example. We will find that from the turn of the century, when unemployment is first recognized as a pressing political concern, dominant perceptions of it are as a problem for *liberal* government. It is in terms of key liberal and patriarchal principles and norms that the issue is discussed: unemployment and under-employment are concerns because they undermine the assumption of the (ideally) self-governing household, of the male breadwinner supporting a family, and of the wage being a sufficient basis to support the life of the wage-earner. Such perceptions are highly significant, for they shape the rationality of proposals for tackling employment questions. For instance, unemployment insurance was favoured precisely because it was not public relief, or a supplement to the wage, but instead, a form of financial support which was assumed to keep the social and ethical principles of the wage intact.

But this is by no means the only way in which the problem of unemployment has been posed. This study will demonstrate how conceptions of unemployment have shifted over the course of the century, how there have been competing accounts of it, but also considerable continuities – as a problem of labour markets and industrial disorganization (Beveridge); as a socio-psychological matter of 'demoralization' amongst industrial workers (during the 1930s); as a risk which afflicts a given population (the insurance view); as a fully economic problem rooted in the structure of the national economy (Keynes) or, more recently, the local economy; and, most recently, as a question of individuals and communities which lack the skills and the capacity to adapt to the 'information-economies' of the coming century. One possible reading of this study is, therefore, as a history of problematizations of unemployment.

This is of course not the first study to historicize conceptions of unemployment. There have been many noteworthy attempts to locate it in terms of a history of economic ideas, and to trace the impact of changing ideas about unemployment on the public-policy making process.[6] There have also been some excellent social histories of the subject.[7] However, there is an important difference between these literatures and the present volume in terms of its ontological assumptions. Following other research in governmentality, this study seeks to go beyond the rather timeworn dichotomy of the material and the conceptual, between institutions and ideas, which still pervades so much empirical work in the social sciences. It insists that the activity of posing unemployment as a problem is no less material and practical than other aspects of its governance. Problematizations of unemployment do not just happen inside policy-makers' and other experts' heads. Rather, we need to see problematization in terms of a heterogeneous and plural *milieu* which combines humans and non-human artefacts; we need to understand governmental thought as an eminently practical activity which is not possible without the existence of all manner of technologies of inscription, description, recording, and representation.

On this note we can turn towards a second analytical emphasis that one finds within the governmentality literature. This body of work is distinctive in the way it has foregrounded the technical and practical aspect of governing. Govermentality research has heightened our understanding of the regulation of social life by focusing attention on the various mundane devices and technologies which enable fields as different as education, crime control, or emotional relations to be constituted as governable domains. If the accomplishment of social history was to found everyday life and popular experience as legitimate subjects of inquiry for historians, then governmentality research seeks to do a similar thing for the world of social technologies. These technologies are important in two ways. First, it is through technical devices that ruling bodies accumulate knowledge about the objects and processes they seek to govern. It is in terms of material inscriptions – charts, graphs, tables, and especially statistics – that reality is constituted as a programmable domain. But technical devices are also important since the ambitions of political authorities to influence the conduct of others are dependent on them. Governmentality research has suggested that such mundane devices as school registers, accountancy practices, and the architecture of public housing should be seen to have power effects because they are linked to aspirations to shape the conduct of others.

In some ways the present study could be read as an attempt to analyse historical changes in the regulation of unemployment at the level of certain key technologies of government and their relevant experts, such as the labour bureau, the insurance technique, the social survey, the employment counsellor. Within existing accounts of the evolution of employment policy, these have been treated as very much of secondary significance when compared with the wrangling of statespersons or the collision of powerful social forces. The emphasis which is placed on the world of political technologies in this study does not rest upon a claim that they are somehow more important, or primary. But it is based on an assumption that there is much we can learn about government by turning our attention to this hitherto neglected dimension of our existence.

Finally we must mention a third way in which research in governmentality offers to enhance our understanding of social and political arrangements: it insists that any account of governmental processes and practices is inadequate if it does not also consider the government of the self. As Mitchell Dean has put it, governmentality 'defines a novel thought-space across the domains of ethics and politics, of what might be called "practices of the self" and "practices of government", that weaves them together without a reduction of one to the other'.[8] In other words it spans two fields which are usually treated in separation – theories of governance and regulation, and theories of the subject and social identity.

This emphasis on the subjects of government is particularly important when analysing liberal forms of government. As Graham Burchell has pointed out, one of the defining features of these forms of government is that they 'set out a scheme of the relationship between government and the governed in which individuals are identified as, on the one hand, the *object* and target of governmental action and, on the other hand, as in some sense the necessary (voluntary) *partner* or accomplice of government'.[9] In other words, there is a development here of Foucault's argument about how we might understand the relationship between power and individual freedoms and liberties. The radical social scientist's argument that freedom under capitalism is bogus or ideological is not always helpful. Nor is the more conventional view that freedom is the limit, the obverse of power. Instead, following Foucault, we can begin to see how government takes place through our liberties and freedoms: how, under liberalism, we are governed as autonomous individuals, possessing various capacities for self-government. Government is said to occur 'at a distance' from formal centres of power precisely because regulation works by harnessing the duties and responsibilities, and forms of practical know-how, which families, firms, individuals, communities, and all other manners of agents come to assume.[10]

By exploring some of the different subjectivities and forms of ethical action which have been assumed by people without work, and presumed and/or encouraged by governing authorities, this study will suggest a new dimension to the study of unemployment. For instance, it will build on the insights of feminist theorists about the patriarchal structure of the welfare state in elaborating how the identity of the male breadwinner has been central to unemployment policies. But it will also draw attention to the plurality of subject-positions which coexist within the field of governing unemployment; it will observe that the unemployed have been governed as moral subjects, as social-citizen subjects, as enterprising, active-citizens, and in other ways besides. It will note how governmental work is done under the auspices of these forms of selfhood. Furthermore, I will demonstrate that these identities are never just top-down impositions by political authorities. In other words, I shall question the social control perspective. Government is a mobile, strategic, and heterogeneous field: official policies frequently incorporate forms of ethical identity and self-government which already existed in other spaces. This is illustrated in Chapter 3 where it is shown that many aspects of social citizenship were prefigured by forms of government improvised by nineteenth-century trade unionism.

To conclude this brief overview of certain key themes within the governmentality literature, it is necessary to offer an important qualification as to the nature of this project. This study uses historical materials for a specific purpose: to explore key changes in the way in which the issue of unemployment has been thought about, and acted on, by those who seek to regulate it. It does not engage in a debate about the historical truth of unemployment, that is, the way things really were. It does not seek to give a more accurate account of the causes of mass unemployment in the 1930s, or the state of the mental health of unemployed people at this (or any other) time. Rather, it is interested in the way in which authorities and social practices – contemporaneous with the periods it is concerned with – produced their own truths about unemployment, and the role that the circulation of such truths played in the government of unemployment. In other words, the use of history in this book is quite instrumental. Historical materials are employed, often quite schematically, to illustrate shifts in modes of perception and governing. The study should not, therefore, be read as a history of unemployment, at least not in any conventional sense. Instead, it could be interpreted as a sociology of the governance of unemployment which relies upon a certain use of historical materials.[11]

GENEALOGIES OF THE SOCIAL

While it is hoped that this book will offer new insights on the government of unemployment, it has other, wider ambitions. It is intended as a contribution towards a genealogy of 'the social'. Given the diverse uses and interpretations of this word, I shall briefly set out how it is understood, and what its significance is within the Foucaultian literature.

The Social

For many social scientists, the meaning of the social is given by its opposition to the natural. It is the sphere of human interactions, relations, institutions, and so on. But for Foucaultian scholars it has a much more specific and finite significance. For Gilles Deleuze, it is 'not an adjective that qualifies the set of phenomena which sociology deals with: *the* social refers to a particular sector in which quite diverse problems and special cases can be grouped together, a sector comprising specific institutions and an entire body of qualified personnel'.[12] Or, as Nikolas Rose, Giovanna Procacci, and Pat O'Malley have all explained, 'the social' is best thought of as a distinctive way of governing, one that is temporally and geographically specific.[13] Until quite recently, 'the social' has been a sort of *a priori* of programmes and strategies of government. Across the 'western' nations, whatever their differences, conservatives, socialists, liberals, social-democrats, and even certain fascists were agreed that to govern well, one had to govern in terms of the social. As O'Malley puts it, the principal objects of rule and the ways of engaging with them were constituted in terms of a collective entity with emergent properties that could not be reduced to the individual constituents, that could not be tackled adequately at the level of individuals, and that for these reasons required the intervention of the state. Social services, social insurances, social security, the social wage were constituted to deal with social problems, social forces, social injustices and social pathologies through various forms of social intervention, social work, social medicine and social engineering.[14]

It is this field of the social that has been carefully and patiently traced in terms of historically situated studies: of schooling, penality, the psy-sciences and practices, popular practices such as drinking, poverty, social and commercial life insurance, and much more. Despite their radically contrasting subject-matters and diverse disciplinary backgrounds, the authors of these studies are linked by their discomfort with the generalizations and systematizations of grand theory, and by a sense that we can learn from the particular and the contextual. The question, then, is: what does this study of the government of unemployment contribute to our knowledge about social governance? A brief outline of the contents and aims of each chapter in this study shall serve as an answer to this question.

The first contribution of this study will be to address a shortcoming in the governmentality literature on the social. Arguably it has paid little attention to the relationship of the social to the economic, and to questions of economic governance more generally.[15] Such questions cannot be avoided by a study of the government of unemployment, however, owing to the fact that unemployment has historically been addressed in equal parts as a social and an economic problem. This theme is addressed most directly in Chapter 1. This chapter argues that what it casts as the discovery of unemployment at the turn of the century – i.e., a shift in the locus of social inquiry from the unemployed labourer to a new object of study: the labour market – is a highly significant event. For it opens up the possibility of governing a troubling array of social concerns – from prostitution and child delinquency to malnutrition and crime – by acting on specifically economic variables such as the labour market and the wage. Chapter 2 develops this point in terms of a specific focus on the technology of the labour exchange, and how it forms the labour market as an observable, calculable, and manipulable plane of the economic.

Chapter 5 then develops our understanding of the place of 'the economy' within social governance in other ways. Not only does it compare the way in which the relation of the social to the economic is posed within different (e.g., welfarist and neoliberal) programmes for tackling unemployment. It also considers the significance of recent mutations in conceptions of the economic for the governance of unemployment – the emergence of relatively new objects of governance, such as the 'local' economy and the European economy.

There is a second substantial way in which this study might be considered as contributing towards a genealogy of the social. For it uses the case of unemployment to clarify what it is we understand by the prefix 'social'. What is the difference between a social and moral problematic? What is the relation between social explanations and structural explanations? What is the relation between the social and the individual. In Chapter 3 in particular, an attempt is made to resolve some of these questions by means of a study of the technology and the rationality of unemployment insurance. Of special interest is the notion of 'involuntary' unemployment which is mobilized by social insurance. The idea that 'involuntary' forces and factors determine the fate of individuals, and that these can become a legitimate target for collective action, is a defining feature of a social approach to government.

Third, this study will explore the uncertainties which surround the project of social governance today, and some of its mutations. Chapter 6 is a case study of a recent initiative within UK employment policy – the New Deal. This scheme exemplifies the current enthusiasm amongst governments for 'welfare to work' programmes. This chapter situates the New Deal at the intersection of arguments about community, social exclusion, and security in an age of economic transformation. It was a hallmark of the post-war welfare state that it treated society as a totalizable object of regulation, a setting for the 'involuntary' and impersonal forces presupposed and constructed by technologies like social insurance. Chapter 6 suggests that today social and employment policy is characterized by its avoidance of questions about the wider social system, in favour of a focus on the 'margins', and its downplaying of the involuntary dimension of unemployment while opting for a very subjective and personalized approach to the problem.

A Note on Genealogy

To conclude the introduction to this book, I want to say something about genealogy, a term which features in its sub-title. What is distinctive about a genealogy as opposed to, say, a theory or a history of the social? What is genealogy as a method and a form of analysis? What implications does the adoption of this mode of analysis have for our comprehension of social, cultural, and political processes? Perhaps a good way to highlight the distinctiveness of a genealogical approach to the social is to compare it with one literature which shares some of its substantive concerns, namely the area marked out by political economy and sociological approaches to welfare states.

At the risk of oversimplifying matters, we can say that there exists an influential current within these perspectives on the welfare state which we might loosely term 'structuralist'. By this I mean a will to analyse social welfare as a sort of sub-system, as one sector within a larger political, social, and economic totality. Within these structuralist approaches the task of the theorist is to draw out the linkages, homologies, supports, but also contradictions, between the welfare system and other regions of the totality – the economic, the political, the cultural and so on.[16] Changes in the welfare system are then made intelligible in terms of changes in other regions of the totality – the globalization of the economy, the rise of post-Fordism, or even postmodernity. As an explanatory device, this approach is quite powerful. However, it tends to portray a highly systematized and rational image of the world.

Genealogy can be contrasted with this perspective in at least two ways.[17] First, in terms of its ontological assumptions: genealogy does not cast its explanations of phenomena in terms of trans-historical or essential structures, epochs, or social forces, be these Capital, The State, The Economy, or Modernity. Instead, it is unapologetically superficial in its outlook. It suspends the question of the deep economic or other causes of a given event, because it holds that there are also interesting things we can learn about the past and the present if we focus on surfaces, that is if we trace out the imagined territories and spaces of government. Whereas it is conventional within the social sciences to treat the social, the political, the economic as given spheres, genealogy reminds us that these entities are themselves categories of government with their own history. As this particular account of governmental strategies will reveal, the distinction between the social and the economic is not, therefore, something which can be assumed, but is instead a division which itself needs to be studied.

Second, genealogy challenges the structuralist perspective in terms of the latter's interpretation of the process of social and institutional change. The structuralist approach tends to work from the general down to the particular. For instance, the rise of welfare to work programmes is interpreted in the light of general, structural changes which occur at the level of the state, capital, international economy, etc. Genealogy is more attuned to the particular, the local, the molecular. It underscores how large changes are the culmination of a multitude of smaller changes, of distinct lines of development which do not evolve simultaneously, and always combine in unpredictable ways. Moreover, it highlights the fact that many of the social forms we inhabit have contingent and accidental origins. It is predisposed to see social forms as 'spin-offs': inadvertent and contingent discoveries which are subsequently captured, rationalized, and pressed into governmental service. Genealogy reveals the present to be a lot less inevitable than we often assume; in this feat lies its political significance.

Given its genealogical disposition, this study of the government of unemployment is not simply an attempt to illustrate or exemplify more general phenomena. It is motivated by the belief that employment questions, along with every other site within the social space, represent specific and irreducible sites where innovations and discoveries have been pioneered. For instance, in Chapter 4 I highlight how unemployment assistance, a technique of nationally uniform discretionary treatment of the unemployed, was invented to deal with the particular circumstances of long-term unemployment. It is only subsequently generalized to deal with other types of population. In this way the fabric of governmental arrangements is composed. But conversely, genealogy is also attuned to the lateral movements, the importation of governmental forms. It cautions against studying the history of employment policy, or any other field, as though it were endogenous or self-contained. This study is not meant to be a history of 'the welfare state'. It is hoped, however, that it will offer insights to the various inquiries which are now grouped around this conceptual object.

CHAPTER 1

THE DISCOVERY OF UNEMPLOYMENT

> Society is built up on labour; it lays upon its members responsibilities which in the vast majority of cases can be met only from the reward of labour ... its ideal unit is the household of man, wife and children maintained by the earnings of the first alone. The household should have at all times sufficient room and air according to its size – but how, if the income is too irregular always to pay the rent? The children, till they themselves can work, should be supported by the parents – but how unless the father has employment? The wife, so long at least as she is bearing and bringing up children, should have no other task – but how if the husband's earnings fail and she has to go out to work? Everywhere the same difficulty occurs. Reasonable security of employment for the bread-winner is the basis of all private duties and all sound action.[1]

Historians are in general agreement that the term 'unemployment' only entered into official and popular usage in the last decade or so of the nineteenth century.[2] Yet the social and political question of work-lessness, and of destitution connected with want of employment, is obviously much older. Almost three centuries ago, Daniel Defoe, in a statement which still resonates today, expressed a condemnatory view of those who attributed their misfortune to an inability to find employ-ment: 'The reason why so many pretend to want work is that they can live so well with the pretense ... [that] they would be mad to leave it and work in earnest.'[3]

This chapter is not a reflection on the rather inglorious history of ideas about worklessness to which Defoe's statement belongs. It is certainly not an account of the changing experience of losing or looking for work either, but something more specific. It is about the emergence, and the construction within governmental thought, of 'unemployment' as a particular kind of socio-economic condition at the end of the nineteenth century, and the implications of this for governmental practices. In Chapters 2 and 3 we then go on to explore some of these implications at greater length.

This discovery of unemployment by a relatively small but influential cadre of social experts, including William Beveridge and Hubert Llewellyn-Smith, has been carefully researched by historians and sociologists.[4] This chapter will argue against the tendency in some accounts of this moment to see it as a turn towards a more social and humane, as opposed to an individualistic and punitive, outlook on the unemployed.[5] It will demonstrate that by employing some of the insights of research in governmentality, particularly about the nature and the mechanisms of liberal governance, new light can be shed on this moment. It is not just that with the discovery of unemployment it becomes possible to see individual misfortunes in terms of the functioning (and malfunctioning) of a larger, impersonal socio-economic system – a system which, it will be seen, becomes itself an object of argumentation, contestation and calculation as to its proper nature. The discovery of unemployment also holds out the possibility of defending and renovating certain key principles and mechanisms of liberal governance, such as the family, by acting at the level of this system. The socialization of unemployment, in the sense in which the social is understood in this study, does not supplant the individual or the familial as poles of government. Instead, it connects them to a new apparatus of government, one involving social insurance, labour exchanges, and other forms of macro-management.

In order to develop this argument that the discovery of unemployment points to new forms of governing population, the main part of this chapter compares discourses about unemployment with the perspective on worklessness which dominated governmental thought in the earlier nineteenth century – what observers at the time called 'the problem of the unemployed'. In short, the latter concerns the administration of the unemployed, whereas in the twentieth century the focus becomes the management of unemployment.

While this chapter is about the construction of unemployment within governmental thought, and not the history of unemployment *per se*, it is nevertheless important that we consider the social and historical circumstances surrounding this process of 'discovery' (but also 'invention'). After all, a genealogy of unemployment has to account for the social conditions under which it becomes possible to formulate new concepts. Why is there little evidence of a socio-economic discourse on unemployment before the end of the nineteenth century? While an exhaustive response to this question would take us beyond the limited aims of this chapter, it is possible to point to at least two critical developments. The first concerns the manner in which a notion of 'employment' becomes thinkable, a concept that will have 'unemployment' as its antithesis, its 'other'.

GOVERNING EMPLOYMENT IN THE NINETEENTH CENTURY

In an important essay Krishan Kumar offers a cogent account of why unemployment becomes a salient political and theoretical issue from the 1880s, and not before.[6] He argues that although unemployment and under-employment were common features of eighteenth and early-nineteenth century social and economic life, the way they were experienced then was not the same as it would be from the end of the nineteenth century onwards.

> Work, employment and unemployment in nineteenth-century England still bore many of the hall-marks of the pre-industrial economy and society. Poverty was caused and relieved in much the same way as the previous century. Work was not so specialized that workers could not turn their hand to a variety of occupations in town and country. Urbanization itself had not yet gone so far that most workers and their families could not have some access to the 'free' resources of the countryside. The contingencies of life, including unemployment and under-employment, pressed as hard as ever; but a mixture of outdoor relief, a diversified labour market, and mutual aid in traditionally-oriented families and communities softened their impact.[7]

He goes on to argue that this situation only began to change significantly at the end of the century – and not earlier, as those who 'antedate the full impact of the industrial revolution in England' suppose.[8] It is only then, through the complex interaction of social, political and industrial developments such as changes in the organization of industrial work, the tightening of poor relief, the removal of children from the family economy (effected in part by compulsory schooling), that the livelihood of most individuals and families becomes almost exclusively dependent upon wages from employment. In this way Kumar explains how unemployment becomes such a burning issue at this time for social inquirers, organized labour, and politics in general.

While I agree with the broad thrust of this argument that the recognition of an unemployment problem presupposes the advent of what John Keane has termed the 'employment society',[9] my sense is that it might be useful to supplement it by interrogating what is understood by 'employment'. For the recognition of a problem of 'unemployment' is influenced by the way in which 'employment' comes to be constituted as a well-regulated form of social and economic activity. In this section

I want to point to some of the ways in which, in the course of the nineteenth century, the notion of employment acquires a fullness, a positivity as an object and target of governmental interventions. Changes in the economic and occupational structure were no doubt an important factor in this respect, most notably the shift from agriculture to industry. However, there are two developments at the level of the regulation of work which I want to examine here. These are the rise of factory legislation, and the impact that trade unionism had on the organization of work. Both were instrumental in shaping modern employment relations. Both these forces actively normalized and socialized employment; they gave rise to a notion of normal employment which would have as its converse a condition of unemployment.

Factory Legislation

Reflecting on the advance of factory legislation Sidney Webb wrote:

> The range of Factory Legislation has ... in one country or another, become co-extensive with the conditions of industrial employment. No class of manual working wage-earners, no item in the wage contract, no age, no sex, no trade or occupation, is now beyond its scope.[10]

In other words, via the spread of factory legislation work became the target of legal and moral norms which framed and codified its conditions, its conduct, the proper identity of its agents, its management, its remuneration, its hours, its location, etc. Work was normalized. On the basis of factory inspection, and as a result of numerous inquiries into the conditions of employment around the country, both statistical and descriptive, a picture of what normal employment was, or should look like, was gradually composed.

Although factory legislation would ultimately contribute to the shaping of what is now recognizable as 'employment', this had not been the intention of the coalition of philanthropic millowners, working-class agitators and Tory evangelicals – known as the Factory Movement – which first proposed and campaigned for it in the period from 1815 to 1831.[11] Their aims were much more limited. The rationality was never a general regulation of the worker or the workplace. Such a prospect was simply too contrary to the socially-ascendant principles of political economy and liberal individualism which held that the state should not interfere in the essentially 'private' employer/employee relationship. However, regulation could be justified in those situations where workers were not 'free agents'. Hence factory legislation began with child labour and it focused upon the burgeoning textile industries of Lancashire and Yorkshire where the industrial employment of children was most pronounced.

Although it was very limited, uneven, and poorly enforced, early factory legislation had certain unforeseen consequences: it 'opened up' the factory. The findings of a number of official inquiries in the 1830s and 1840s brought the dreadful conditions of factory work to the attention of a wider public. They made the factory available as an object for campaigning around, reforming, improving. In this way factory legislation spread – through the textile industries, and by the early 1870s it applied to all factories, mines, and increasing numbers of workshops. The exact details of how need not concern us here, except to say that reformers attempted to use competition between employers to level standards in an upwards instead of a downwards direction.

But factory legislation also spread in terms of the categories of person that would fall within its remit. From children it was extended to all young persons, and by the 1840s it applied to women whose situation as 'unfree agents' was deemed comparable to young persons.[12] Although most of this legislation was ostensibly aimed at the protection of women, young persons, and children, ultimately it transformed the working conditions of the adult male worker also: in many cases he worked in factories which now had to conform to the new standards.

One should not assume a simple uniformity in the aims and objectives of the various Factory Acts which mark the nineteenth century. For a gradual shift in their political rationality can be discerned: from moral to social regulation. It is a shift that will be encountered at several places in this study. At the start of the century, legislation was concerned to promote the moral conduct, well-being, and development of individuals. For instance, the Health and Morals of Apprentices Act of 1802 prescribed that millowners provide separate accommodation for boys and girls.[13] Early factory legislation was framed around a pastoral view of social relations; it was often supported by Tory philanthropists[14] who would have seen it as an instrument for re-establishing the bonds of community in the face of industrial turmoil.

However, by the 1890s factory legislation was being invested with a fuller social (or societ-al) rationality. Increasingly it was to be a means of protecting society which, by this time, was coming to be understood as a national community. As the likes of Sidney Webb saw it, factory legislation was to be about 'the application of the principle of the "national minimum" in the standard of life, to be prescribed by the community, and secured by law to every one of its citizens'.[15]

Factory legislation was certainly not universal in its coverage by the start of the twentieth century. Historians and sociologists of work have pointed to the vast array of trades which escaped regulation or diverged from the model.[16] Employment patterns were not transformed universally. The point is, however, that by the end of the nineteenth century, social observers possessed a mental image of the form that employment relations should take. This explains why casual employment, which had for long appeared quite unremarkable, could be problematized at this time. I shall return to the casual labour question later in this chapter since it is central to the formation of the unemployment problem.

Trade Unionism

A second line of forces which will contribute to the construction of a model of normal employment is associated with trade unionism. In their monumental analysis of British trade union life, *Industrial Democracy*, Sidney and Beatrice Webb anatomize a range of methods which trade unions had traditionally used to regulate conditions of employment.[17] They highlight three sets of practices – mutual insurance, collective bargaining, and legal enactment. Varying combinations of these practices, they argue, enabled unions to impose certain norms upon working life: e.g., concerning a standard rate of pay for a job, the length of the working day, safety and sanitation standards, and conditions of entry for a trade. In many instances there are convergences with the movement for factory legislation. This is especially so after 1867 as working men were brought within the franchise. This enabled trade unions like the Amalgamated Association of Operative Cotton-spinners to agitate for such measures as the Nine Hours' Bill in 1871.[18]

What is interesting about trade union tactics for the purposes of this study is that they were seen to bring 'organization' to the labour market. This is evident if we briefly consider the way in which the technique of mutual insurance functioned. In their magazine, the Flint Glass Makers express the objective of mutual insurance in a very succinct fashion: 'Our wages depend on the supply of labor [*sic*] in the market; our interest is therefore to restrict that supply, reduce the surplus, *make our unemployed comfortable, without fear for the morrow – accomplish this, and we have a command over the surplus of our labor, and we need fear no unjust employer.*'[19]

Similarly, the General Secretary of the Associated Shipwrights Society reminded his members:

> It is utterly impossible ... to secure trade protection when a third or a half of your trade are walking about idle and starving. And unless members of the trade were prepared to buy up, more or less, its surplus labour in the market, it never could have the actual trade protection desired.[20]

Through the payment of a regular 'out-of-work donation', then, unions sought to alleviate the pressure on their unemployed members to take work on terms that would undermine the so-called 'standard rate' for a job. Two things need to be mentioned in this respect. First, that mutual insurance therefore functioned to standardize employment: it made it possible for workers to assert that a given job would not be performed at less than the 'going rate'. But second, in standardizing employment, the technique of mutual insurance actually contributed to the production of the identity of the unemployed. Without the 'out-of-work donation' the worker would be compelled to take work on unfavourable terms almost immediately, or worse, resort to begging, crime, pauperism, or casual employment to survive. In other words, it can be argued that the status 'out-of-work' was actually invented by trade unionism and served strategic purposes. This condition is invented and not natural in the sense that mutual insurance carves out a space of security such that the normally regular worker can survive without work, at least for a short period of time, rather than become, say, a casual worker. It is strategic because it is generally in the interest of the union that the individual be temporarily 'unemployed' rather than casualized.

However, most workers in the nineteenth century did not belong to unions. The total membership of trade unions at the end of the 1870s was no more than 500 000. Most of these were skilled workers and artisans grouped in craft unions. The 'new unionism' which flourished in the late 1880s saw the organization of unskilled and general workers, and this helped to push the membership of the union movement towards 1.5 million by 1892.[21] Nevertheless, vast numbers remained outside the regular employment system I have described.

This was particularly true of women workers. As a result, their want of employment was made especially difficult to define and relieve, since 'the application of the remedies [for unemployment] is easiest in those trades where Unionism has already defined and regulated the area of employment, and hardest where labour is still casual, uncertain and unregulated'.[22]

The problem for so many trades in which women were employed was that there existed no clear mechanisms for regulating membership in them. Women typically worked in unskilled[23] and unorganized trades whose boundaries were thus very porous, trades which became saturated during depressions as a result of the huge reserves of female labour normally employed in domestic work.[24] For the trade unionist J. R. Brooke, this difficulty could only be resolved if '[w]omen's Unions can cover the ground in any trade so that employment in that trade is mainly confined to members of the Unions'.[25]

There is an important lesson for the purposes of this study which can be drawn from the briefest reflection on the situation of women's work in the late nineteenth century. It is that the 'organisation' of a trade – which is tantamount to its de-casualization – is a precondition for the regulation of the worker in terms of unemployment. To be 'unemployed' in the strict sense of the term presupposes that a worker has some sense of ownership, some sort of durable connection to her or his job which persists even when employment is interrupted. Later in this chapter I shall focus on what proved to be a particularly influential programme for dealing with unemployment, a set of proposals associated with the likes of Beveridge and the Webbs calling for the 'public organisation of the labour market'. As J. R. Brooke recognized, as a policy of de-casualization, this programme sought to generalize what the trade unions had pioneered:

> The bold and ambitious proposal to deal with unemployment, by organising with State machinery the whole of the labour market, which to-day holds the field unrivaled, could never have been put forward but for the progress and success of Trade Unionism in organising separate trades on an independent basis. That independent organisation is equally indispensable in the case of women. Before unemployment can be lessened, or the distress arising from that which inevitably remains satisfactorily relieved without recourse to the Poor Law, *employment itself must be defined and regulated.*[26]

What this statement seems to suggest is that regulatory forms and devices are not always imposed upon society in a straightforward fashion from above, by Capital, or The State, as certain 'social control' interpretations of Foucault sometimes imply. In rejecting certain totalizing and structural theorizations of power Foucault called instead for 'an ascending analysis of power, starting … from its infinitesimal mechanisms, which each have their own history, their own trajectory, their own techniques and tactics, and then see how these mechanisms of power have been – and continue to be – invested, colonised, utilised, involuted, transformed, displaced, extended, etc., by ever more general mechanism and by forms of global domination'.[27] The techniques for 'organizing' trades are nice examples of this reversibility, of the indeterminacy of techniques of government. Pioneered in a specific setting to meet particular objectives, they are capable of being re-deployed in the form of a more systematized state policy.

Employment and Unemployment

To conclude this section, we can speculate about another level at which employment and unemployment are linked. What seems to happen in the course of the nineteenth and early twentieth centuries is that work becomes more generic, both in terms of the way it is regulated, and, with the spread of the factory system, in terms of its substance. In the context of the many surveys, commissions, and investigations into working conditions which were so characteristic of the mid- to late-Victorian period, a multitude of discrete trades and occupations come to be arrayed, compared, and linked to one another on the plane of 'employment'; they all become so many instances of a *general* condition of employment. Under these circumstances it will be possible to think of non-work similarly as a general condition, as *un*-employment, rather than a problem endemic or particular to a given trade.

Having surveyed changes in industrial life and how these establish certain conditions under which it will be possible to pose a problem of unemployment, I want to turn now to a more detailed account of how a problem of unemployment is formulated at the level of the 'social question'.

THE 'SOCIAL QUESTION' AND UNEMPLOYMENT

Aside from the emergence of a notion of 'employment', there was a second set of circumstances framing and shaping the emergence of a discourse on unemployment – a loose collection of concerns and fears about poverty and social order that Victorian society knew as 'the social question'.[28] The raising of the social question coincided with the Great Depression, conventionally dated from 1873 to 1896. This was a period which saw the undermining of the Victorian belief, at its zenith at the middle of the century, that the social and economic system comprised a self-regulating order best served by a combination of a limited state and the vigorous promotion of self-help and *laissez-faire* capitalism.

There were several aspects to the social question. Not the least significant was a series of revelations about the extent of poverty in the heart of the great towns and cities, and about the conditions of slum life. Public opinion had assumed that the general improvement in standards of living which occurred during the 1850s and 1860s meant that chronic poverty was now confined to a small 'residuum' of people who were incapable of 'improvement'. However, the revelations of a new genre of sensationalist journalism, the more diligent surveys carried out by the growing cadre of social inquirers, and a series of official investigations all documented poverty on a frightening scale.[29]

The Victorian social order was based on a conception of the working classes which saw three distinct strata. At the top was a 'labour aristocracy' of skilled men and their families, who had forged a distinct social, political, and cultural identity based upon a network of institutions such as their trade unions, friendly societies, and mechanics institutes, and an ethos of self-reliance, thrift, respectability, and independence. At the bottom was the residuum, the 'dangerous classes', the slum-dwellers who had turned their backs on 'progress'. This stratum is the antithesis of all that is considered 'social' and respectable: its members are improvident and lack 'character'; they survive on the basis of occasional work, crime, prostitution, and begging; they revel in gambling, promiscuity, vice, and drink.[30] And in the middle there was an intermediate stratum of semi-skilled workers, tradespeople, sweated workers, seasonally or casually employed, struggling to get by, but vulnerable to trade cycles and recessions because they lack the social institutions and resources of the labour aristocracy.

The fear was that with the spread of casual work, the periodic downturns which were increasingly afflicting industry, the mass of poor rural workers streaming into the cities, and overcrowding in evidence in urban centres like London and Liverpool, the social and spatial boundaries which had separated the 'respectable' from the 'rough' were becoming blurred. The intermediate strata were increasingly vulnerable to pauperism. This insecurity touched the labour aristocracy as well, as its influence over the production process began to be undercut by employers looking to squeeze out profits in response to heightened competition within domestic and foreign markets.

There is a radical political dimension to the social question as well. The last decades of the nineteenth century saw a revival of socialist organizations and ideas which had been dormant since the defeat of Chartism. These ideas found a ready audience amongst many semi-skilled workers who for the first time began to organize themselves into new types of mass trade union to demand better working conditions.[31] In 1893 the Independent Labour Party was formed to represent newly enfranchised workers at the national level.

But significant for this study is the fact that socialist appeals also found an audience in a new form of collective identity which first became widespread during the 1880s, 'the unemployed'. Now, collective and at times violent protest on the part of people desperate for work was not an uncommon feature of the early nineteenth century. For instance, Stevenson documents how, in 1824, handloom weavers in north Lancashire protested the widespread adoption of power looms in the cotton industry, attacking more than twenty mills and smashing over 1000 looms.[32] Similarly, in their celebrated study of the Captain Swing disturbances which swept through rural areas from 1830 to 1832, Hobsbawm and Rudé record the fact that agricultural workers frequently engaged in violence, large-scale collective action, and clandestine acts of arson as they protested worsening work and social conditions.[33]

But while people without work, or needing more work, had a long and painful history of protest, it was only from the start of the 1870s, and on a wider scale in the 1880s, as Flanagan has argued, that they start to become organized, identify themselves as 'the unemployed', and make political demands in this name.[34] It was only from this time, and not before, that the unemployed acquire certain features of a political movement, including authorized spokespersons and definite demands. Socialist organizations like the Social Democratic Federation played an important role in this process. For their exhortations encouraged those without work to see themselves as the unemployed, and not simply misfortunates, beggars, supplicants, or the poor. In this way, such political organizations turned 'unemployed' into a noun, made it signify a distinct collectivity, and invested it with political purpose.

As the century draws to a close what the social question asks is how to secure a social order which seems to be cracking; how to fashion new social relations and political institutions capable not only of addressing poverty and industrial antagonism, but at the same time accommodating the demands that various groups are making that they be addressed as citizens. As such, the social question will provoke a profound *transformation* in the way that poverty is governed. This will entail a reordering of the relations between state, society, and the individual, and the construction of social policy in its modern form. It will also involve the construction of a new object of governance, 'unemployment', which will be pivotal to the way in which social policy will operate.

But the specificity and the novelty of 'unemployment' and the new possibilities for governance which it suggests at the end of the century cannot be fully appreciated without some understanding of the existing ways in which the poor, and in particular those without work, were governed. In the following section, then, I examine what Victorian society understood by 'the problem of the unemployed'. This designated an approach to governance which centred upon moral individuals. It is therefore consistent with the wider Victorian conception of 'the poor'. Once it is possible to conceive of an economic condition of 'unemployment', which is distinct from its bearers, the possibility of other ways of acting on poverty is opened up. It is therefore important to distinguish between the nineteenth-century problem of the unemployed, and the emergence of a concept of unemployment.

'THE PROBLEM OF THE UNEMPLOYED'

The discourse on the problem of the unemployed is an extension of liberal discourses and practices regarding poverty. It is structured by the social, political, and ethical concerns of the agencies which first address the social implications of the unemployed problem – in essence, the philanthropies and the Poor Law guardians. It is therefore marked by their characteristic concerns, namely an individualistic, discriminatory treatment of distress which is wary of encouraging the 'demoralization' of its subjects, and which seeks to place 'character' at the centre of its relieving practice. From the mid-1880s, when the Trafalgar Square riots announced the arrival of the unemployed as a self-conscious political actor, until well into the 1900s, a whole slew of pamphlets and tracts are written about the unemployed problem. Of signal importance to this literature is an appropriate scheme of classification for its target population.[35] The words of one of the earliest tracts on this matter are insightful:

> Without some method of classification ... nothing can be accomplished ... [T]o know the real constituent elements of the mass we have to deal with is the first condition of success in acting upon it, and in no way ... shall we be better able to separate the body of the really industrious but unemployed poor from the clamorous horde of idle, dissatisfied and incompetent folk who cumber our labour market and prey on the best sympathies of the benevolent, than by such method of registration as is here shadowed forth.[36]

At one level 'the unemployed' will refer to all those who are in distress through some failure to get (enough) employment. However, most inquiries then differentiate the unemployed into two basic classes, 'those unable to work, and ... those unwilling to work'.[37] The former are seen as the 'genuine' or 'industrious' unemployed and are viewed like the 'deserving poor'.[38] They are the 'competent victims of trade fluctuations'; their distress is due not so much due to 'personal failure' as to 'exceptional' circumstances, like a harsh winter, or the collapse of a trade. They are 'deserving' because it is evident that they have already proven their qualities as citizens through the steps they have taken to help themselves – whether through familial thrift, trade organization, or mutual assurance.

The 'undeserving' unemployed are all those who do not work because of some failing of character, will, or physique. By the 1900s they are frequently addressed as the 'unemployable', with new discourses like social eugenics explaining their condition in socio-biological terms. Unlike the 'deserving' unemployed, 'those who are unwilling to work must be disciplined'.[39]

This discourse about the unemployed finds its practical accompaniment in a structure of administrative intervention which takes shape in the period from the mid-1880s to the end of the 1900s. The assumption was that the undeserving unemployed should be dealt with by the harsh and tutelary methods of the Poor Law. At the same time, provision for the genuine unemployed was made by a loosely co-ordinated alliance of charities and local authorities, organized on a city by city basis. The main form of assistance which it offered was the 'make work' scheme which often consisted of trenching, ditching, and other types of 'spade labour'. Typically, such municipal work would be financed by the Mayor or Provost of the town making an appeal for funds to the local community. In addition, the various local charities organized soup kitchens, provided clothing and meals for children, and sought to assist the able-bodied unemployed and their families to emigrate.[40] The Salvation Army was particularly active in this latter respect and had by the end of the nineteenth century established an international network of offices for the purpose.

Gradually a legal and administrative code emerged to regulate this form of governance for the unemployed. A milestone in this respect was the circular first issued in 1886 by the Local Government Board (known as the 'Chamberlain Circular', after Joseph Chamberlain who was its president). This instructed local authorities to try to schedule municipal work for times of slackness and to co-operate with Poor Law guardians to make such employment available to the genuine unemployed on a non-pauperizing basis. But the apogee, and in many respects the culmination of this approach to administration, came with the passage of the Unemployed Workmen Act 1905. This authorized the establishment of 'distress committees' in all large towns and cities. These were composed of representatives of local councils, charity workers, and Poor Law guardians. Distress Committees were financed through a combination of rates and voluntary contribution. Their role was to co-ordinate the various types of voluntary support for the unemployed, but mainly to assess applicants for relief work.[41]

While the measures that culminate in the Unemployed Workmen Act are significant in marking the entry of the state into the unemployed question, they cannot be said to signal a break with nineteenth-century, disciplinary approaches to poverty. Their object remains the individual in distress, their method, the assessment and promotion of character. This is evident from the Local Government Board's guidelines for the administration of relief works:

> A Record Paper should be filled for each case ... preference is to be given to persons: (a) Who have in the past been regularly employed, have resided in the area for a continuous period of twelve months at least, and have been well-conducted and thrifty; (b) who have dependants; and (c) who are qualified in respect of age and physical ability for the work offered ... Verification of the applicants' statements has to be obtained by a visit to the home and by inquiries of the guardians and other persons where the circumstances so require.[42]

Although there is legal and administrative acknowledgement of a new category of person, 'the unemployed', in the absence of an actual technique for determining the identity of the unemployed, there is no alternative but to rely on the extant and highly imperfect techniques of the Poor Law and charity, namely an assessment of character and worthiness. Within this system, a person's employment history still figures as evidence of their character. It will be seen that with the labour exchange and unemployment insurance system administrative authorities were furnished with a dedicated technique for the administration of the unemployed.

As a form of governance 'the problem of the unemployed' encountered a number of serious obstacles which it was unable to resolve. First, the system of relief works was inadequate. Relief works were shunned by the class of respectable unemployed worker for which they were designed. In the eyes of the respectable worker, such measures were tainted by their association with the Poor Law and charity. They were also detested precisely because they pried into the personal and domestic circumstances of the individual. Nor was the unskilled, manual labour they offered deemed suitable for artisans and skilled workers.

This fact illustrates nicely the point I introduced at the outset of this study: practices of government work hand-in-hand with practices of self-government. Social reformers were influenced in their search to prescribe new forms of administration for the respectable unemployed by this fact: for their methods to be successful they would have to win an element of consent from their subjects. In other words, the form of ethical self-understanding of the respectable unemployed did make an impact on the development of governmental forms.

But there was another reason why relief works 'failed'. They were locally-organized and largely dependent on voluntary contribution. Since the middle class, the principal source of their funds, was also affected by recessions, relief funds were prone to becoming exhausted just when they were most needed.[43]

If relief works were ineffective at helping the 'genuinely' unemployed, what they did help to reveal was the existence of a vast mass of people who were not so much *un*-employed as permanently *under*-employed, whose distress was not temporary but chronic. For relief works schemes were overwhelmed by applications for work from casual workers. One major survey concluded that 'the published experience of the last twenty years is unanimous that the man with an uncertain hold on the labour market is the problem which the community has to deal with if it wishes to deal with '*distress* due to lack of employment'.[44]

It was through reflection on the problem of the casual worker, as much as on the unemployed, that it became possible for social experts to formulate a more general concept of unemployment, one that enabled both these figures to become objects within a more fully socio-economic form of explanation.

The Problem of Casual Labour

The casual labour problem marks the point at which the problems of poverty and pauperism begin to be linked to forms of employment.[45] Within this intellectual and empirical space of inquiry, the relations between labour markets, forms of employment, forms of social and moral life, and of subjectivity will be established. Unemployment policy will be devised as one way of organizing their interrelations according to a model of normal employment and its social responsibilities. We have already seen how this notion of normal employment takes shape gradually over the nineteenth century in the context of factory legislation and trade unionism. This normalization of the field of employment provides the setting in which seemingly 'irregular' forms of employment like casualism can be posed as problematic. In other words, in so far as early unemployment policy will make 'de-casualization' one of its principal objectives, it represents the extension of this programme of normalization to the frontiers of work and non-work.

As early as the 1850s, Henry Mayhew's investigation of 'London labour' had pointed to low wages, sweating, and seasonal and casual labour as the primary causes of chronic poverty.[46] However, the view that the demoralization of the poor was primarily the result of indiscriminate charity was not seriously challenged until the 1880s.[47] Above all, it was with Charles Booth's 'Poverty Surveys' of London that factors of employment were used systematically to explain poverty. Booth's surveys reveal that the condition of a large proportion of the families in, or destined for, pauperism can be explained because their principal wage earners receive very low wages, or because they don't work regularly, i.e., they are casual labourers. Of those that don't work regularly, this is either because they can't find regular work, or they have become physically and morally incapable of working regularly.[48]

These two dimensions of the problem are in fact related. Studies of dock work, which Booth interpreted as a 'distress meter' since the problem was particularly acute there, revealed a casual system of employment arising from the employer's desire for a flexible supply of unskilled labour. Each employer kept a surplus of hands from which casual workers were hired by the week, day, or even a few hours depending on the state of demand. Casual labourers are not so much unemployed as under-employed; their time is divided up between working and looking for work. This constant struggle for work with its irregular income led to the moral and physical deterioration of the casual worker to the point where they were incapable of performing regular work. In this way the docks were understood as illustrating how casual labour was a critical relay in the process of demoralization.[49]

It is worth looking more closely at what was written about the casual labourer. For this figure is the antithesis of the regular worker. In the problematization of the figure of the casual worker we see revealed a set of tacit presuppositions about the 'social' responsibilities which are attached to employment. To put it another way, casual labour reveals how the employment relation is a mechanism of 'government at a distance' – a concept mentioned in the Introduction – under various regimes of liberal rule. For the wage is at the centre of a set of assumptions and practices (saving, budgeting, etc.) through which wage-earners and their families take responsibility for various aspects of their own livelihoods – not simply because they are ordered to do so, but through notions of self-respect and obligation. How does casual labour illustrate the governmental functions of the employment relation?

First, as a form of employment, casual labour is seen to be inimical to the formation of self-reliant subjects, the 'private' correlates that all systems of liberal rule require if they are to be practicable as modes of government. This is most evident in financial matters. The most immediate problem for casual workers is that 'their average earnings for the year are so low that even with careful management they are unable to procure for themselves and their families the necessaries of healthy life'.[50] Efficient household budgeting had long been proffered as a technique for governing poverty. Yet as the Minority Report of the Royal Commission on the Poor Laws acknowledges, even the best housekeeper cannot budget upon a day-to-day basis – this being the way in which casual wages are earned.[51] Casual earnings are therefore not conducive to thrift. Furthermore, they provide no margin for saving. The Charity Organisation Society (COS) was forced to admit that more and more of London's workers

> were in receipt of wages ordinarily so small, or had opportunities of labour so precarious, that they had no competence out of which they could save for bad times, and thus at any period of unusual pressure they were brought down to utter penury.[52]

But casual labour is more than a problem of economic security. In its very organization it represents the failure of mechanisms that were crucial to the formation of 'character', and thereby, responsible and reliable individuals. One COS official explains that:

> The men flit from odd job to odd job; their 'characters' are not 'taken up'; when no records are kept, strenuous efforts to maintain a high moral standard do not necessarily secure a man a preference; and complete failure to maintain the ordinary standard of his class creates no prejudice

> against him in the eyes of a fresh employer. The world of work to the
> typical casual man is governed by chance; for the good are not more
> successful in securing work than the evil. No class within the community
> could withstand the demoralizing influence of such a view of life and such
> a system ... the clergy, the bar, or the professions generally.[53]

With casual employment, the tie that should join ethical conduct and
consequences for an individual is sundered. Since no account is taken
of the worker's performance they cannot be called to account for it
(nor get credit for it). So the casual worker has little incentive to act
responsibly. Accordingly, the kernel of many 'de-casualization' schemes
will be some technique for 'taking up character', making it legible and
visible so that it can operate as a site of self-investment and external
review.[54]

It will be seen later in this chapter that a line can be traced from this
concern with character to the emergence of the labour exchange and
the way it will archive the employment history of its population. Only it
is not a person's character that is given a hard, measurable, and governable form by such devices as the reference letter, the insurance stamp
booklet, and the labour exchange records. More specifically it is a
descendant of the notion of character, the 'employment record', that is
formed there. With this construct official practices are brought into line
with the ethos of the self-respecting worker – that his personal, familial
circumstances are private affairs.

Finally, on the subject of casual labour it should be noted how it is
also a problem for family life. Casual labour is held to undermine the
sexual division of labour around which the working class family is to be
organized.

> [The] chronic Under-employment of men is coincident with the employ-
> ment in factories and workshops, or on work taken out to be done at
> home, of a large number of mothers of young children who are thereby
> deprived of maternal care; with an ever-growing demand for boy-labour
> of an un-educational kind; and actually with a positive increase in the
> number of 'half-timers' (children in factories below the age exempting
> them from attendance at school). Thus we have, in increasing numbers
> (though whether or not in increasing proportion is not clear), men
> degenerating through enforced Unemployment or chronic Under-
> employment into parasitic Unemployable, and the burden of industrial
> work cast on pregnant women, nursing mothers, and immature youths.[55]

Female casual labour is interpreted as a kind of second-order demoral-
izing force because it deadens the man's need to work where marriage
is meant to sharpen it. As one investigation of the casual problem will
put it:

[W]hen the wife has 'set to' and is earning there is too often a tendency to slacken in the pursuit of work. The great influence of women's earnings in encouraging slackness among their husbands has been remarked upon in many quarters.[56]

Yet since most thinking about casual labour was guided by the male breadwinner norm, the problem of 'women dependent on their own earnings' was given little consideration. A national conference was organized by the Women's Industrial Council (WIC) to highlight this question in 1907.[57] Many of the participants stressed that unemployment could be harder on women in this category than it was for men. Not only were their wages lower, and women's trade unions and forms of mutual assistance almost non-existent, but most of the schemes to assist the unemployed presumed that those without work were male. In the Birmingham area, for instance, where most women's work was very seasonal, most distress committees assumed winter to be the slack period. As true as this may have been for many men, it was by no means the case for women's employment.[58]

The critical distinction the WIC conference urged was between women 'dependent on their own earnings' and married women. The conference participants endorsed the basic principle of the single family wage, but with the caveat that not all women were dependants, and in so far as they were not, in as much as they were self-supporting wage-earners, they had a right to assistance when unemployed. Moreover, the single family wage was seen as a practical measure that would reduce competition in female labour markets; for women who are 'habitual wage earners', a major problem was seen to be 'the wives of men out of employment – women who would not be, and ought not to be, in the labour market if their men-folk were either at work or sufficiently paid when they were at work'.[59]

It was along these lines that many proposals for de-casualization were to advance. From Booth to Beveridge, casual labour was seen in large part to be a problem of the maldistribution of population in relation to employment. One axis for its redistribution was provided by the principle of 'efficiency'. Paid employment was to be concentrated on the more efficient workers while the 'less efficient' were to be variously detained and retrained. However, a principle of gender identity provided a second axis. Both Beveridge and the Webbs envisaged a mode of 'social' government that operated in terms of a clear delineation of the spheres of family, social policy, and industry. This entailed a concentration of wage-earning activity on able-bodied men – what one might term the 'masculinization' of industrial labour – and its complement, closer regulation and support for women's maternal and domestic work. The Webbs even suggested 'boarding out' a widow's children with their mother on the condition that she abstained from industrial work.[60]

From issues of demoralization to vagrancy, 'boy labour' to hooliganism,[61] moral character, and prostitution,[62] casual labour became central to the 'social question' at the turn of the century precisely because it came to explain such diverse social problems. When it was first studied in detail by social inquirers like Charles Booth it was understood to be a problem endemic to certain trades. However, for Beveridge it was a *general* problem of the labour market. Comparing his analysis with Booth's, Beveridge wrote:

> All that is new here is the emphasis laid on the *general* character of the evil. Every trade tends to be chronically overstocked with labour in proportion as the demands of separate employers are fluctuating.[63]

In this way the focus of inquiry shifted. Where once it was a matter of relating a casual form of life to the anomalies of certain local labour markets, with Beveridge the labour market emerges as an object to be theorized in its own right. Unemployment begins to be conceptualized as an economic condition at this juncture where economic systems supplant problematic figures and forms of life as the primary objects of theoretical and empirical scrutiny.

THE DISCOVERY OF 'UNEMPLOYMENT'

So far I have noted the ways in which the problems of the unemployed and of casual labour were posed. In this section I want to trace briefly how, at the level of theoretical and empirical practices, a concept of unemployment is first formulated, and how it will fill the problem-space formerly occupied by the casual worker and the unemployed. With the opening up of a problem-space of unemployment it will become possible to think of approaches to the social problem, the government of population and individual in terms of a new object of regulation – the labour market.

While he set out to measure the extent of poverty in London, what Charles Booth somewhat inadvertently discovered was the extent to which 'questions of employment' were fundamental to the social question. Yet, despite his pioneering interest in labour markets, Booth's work belongs to the prehistory of theories of unemployment.

For Booth, casual labour pointed to a problem of 'overcrowding' in the labour market. (It is interesting how he seems to take this notion of 'overcrowding' from discussions of the late nineteenth-century housing crisis in the cities.) He expressed this in terms of his famous system of classes. He identified a 'class B', 'the very poor', which was incapable of working regularly, yet whose competition for work nevertheless deprived the more efficient classes above it from getting enough work and income. In this way, class B exerted a downward pull on these other classes. Booth's solution was consistent with other disciplinary approaches to the social problem: he called for labour colonies to be used to quarantine and recondition the members of this class.[64]

Booth explains why social inquirers found it so difficult to count the numbers of the unemployed. He states that 'the total number of the superfluous is the true measure of the unemployed'. Yet this surplus is disguised by the workings of the casual system which makes workers under-employed rather than wholly unemployed. However, he is unable to formulate a concept of unemployment. This is perhaps because he is still too close to the older problematic of the unemployed, with its mania for classifying types of person.

The task of making this final break from the problem of the un-employed to unemployment was to fall to a younger generation of social inquirers. In the case of Hubert Llewellyn-Smith and Beatrice Webb, they served their apprenticeship as social inquirers under Booth. Many of this generation – most significantly Llewellyn-Smith and Beveridge – came from Oxford University to work in the settlement movement in the poorest parts of London and other large cities.[65] With the social philosophy of new liberalism, and its repudiation of the liberal political economist's atomistic view of society, they combined a commitment to empirical, statistical analysis.

Llewellyn-Smith's contribution to the conceptualization of unemploy-ment lay with his novel taxonomy which cross-tabulated the different types of unemployed worker with the various types of trade 'fluctu-ation'. The latter ranged from the seasonal variations which afflicted trades like construction, through the stops and starts of dock work, to the seven-year cycles which governed employment in the great ship-yards. The aim of this analysis was to 'break up into their elements the congeries of industrial and social problems which are lumped together in common language as "the problem of the unemployed"'.[66] According to Harris, this analytic of fluctuations provided the basic framework for the study of the labour market for many years.[67]

However, it was only with Hobson and Beveridge that the typology of unemployed was fully displaced by a perspective which centred upon the economic. The new liberal economist and journalist J. A. Hobson was probably the first thinker to do this. As early as 1895, Hobson used the term 'unemployment' to describe 'all the forms of involuntary leisure suffered by the working classes'. He went on to state that his 'more scientific definition would, however, identify unemployment with the total quantity of human labour-power not employed in the production of social wealth, which would rank, under present conditions, as superfluity or waste'.[68]

Hence Hobson treats the unemployed in abstract terms: as a quantity of surplus labour ascribable to the workings of the industrial system. 'Personal causes, no doubt, explain in a large measure who are the individuals that shall represent the 10 per cent, "unemployed", but they are in no true sense even contributory causes of "unemployment".'[69] He was therefore critical of the tradition of the factual, empirical approach which stressed the different types of unemployment and unemployed worker – casual, seasonal, cyclical and so on. These only fragmented the problem and obscured the general, underlying principles. What Hobson advocated was 'a unified, organic treatment' of the question.[70] Hobson challenged orthodox liberal economics by suggesting that a situation of general over-production was not impossible. He ascribed this to a maldistribution of consuming power at the level of society: certain elements within the middle class, such as landlords and other rentiers, were in possession of savings which they kept idle. The solution to unemployment therefore required the implementation of policies (e.g., of personal taxation) which would redistribute purchasing power to the wage-earning classes who would spend it and boost the economy.

Like Hobson, Beveridge also sought to map the unemployed onto a space of variables and processes which are fundamentally economic; 'the inquiry must be essentially an economic one ... into unemployment rather than into the unemployed'.[71] But if Hobson linked unemployment to a dimension of economic life which Keynes would later theorize as the 'macroeconomic',[72] Beveridge instead situated it in the workings of the labour market.

Beveridge's argument, presented at length in his 1909 book, held that unemployment was a basic and general feature of the industrial system. It was in fact a normal feature of the labour market and economic life within the dynamic framework of capitalism. 'The problem of unemployment is the problem of the adjustment of the supply of labour and the demand for labour.'[73] The labour market was subject to constant (but always temporary) maladjustments which Beveridge attributed to three main causes: labour's failure to shift efficiently from 'decaying' trades to new ones; the retention of large reserves of surplus labour by employers in their bid to manage unpredictability in the economic system (this was the source of the casual labour problem); and swings in the trade cycle.

Beveridge proposed a policy of 'public organisation' for the labour market. This will be discussed at greater length in the following chapter. In many ways, it provided the theoretical rationale for the Liberal government's attempts to move unemployment policy beyond the 'relief of distress' paradigm which, I noted, underpinned the Unemployed Workmen Act 1905. But basically, 'public organisation' was based on two governmental technologies – the labour exchange and unemployment insurance. While a system of labour exchanges was to co-ordinate the supply and demand of labour across the entire economy, unemployment insurance was to effect a partial collectivization and temporal reallocation of labour's income, spreading it across the economic cycle. In this way Beveridge suggested a new line of development for social governance, arguing that the centre of gravity of the prevention of pauperism and social breakdown could be shifted from the traditional mechanisms of social policy onto the sphere of 'industry'. It was through the more efficient organization of the industrial sphere, rather than the relief system, that the liberal objectives of encouraging self-reliance, thrift, and individual security were to be sought.

There is one final point to be made about the early theorization of unemployment. As Harris has noted, it was carried out for the most part by a community which included very few professional economists.[74] Most of the intellectual work which set the foundations for our understanding of unemployment was done by individuals like Beveridge, operating in the tradition of empirically-based, ameliorative and administrative reform. Why did the emerging profession of economics contribute relatively little to understandings of unemployment before the First World War? Katznelson's analysis of the internal structure of turn-of-the-century social knowledge is insightful here. He suggests that economists' failure to confront unemployment at a theoretical level, i.e., as a *problem* for their discipline, was not a sign of their lack of social concern. The case of Alfred Marshall is illustrative of this. Marshall was a committed and leading New Liberal. His ambition was to found economics as a profession (he campaigned to institutionalize its teaching at Cambridge) and to link it to a rigorous objective and scientific analytical technique in order that it could serve more effectively in the promotion of social improvement. However, the paradox was that in making economics mathematical, individuals like Marshall almost inadvertently distanced it from the social field. Katznelson summarizes this moment well:

> Just at the moment when, in the late nineteenth and early twentieth centuries, the social tensions of markets and citizenship intensified under the impact of economic depressions, the radical transformations in industrial size and class structure entailed in the second industrial revolution, international rivalries for markets, a new geopolitics characterized by imperial ventures and, ultimately, by total war, the academic discipline of economics lost a good deal of its capacity to function as a practical policy science. In part this was a matter of distancing from practical affairs, in

part a flight to abstraction, in part a deliberate decision in favor of the ambitions of science at the expense of moral discourse.[75]

When unemployment finally emerges as a fully theorized object within economic discourse – and no more so than with Keynes' macro-economic explanation of this phenomenon – it will bear the imprint of this Marshallian moment. For unemployment will appear as a highly abstract, mathematical, almost 'metaphysical category',[76] and hence an object quite distinct from the social problem of unemployment with which social policy experts are concerned. For the main part of this century unemployment will exist as a problem that is defined as equally 'social' and 'economic'.

The first section of this chapter discussed certain conditions of possibility for the emergence of a discursive space, one in which theorists and social experts could offer contending theories about a new object: unemployment. One such condition, as we have seen, was the emergence of a concept and practice of regular employment. A condition of employment could only be delineated from one of unemployment once work came to be concentrated in the socio-spatial form of the factory or office, compressed into a normal working week, and set within a modern, bureaucratic system of employment relations. It was seen how the spread of factory legislation and certain trade union practices contributed to such transformations in the form of work.

This chapter has also demonstrated how the investigation and theorization of unemployment needs to be seen as a response to the late nineteenth-century social question. This was a period of public anxiety that the structure and stability of the Victorian social order was under threat. If society felt itself menaced by rumours of a growing criminal element or by deep, impersonal forces pulling it apart, then social experts like Beveridge and Booth provided what Helga Nowotny has called 'knowledge for certainty'.[77] They mapped and named the unknown, rendering it thinkable, debatable, and manipulable. This project was carried out by eugenicists, penologists, philanthropic inquirers and many other emerging forms of social expertise. The particular contribution of theorists of unemployment was to project the social problem on to a space of economic processes and categories. In this way they suggested how the economy could be mobilized to promote social objectives. For example, by organizing the labour market it was held that the various social dangers associated with casualism – child employment, improvidence, indigence, family breakdown – could be combated.

Lastly, this chapter has outlined the nineteenth-century discourse on 'the problem of the unemployed'. It noted that this is basically a problematic of 'relief': as with other disciplinary forms of governance, the morals and habits of the poor are its primary targets. Subsequent chapters will develop the point made in this one: that the discovery of unemployment signals a shift within discourses on the governance of poverty and society. For this moment opens up the possibility of forming and acting on new objects of regulation like the labour market (Beveridge) or the macroeconomy (Keynes). But these chapters will also show that there is a sense in which debates about unemployment never quite transcend 'the problem of the unemployed'. Its characteristic emphases – distinguishing between types of unemployed, punishing the workshy, etc. – will be articulated within various unemployment policy regimes during the twentieth century.

CHAPTER 2

INVENTING UNEMPLOYMENT: THE BIRTH OF THE LABOUR EXCHANGE

The last chapter examined the discovery of unemployment, tracing its formation as a *conceptual* object. This chapter deals with roughly the same time period, but begins to trace the construction of unemployment as an object of regulation. It does this in two stages. First, through a consideration of some of the most significant political programmes which, in competition with one another, sought to define the terms of a modern policy for unemployment. These programmes help to demarcate the field of possible ways of acting on unemployment. The relation between this field and the famous Liberal social legislation of the 1908–14 period is discussed. Second, as a way of demonstrating the strengths of a governmentality approach to social policy questions, a seemingly mundane administrative device is analysed: the labour exchange. Its significance lies not just with the fact that it brings a new regime of routine and comprehensive visibility to unemployment and the labour market. The labour exchange is also interesting as a prism through which to view new relationships of citizenship, power, and knowledge which take shape at the start of this century. These relations will be key features of welfare state governance.

THREE PROGRAMMES FOR GOVERNING UNEMPLOYMENT

I have explained how unemployment becomes an object of theoretical controversy. It is of course at the same time a site of political argumentation. Since political discourse is a powerful factor in establishing the horizon for what is thinkable in terms of policies, here I want to survey the main political programmes addressing unemployment at the turn of the century. The most influential of these was the campaign for the 'public organisation of the labour market' (POLM) which was advanced by a loose coalition of new liberals, social-imperialists, and Fabian socialists. It will be seen that this programme informs the construction of an actual unemployment policy before 1914. Before turning to POLM, however, I want to review two other programmes – those associated with organized labour, and the movement for Tariff Reform. While it might seem that these projects were 'defeated' by POLM, my argument will be that political programmes are never actualized in any straightforward way. It is possible to discern residual traces of the schemes proposed by Tariff Reformers and organized labour within the unemployment policy regime of the early twentieth century.

The Labour Movement and the 'Right to Work'

The turn of the century did not just see the beginnings of a perception of unemployment as a socio-economic phenomenon. It also saw a growing awareness on the part of politicians, social experts, and the public, that unemployment was a national, not a local issue. Several developments contributed to this new scale of perception. One was the realization that previously localized markets for goods and labour were increasingly interdependent so that there was a tendency for depressions to spread nationally. Another was the fact that social scientists were developing quantitative devices – such as statistical sampling – for representing and recording poverty and unemployment on a national scale.[1] But while both these factors were significant in enabling the 'nationalization' of the unemployment question, one should not ignore political dynamics – the force of electoral competition between the political parties. With the enfranchisement of working-class men, which began in 1867, unemployment gradually became an issue around which political parties were to compete.[2]

Richard Flanagan has shown how the fledgling Labour party advanced the issue of unemployment as part of its bid to become a mass party of the working class in the 1900s.[3] Along with other socialist groupings like the Social Democratic Federation and the Independent Labour Party, it had given qualified support for the Conservative's Unemployed Workmen Bill 1905. The understanding was that, however imperfect, such a measure began to acknowledge the state's responsibility to the unemployed, and could be improved by various amendments. But by 1907 the labour movement was shifting its attention to its own legislative proposals. Central here was the Right to Work Bill which, according to Ramsay Macdonald, 'recognizes the right of the unemployed workman to demand an opportunity to work'.[4]

The labour movement in fact held conflicting definitions of the unemployed, reflecting some of its own inner tensions. The response of the ILP to the partial and highly moralistic Unemployed Workmen Act had been to proclaim a very expansive conception, that 'the unemployed of both sexes and of all ages and conditions ... must be organised ... not merely the respectable, but the loafers and the wastrels'. As was seen in the previous chapter, there was sympathy within the ILP at this time for the view that women – though not *married* women – had a right to work as well as men.[6]

But when Labour came to propose its own Right to Work Bill in 1907–8, it was the more conventional, restrictive definition of the unemployed which it upheld. The Bill was strictly to exclude the undeserving elements; Ramsay Macdonald told the House of Commons how he 'hoped it would not again be said that the Labour Party had any sympathy with the loafer and shirker who tried to batten and fatten on public funds'.[7] In other words, Labour narrowed its definition of the unemployed as part of its bid to establish itself as a respectable, parliamentary force. This episode should remind us that the recurring concern to distinguish deserving from undeserving elements of the poor and the unemployed is not just a reflection of political and social authorities' desire to discipline the poor. It can also serve wider political purposes. In the age of plebiscitary politics this invidious distinction will function as the way in which parties and politicians of left and right seek to appeal to the electorate around social values of respectability, thrift, merit, and so on.

Now, the previous chapter noted that the Unemployed Workmen Act was associated with the discourse of 'the problem of the unemployed'. At best this Act bolstered and extended the various local efforts of charities and municipalities to relieve 'distress from want of employment' by situating these initiatives within a new legal and administrative framework. To what extent was the Right to Work Bill significantly different? The Right to Work Bill called for the creation of local unemployment committees which would monitor the labour market situation, provide labour exchanges, vet applicants for public works (e.g., reporting on cases where individuals refused to work), and assist in emigration. These committees were to be co-ordinated by a central authority which would plan schemes of public employment.[8]

What is interesting about the Right to Work campaign, then, is its proximity to the approach to the unemployed embodied by the Unemployed Workmen Act. To be sure, it is more sympathetic to trade union principles (such as paying the standard rate for public work); it looks to public funding whereas the Unemployed Workmen Act relied considerably on charitable donation; and it seeks to place experts drawn from labour and industry on its various committees rather than charity workers and Poor Law guardians. But as an administrative technique, it is basically the same. It relies upon the provision of public employment to address the unemployment problem. The case of the Right to Work campaign illustrates quite nicely the relative *scarcity* of governmental techniques, the fact that ideologies may oppose one another, yet rely on the same basic mechanisms to give effect to their governmental ambitions. For any given period or political problem, there exists a fairly limited range of ways of governing. Competing political programmes are often obliged to share them. New periods in politics often coincide with the invention of new techniques: social insurance is one, Keynesian economic management another.

Not surprisingly, the Right to Work Bill made little progress in a parliament in which Labour was a distinct minority. As Nikolas Rose has pointed out, 'rights' always require some form of technique by which they can be operationalized – made adjudicable, and so on. Public employment was incapable of operationalizing a right to work. But this does not mean that the Right to Work episode will not influence the course of the governance of unemployment in the twentieth century. It does in several ways.

First, the right to work idea resonated with the protests of the unemployed which broke out nationwide during 1907–08, a time of rising unemployment. It was hence part of the movement which provoked the Liberal Government to reconsider the unemployment question in 1908 and implement the kind of measures I shall discuss shortly.[9] Second, one should note that there is a mutation in the technology of public works. As long as it was set within the framework of orthodox economic policy, public works was very limited in what it could achieve in terms of job creation. However, with the shift in economic policy practice of the 1940s, most closely associated with Keynes' reformulation of economic theory, this technique is accorded a new efficacy. It ceases to be merely a method of temporarily and directly employing the unemployed. Instead, along with monetary and taxation policy, public works becomes an instrument capable of acting on aggregate demand in the national economy. In other words, public works becomes an instrument for governing the macroeconomy, and acting on the unemployed *indirectly*. Finally, it is evident that once the question of rights is introduced into debates about unemployment, it does not simply disappear just because it cannot be operationalized by the available technologies. Instead, it seems to migrate, provoking experimentation with, and attaching itself to new technologies of governance like social insurance, and full employment policy. In the twentieth century it gives both a democratic inflection.

Unemployment and Tariff Reform

I have already noted how the Labour Party fostered a politics of the unemployed in its bid to establish itself as a mass political movement. A comparable process was in evidence at other points across the political field. The urgent need to consolidate its working-class support led Conservatism to engage with the social field also. But there were other concerns structuring this engagement, besides a desire to cultivate popular electoral support. For Conservatism's articulation of the social question at the turn of the century largely took the form of social imperialism.

Social imperialism was a complex discursive formation which in fact cut across the political field. If its centre of gravity was on the right, it was nevertheless capable of temporarily accommodating Fabian socialists like the Webbs and Bernard Shaw, as well as ex-Liberals like the former Prime Minister, the Earl of Rosebery. Social imperialism was a response to the perception that Britain was ill-prepared to compete economically and militarily in the new age of imperialism with its traditional rivals like Germany, and with new industrial powers such as the USA. Britain's humiliating defeat in the Boer War was a focal point for such anxieties. Social imperialism represented 'a socialism of the Right, of order, social hierarchy, and bureaucratic control'.[10] It disparaged party politics and instead celebrated technical-administrative solutions focused upon a programme of 'national efficiency'. It called for a regeneration of society, industry, and the political system which would be organized from above – by a new breed of administrative experts, industrialists, and professional managers. In this way, a strand of Conservatism was accommodated to the idea of using the state to promote new social and economic objectives, particularly a larger role in technical education, and the regulation and planning of certain aspects of the economy.

Social imperialism's principal mode of intersection with the social field took the form of the campaign for Tariff Reform, launched in 1903 by the ex-Liberal Joseph Chamberlain.[11] In his bid to equip the Conservative party for mass politics, Chamberlain sought to popularize a link between foreign trade and the unemployment problem. Tariff reformers called for a protectionist trading system centred on the British Empire. Employment was to be steadied within this new political-economic space, while imperial solidarity, defensive strength, and domestic social reform would be financed by the foreign competitor rather than by higher domestic taxes.[12] As Chamberlain put it, 'those who try to induce you to believe that everything depends upon the price of corn are deceiving you. What you have to find is employment – plenty of employment at the best wages you can get for that employment'.[13]

Tariff Reform proved attractive to certain industrialists, especially within iron and steel, who favoured protection at a time when competition from the emerging industrial powers was beginning to pinch. But despite the imposition of the McKenna duties in 1915, British commercial policy did not move strongly towards protectionism until the 1930s.[14] With the international trading system crumbling, Britain imposed a general tariff in 1932. But in the period leading up to the First World War, the social pressure for tariff reform was checked by a series of factors, including the deeply embedded liberal orthodoxy of institutions like the Treasury, the revival of the economy between 1900 and 1914, and by an electorate (apparently associating protectionism with dearer food),[15] which decisively rejected the pro-tariff Conservatives in 1906.

Nevertheless, like the right to work, tariff reform had a legacy for the governance of unemployment even if it never successfully captured the policy agenda. One notable feature of Tariff Reform was its location within a populist discourse on unemployment which would periodically resurface in the course of the century – a discourse and a politics which, in its bid to win support from what it perceives as the disaffected base of society, associates unemployment with a variety of threats posed to the integrity of the nation. In the case of Tariff Reform, it is the penetration of nation/empire by foreign commodities which becomes the problem. But equally this discourse can take more overtly racialized forms, such as when unemployment and social disorder are blamed upon the presence of 'aliens' and 'immigrants'.[16] While this discourse draws a link among the movements of trade, people, and unemployment, it has not successfully underpinned such associations with its own theory; it has not produced novel concepts or new economic categories.[17] This is perhaps a sign of the strength of liberal orthodoxy within economics.

Public Organisation of the Labour Market

There is one last political programme for governing unemployment which I want to review here. The campaign for the POLM is arguably the programme which was to prove most influential on the course of actual policy development.

The most concise programmatic statement of the POLM agenda was the Minority Report of the Royal Commission on the Poor Laws which was drafted by Sidney and Beatrice Webb. However, the theory on which it was based was mostly supplied by Beveridge's work on unemployment. This was highlighted in the previous chapter. The aspect of POLM which I want to bring out here is how it is propounded as an alternative mode of governing poverty and unemployment from that expressed in the discourse on 'the problem of the unemployed' and associated more generally with the Poor Law.

The objective of Poor Law and philanthropic practices had long been the prevention of pauperism. However, according to the Webbs, strict adherence to the Poor Law's deterrent principles (or conversely, their lax application) was in fact manufacturing pauperism:

> So long as the conditions afforded by the Poor Law authority are 'deterrent', few will apply for maintenance ... even at the cost of foregoing the treatment they really need ... As a Destitution Authority, it is inherently incapable of bringing pressure to bear on the lives and wills of these people, at the time when such pressure may be effective, namely long before they have become destitute, at the time they are taking the first step towards the evil parasitism to which they will eventually succumb.[18]

Furthermore, from the Chamberlain Circular to the Unemployed Workmen's Act, those methods of relieving the unemployed beyond the Poor Law were likewise held to be fundamentally flawed. Their most obvious failing was that the non-pauperizing, public relief work they offered for the temporarily out of work was invariably overrun by casual labour. Not only was the problem of the 'bona fide' unemployed left ostensibly unresolved, but the problem of casual labour was exacerbated. As Beveridge pointed out, the provision of temporary relief work was yet one more way of propping up casual life. Moreover, it blurred the moral distinction between a condition of self-support through wage labour and dependence on charity. For these reasons, the extant machinery of social policy was found to be unsuited to the problem of unemployment.[19]

What sort of alternative did POLM suggest? In essence, POLM sought to shift the locus of 'prevention' from relieving practices, where it had been located in the nineteenth century, to industry – or more specifically, the labour market. If unemployment was a problem of industry, then it was this sphere which had to be organized by the state along preventative lines. As such, POLM represented a critical meeting place where new liberal political philosophy intersected with practical questions. For the New Liberals had called for 'the conscious organisation of society and an enlarged conception of the State' in order to tackle 'that "huge unreformed monster" the social question'.[20]

But how is the organization of the labour market supposed to address the problem of unemployment? As Beveridge saw it:

> The problem of unemployment is the problem of the adjustment of the supply of labour to the demand for labour. The supply of labour in a country is, in the widest sense, the supply of population ... At the

threshold, therefore, of the present inquiry lies the general question as to the relations of population and industry.[21]

For Beveridge unemployment policy turned on the government of the relations between 'population' and 'industry'. It had to recognize, to begin with, that the three principal economic factors associated with unemployment – cyclical and seasonal variations in industrial activity, the need for reserves of labour, and the rise and decline of specific industries – were all *necessary* features of industrial life under capitalism. There is, as such, no 'cure' for them within the remit of 'practical politics'. The first problem of unemployment policy then was: how to palliate their deleterious social consequences, how to buffer population from industry's shocks and disturbances? The second problem of unemployment policy ran the other way: how to provide industry with an adaptable, mobile and efficient working population? This two-way relationship was to constitute the field of unemployment policy as Beveridge saw it.

The relationship of population to industry could be posed in this way because governmental technologies capable of forming and linking these entities in new ways could now be envisaged. For POLM, these technologies were principally the labour exchange system and some form of unemployment insurance. In each case, what was suggested was that industry must and now could be made to secure the population in the way that liberal political economy had always imagined it would; Beveridge described his programme as a 'policy of making reality correspond with the assumptions of economic theory'.[22]

How are these administrative techniques to function in the governance of unemployment and poverty? Let us take the labour exchanges first. These were to counter the pervasive casual employment which, as demonstrated in the previous chapter, occupied a central place in thinking about unemployment and social problems by the turn of the century. A national system of labour exchanges, traversing the country, was to 'organise' the labour market.

> [A]ll the irregular men for each group of similar employers should be taken on from a common centre or Exchange, and ... this Exchange should so far as possible concentrate employment upon the smallest number that will suffice for the work of the group as a whole; ... successive jobs under different employers should, so far as possible, be made to go in succession to the same individual, instead of being spread over several men each idle over half his time.[23]

The objective of this policy of 'de-casualization', then, was to use an administrative technique to polarize the employment spectrum where

casual labour represented the grey area impeding a proper differentiation of the industrious worker and the unemployable. It was to
separate out a body of workers capable of working regularly, from a
surplus which was deemed to be in need of restorative treatment,
retraining, and possibly retirement. It was to fabricate regular work
regimes for the majority, so that they would be capable of governing
themselves and their families on a properly independent basis. And it
was to reveal the less-efficient members of the workforce who must be
the subjects of greater discipline.[24]

Beveridge thought that some system of insurance could offer a
'second line of attack on the problem of unemployment'. Whereas
labour exchanges were aimed at the casual problem, unemployment
insurance was directed towards the labour aristocracy who, it will be
argued in Chapter 3, actually invented this technique. Beveridge
interpreted the insurance principle quite broadly as

> any process whereby each of a number of workmen sets aside something
> of his wages while earning in order to obtain an allowance in case of
> unemployment ... Its essence is for the individual workman an averaging
> of earnings between good and bad times, and for the body of workmen
> a sharing of the risk to which they are all alike exposed.[25]

If certain socialist programmes sought to abolish the wage principle as
part of their response to poverty and worker insecurity, unemployment
insurance represents a technique for social-izing it. It maintains the
capitalist wage mechanism intact, at the centre of a set of liberal
assumptions and practices concerning self-support, individual reward,
and the proper distinction between the public and the private. But at
the same time, it makes the wage serve social functions, namely provide
for the unemployed worker(s) in times of temporary depression. The
contribution that social insurance will make to the governance of
unemployment is discussed more fully in the next chapter.

In concluding this discussion of POLM, it is worth noting how POLM
signals a shift in the status and significance of poverty within political
and economic discourse. For classical political economy and the liberalism of the architects of the New Poor Law, poverty was a fixed datum.
It was the natural and inevitable condition of the vast majority of
the population. It was also a necessary condition: the spur to labour.
'Without a large proportion of poverty, there would be no riches, since
riches are the offspring of labour, while labour can only result from a
state of poverty.'[26]

However, by the start of the twentieth century, when viewed through
the lens of new liberalism – or, for that matter, social imperialism –
poverty and unemployment are no longer the precondition of the

wealth of the nation. Instead, they are registered as a cost, one whose magnitude 'first in the millions of days of enforced idleness of productive labourers, and secondly in the degradation and deterioration of character and physique ... can scarcely be exaggerated'.[27] Accordingly, the power of the state comes to be linked up with social problems like poverty and unemployment. This point must be kept in mind as we turn to examine the developments by which unemployment comes to be placed at the centre of the modern social policy system.

FROM PROGRAMMES TO PRACTICES: THE BIRTH OF THE LABOUR EXCHANGE

The previous chapter showed how an economic understanding of unemployment is formulated in the context of wider debates about the social question. It concluded with the argument that this event is significant for a history of the regulation of poverty since it opens up the possibility of acting on the social by manipulating the labour market. This chapter has surveyed three different political programmes which propose ways of governing unemployment. Having shown how unemployment is formed as a theoretical concept, and as the object of political debates, in this final section I want to turn to a different question. How is unemployment formed as a regulable object? How is it institutionalized so that only certain experiences and situations will count as 'unemployed' and not others? How does it become the object of administrative techniques? How is it applied as a regulatory category to individuals and populations? How are new forms of expertise brought to bear on this object?

One way to understand the constitution of unemployment as an administrative field is in terms of the governmental technologies which make it visible and manipulable. An important respect in which the present study differs from other research in the area of unemployment is the manner in which it can be read as a history of unemployment policy written from the perspective of these technologies. The rest of this chapter considers the labour exchange in this light.

Labour Exchanges and Liberal Social Policy, 1908–1911

The legislation to initiate the labour exchange system passed uncontroversially through Parliament in 1909. By February 1914 there were 423 exchanges in the United Kingdom which registered more than two million workers per year.[28] Churchill's arrival at the Board of Trade had provided the political impetus for the undertaking, and he had recruited Beveridge to the Board as his chief architect. Along with social insurance, the technique of the labour bureau was already widely established in Germany; Churchill, Beveridge, Lloyd George, Llewellyn Smith, and leading civil servants all made study-tours there in the 1900s. As Churchill had explained to his Prime Minister: 'Underneath ... the immense disjointed fabric of social safeguards and insurances which has grown up by itself in England, there must be spread – at a lower level – a sort of Germanised network of state intervention and regulation.'[29]

A system of labour exchanges formed part of the social policy reforms that were pioneered by the Liberal Government between 1908 and 1911. In a flurry of legislative activity which gathered pace as Asquith became Prime Minister in 1908 and Lloyd George first entered the Cabinet,[30] the Liberal government created a range of institutions which were to transform the governance of poverty and welfare. As well as the labour exchanges there was a compulsory scheme of social insurance for unemployment and sickness (1911), a system of trade councils to regulate the low-paid, 'sweated' industries (1909), and a scheme of non-contributory old-age pensions (1906). Equally important were the first steps towards a graduated income tax which Lloyd George introduced in his budget of 1908 since these were to pave the way to the social-ization of fiscal policy.

These reforms are significant for a history of the regulation of poverty and social policy for several reasons. First, they represent the central state's first foray into the field of social insurance. As such, they mark the beginning of a new mode of relationship between states and individuals around poverty. Individuals are no longer addressed solely as paupers, beggars, or supplicants, but also as citizens bearing certain entitlements with regard to the social field. This matter is pursued at greater length in Chapter 3. Second, these measures circumvented the vexing matter of what to do with the Poor Law. Rather than reforming it, these reforms set in place new national bureaucracies which were to take their subjects out of the Poor Law's orbit.[31] And as national organizations, these bureaucracies gave recognition to the fact that issues like unemployment, and the welfare of the workforce, were matters of national, not just local, significance. Third, they built upon changes which had already been initiated at the end of the previous century, such as the creation of a system of workmen's compensation for industrial accidents, or the various social functions, like child welfare services and public housing, which local authorities had come to perform. As such, they betoken not a turning away from the ethos of voluntarism and self-help individualism, but rather an acknowledgement that for liberal individualism to serve as a viable formula for government, its subjects will require forms of support and assistance from the state. In other words, the state will have to resource the individual and the community before the latter will be in a position to exercise liberal freedoms and responsibilities.[32] Fourth, the Liberal reforms see the creation of central agencies which will bring official expertise to bear on a permanent basis upon the social question.[33]

These reforms have been widely interpreted by the social policy literature as initiatives which laid the foundations for the modern welfare state. By taking the example of the labour bureau, and by analysing its technical aspect, the following section seeks to offer a different perspective on some of the new relations of welfarism and social citizenship which were being anticipated by these social policy measures. For the bureau offers us a diagram: it explicates relations and forms of governance which become so prevalent that we have come to take them for granted. But in studying the bureau we will see something else as well. The social policy literature treats unemployment insurance and labour bureaux as *responses to* the problems of unemployment and poverty. But they can also be regarded as constitutive of the problems they seek to act on. The labour bureau does not simply find unemployment already there. It produces unemployment, as well as a particular set of social and administrative relations, in a particular form. In a sense, we are talking about the invention of unemployment.

The Labour Exchange as a 'Diagram'

The main political argument for labour exchanges was that they should address the casual employment problem which was seen as central to the unemployment question. They were to be instruments for making the labour market work more efficiently, weeding out the 'unemployable', and providing industry with a better grade of worker. They were therefore a practical correlate of the wider debates about 'national efficiency' which circulated in the 1900s, and provided a common ground for new liberals and social imperialists. Labour bureaux had a second purpose which was to monitor the labour market and provide an infrastructure for the administration of unemployment insurance.

The labour exchange failed to make a powerful impact, at least as far as the objective of de-casualizing trades like dock work went.[34] However, it is not the success or failure of the labour exchange at fulfilling the explicit ambitions of its designers that interests me here. What is more to the point are other developments in the government of labour, poverty and population which it can illuminate, and the transformation in which it is subsequently involved. In what follows I shall argue that the labour exchange offers us a 'diagram', the 'bureau', for understanding these changes. François Ewald has suggested that insurance offers us the diagram for explicating twentieth-century government.[35] Yet government is surely too complex and diverse an affair to be captured by a single diagram. Its interpretation requires numerous diagrams, of which the bureau is but one. A significant one, never-theless, given that the welfare state is surely as much, if not more, about bureaucracy than it is insurance – especially for the populations who fall beyond the latter's scope.

The Bureau and the Social Citizen

First, one can ask, what sort of relationship between individuals and social experts does the bureau presuppose? The following observation by the system's first general manager is telling:

> [T]he system is industrial and not eleemosynary [charitable]. Every attempt has been made to free the Labour Exchanges from any form of association with the Poor Law, charity, or the relief of distress, and to give them the character of a piece of industrial organisation of which any man may avail himself and with as little loss of self-respect as is involved in using the post office or a public road … The questions asked of work-people at the Exchanges relate solely to their industrial qualifications and not to their poverty, family circumstances, thrift, or similar matters.[36]

Clearly, this particular piece of governmental technology has its con-ditions of emergence in the failure of Poor Law and public relief approaches to the unemployed. The unorganized, molecular resist-ances of all those 'respectable' workers who rejected the offer of work or assistance as long as these involved the discrimination of the guardians and 'benevolent persons', as long as they attracted the stigma of the Poor Law; the strategies of other groups who organized them-selves as the unemployed and demanded to be treated as workers and not as supplicants when they besieged the workhouse;[37] these myriad acts of refusal and contestation mean that relieving functions, if they are to have any purchase on the situation of the poor, will have to seek out a different social and cultural form. One of the forms they find is the labour bureau, a social form which – by presenting itself as an industrial and not an 'eleemosynary' intervention, as a 'public service to the citizens'[38] – seeks to win the acceptance and compliance of the in-dustrial worker. Certain commentators have rightly highlighted the disciplinary functions of the labour bureau.[39] However, this singular emphasis on it as an instrument of power misses the point that the bureau also encodes popular resistance to prior forms of control. To some extent, at least, it acknowledges the *power* of the subordinated.

As a new setting for administrative practices the labour bureau seems to contribute to a bifurcation in the identity of its subject. Organized charity evaluated individuals in terms of their 'character' – a rather totalizing and holistic conception of the self. However, the bureau operates in terms of a splitting of the self so that there is now a formal distinction between the public, industrial aspect to a person's character, and their private self. In the former sphere individuals will be represented and assessed in terms of their industrial records not their character; they will become subjects of interventions like vocational guidance, unemployment insurance, industrial training, and industrial psychology, which act on this circumscribed aspect of their existence, but which are not to intrude upon the 'private' sphere of domestic and familial relations. When the labour exchange does become a setting for inquiries into 'personal' matters – as it will between the wars when the payment of unemployment insurance benefits will depend in part upon the worker's domestic situation – this will provoke considerable antagonism.

Information-Exchanging Machines

Perhaps the most significant thing about the bureau for the purposes of this study is its function in the production of new types of knowledge about unemployment. As an interface with the unemployed who pass through its door it was to make available to the state and its experts a new cache of social and economic knowledge.

This social knowledge is principally a biographical account of the unemployed, taking the form of millions of standardized forms, insurance cards, and dossiers accumulated by the labour exchange system. Combined with the new statistical techniques of sampling which were being developed by such statisticians as A. L. Bowley by the mid-1900s,[40] this record meant that it would be possible to analyse the unemployed population on a national basis, breaking it down by region, sex, industry, age, and so on. In this way, various sub-categories of the unemployed are produced – youth unemployed, unemployed women, etc.[41]

But as well as a knowledge of the social profile of the unemployed, the data produced by the bureau offered a major development in the statisticalization of unemployment, and a new type of representation of the labour market. The Majority Report of the Royal Commission on the Poor Law had expressed excitement at this prospect, anticipating that a national labour exchange system

> would give practically accurate data and records of the amount, character, and intensity of industrial depression or unemployment. It would afford the central as well as the local authority a vantage ground from which to watch over and deal with the results of distress from want of work.[42]

Previous methods for tracking unemployment, like trade union benefit returns and Poor Law relief records, were specific to a trade or locale, or like social surveys were essentially 'snapshots'. They offered a partial or static depiction of the situation. The system of bureaux holds out the prospect of being able to 'see the whole labour market and all the jobs that offer'.[43] In this respect it comes close to fulfilling the aspirations Booth invested in his Poverty maps, where, in contrast with the narrative descriptions of the poor produced by his contemporaries, 'it is in effect the whole population that comes under review'.[44]

Like the countless other inscription devices which theorists of government have highlighted (e.g., maps, tables, charts, and reports), the function which these labour market statistics serve is literally one of *re*-presentation. These rather prosaic technologies are essential to the practice of governance because they make complex and disparate social processes visible at a political centre, such as the Labour Department of the Board of Trade, where they can form a basis for political debate and calculation. For instance, we find the Webbs suggesting that the data provided by the labour exchange could be used by planners to help them schedule public work so as to 'regularize' fluctuations in the business cycle.[45]

But on what basis can the bureau aspire to produce this global perspective? We need to recall its function as a 'service to the citizen': it offers information on job vacancies and, increasingly after 1911, it will administer unemployment benefits. It offers the unemployed incentives to render information to it.[46] In this sense it functions as a sort of information exchanging machine. The bureau places intelligence about industry and population in a reciprocal relation: it dispenses information to its users – constituting an 'organized and intelligent fluidity of labour'[47] – while at the same time it processes their countless signals to produce a moving picture of the labour market at all its levels.

In this way the bureau is a diagram highlighting the transactional aspect of emerging forms of social governance. In labour exchanges, but also in all the other sites, such as Tuberculosis Dispensaries, child welfare clinics, and citizen's advice bureaux, where basically this same technology is deployed from the start of this century, we have an interface where knowledge about individuals and populations is accumulated and made available to programmers for regulating the social and economic machine.

These various bureaux can be understood in terms of practices of 'government at a distance'. They are dispensing information to their respective populations, concerning opportunities in the labour market for young people, or sanctioned forms of child-rearing practice. Unlike more overtly despotic and penal approaches to the poor, such information-exchanging machines presuppose an individual who is already well socialized, already conscious of his or her social responsibilities. They presuppose individuals who have been well drilled by the various bourgeois and popular forms of responsibilization which infiltrated the social body in the nineteenth century. Although we should not ignore their capacity to discipline, categorize, segregate (e.g., weeding out the 'malingerer'), it is important to note that the bureau seeks to govern unemployment by enlisting and promoting the aspirations of the individual to find work; it governs *with* the unemployed.

Seeing and Governing Unemployment

The labour exchange system produces a space in which unemployment is made observable – not unlike the way that for Foucault the asylum, the clinic, or the prison help to make possible the specialist classifi-cations, knowledges, and practices which constitute madness, disease, poverty, and delinquency as positivities. The counterpart to this new visibility accorded to unemployment is the advent of experts authorized to administer and speak about it. It means that the Labour Department, and its successor, the Ministry of Labour, will become the repository of an official expertise about unemployment. The bureau is a site where power and knowledge enmesh in a circular relationship. The Webbs illustrate this nicely:

> [A] demonstrably perfect and popularly-accepted *technique*, either with regard to Unemployment, or with regard to the treatment of the Unemployed, has not yet been worked out. No such *technique* can ever be more than foreshadowed until it is actually being put in operation ... [A] century ago, no one knew how to administer a fever hospital ... Yet it was only by establishing hospitals that we learnt how to make them instruments of recovery for the patients and of a beneficent protection for the rest of the community ... What has been effected in the organisation of Public Health and Public Education can be effected ... in the Public Organisation of the Labour Market ... We have still to work out by actual practice the appropriate *technique*.[48]

Having compared the labour exchange in its relation to unemployment with the enclosed spaces Foucault offers as conditions of possibility for madness, medicine, and so on, we should note a significant difference. Foucault's prison–workhouse–asylum series functions by quarantining and confining problem populations; it operates a tactic of physical con-finement. This is not really the case with the labour exchange. Instead, it belongs to an architecture which, as Robin Evans has explained,[49] flourishes after 1840. The bureau belongs to a series of building types and other spaces which includes the public bath, street improvements, the public library, the model dwelling, the maternity clinic, and the Board school. The emergence of these new spaces signals the shift from reforms which target those on the margins of the social body to interventions which tackle society itself.[50] These are the spaces not of 'aberrant' sub-populations, but populations with the potential for aberration from any one of the myriad norms which come to striate the social body.

It is not that there is no longer a use for the more archaic spaces of confinement. It is instead the case that they are accorded an auxiliary role. The labour colony becomes a place of last resort for the recalcitrant, for the small core of unemployables. But even then, this older tactic is influenced by the new: the labour colony of the nineteenth century becomes a source of retraining and recuperation as belief in the redeemability of subjects strengthens.

What this study offers is not a more accurate or more truthful analysis concerning the phenomenon of unemployment – its causes, consequences, or policies. For unemployment is not being treated here as a pregiven thing-in-itself. The aim of the book is instead to account for some of the social, epistemological, institutional, and other types of conditions under which it becomes possible to speak of a problem of unemployment; the rules governing what can be said about it and by whom; and the techniques which will be used to govern it. The first part of this chapter reviewed some of the ways that unemployment is constructed within political discourse. The second part, through its analysis of the labour bureau, has demonstrated that it is not just through narrative or rhetoric, however, that unemployment can be said to be constructed. At the same time that it seeks to govern unemployment, the labour exchange also plays an active and creative role in as much as it makes this phenomenon visible. It constructs its object at a technical level.

However, the birth of the labour exchange gives us but one site where unemployment could be said to be 'invented'. In the next chapter we encounter the technology of social insurance: the application of insurance concepts and techniques to the problem of joblessness will shape what it is we understand by unemployment.

CHAPTER 3

GOVERNING UNEMPLOYMENT AS A 'RISK'

The premise of this volume is that an exploration of some of the different ways in which unemployment has been problematized can furnish us with important insights about social governance. This study is also motivated by the claim that valuable insights about governance are possible through focusing attention at the level of the technical, at the means by which issues are rendered governable. Since the evolution of unemployment policy has been narrated many times in terms of the history of ideas, then a study which traces changes at the level of governmental techniques is timely.

Such a project would obviously be radically incomplete without a consideration of the place of social insurance within the history of governing unemployment. Accordingly, this chapter covers the same time period (roughly the 1890s to 1914) as the previous two, when public debate was grappling for appropriate models to visualize the nature of unemployment, and to devise mechanisms for addressing it. Whereas the previous chapter highlighted the labour exchange, this one examines the effects of the deployment of unemployment insurance. To put it another way, it is about governing unemployment as a *risk*.

The objectives of the chapter are threefold. First, it will try to demonstrate that the advent of social insurance consolidates a sociological as opposed to a moral perception of the nature of unemployment. It does this by governing unemployment as a 'risk', as a *probability* pertaining to a given population just like mortality, sickness, injury, etc. The second objective of the chapter is to show how social insurance also redefines unemployment at a more routine, practical level. For unemployment insurance, considered as a system of social administration, embodies a set of norms and practices for deciding the question of who and what is to count as 'unemployed'. Finally, the chapter will offer a series of reflections on unemployment insurance and subjectivity. The aim is to highlight the fact that insurance practices assume and enjoin particular forms of individuality in their subjects. We should, therefore, be suspicious of arguments which simply equate social or welfarist governance with collectivism, and neoliberalism with a renewed individualism. These equations miss the fact that both these strategies govern at the level of the individual and the population simultaneously, albeit in strikingly different manners.

But before I turn to these analytical questions, I shall provide a brief summary of the historical context for the inception of unemployment insurance in the UK.

SOCIAL INSURANCE FOR UNEMPLOYMENT?

The previous chapter identified the period between about 1895 and 1914 as something of a turning point in terms of social legislation, and highly significant for the purposes of this study. For this period saw the creation of a national labour exchange system, an important technology for the way it was to enhance the status of unemployment as an empirical entity, and constitute the labour market as a national object. But labour exchanges were hardly the centrepiece of these Liberal reforms. That accolade must go to social insurance.

The key Act was the National Insurance Act 1911. For John Williams and Karel Williams this marks a major step in the emergence of 'a cautious strategy of giving very limited sums of money to the poor'.[1] This is a nice phrase since it captures the novelty of a response to mass indigence which we take for granted today. The 1911 Act was not the first national scheme to 'give money to the poor'. For instance, there had been the Old Age Pensions Act of 1908. However, this was not insurance-based: it was non-contributory, and eligibility for a pension was conditional, among other things, upon a person's previous good conduct.[2]

The 1911 Act provided coverage for two areas: national health and unemployment insurance. From a political perspective, the former was by far the more contentious, since it had to negotiate the vested interests of the friendly societies, the commercial insurance industry, and the medical profession.[3]

But if state-organized insurance for sickness was the more controversial, the use of this method for the purposes of relieving unemployment was a more innovative and daring measure. Policy makers had studied German social insurance in particular when devising national health insurance. Bismarck's Germany had also provided a template for the labour exchange experiment.[4] But no state provided social insurance for unemployment. The consensus was that unemployment was too difficult to verify, and there was little precedent for it. Nevertheless, although there were no state unemployment schemes available for British policy-makers to study, there were other initiatives within the larger field of unemployment insurance which they could look towards.[5] The setting for the first of these was the labour movement.

Although there existed a flourishing commercial insurance industry in nineteenth-century Britain, and alongside it a non-commercial sector comprising benevolent societies and friendly societies,[6] the only bodies with experience at running some sort of insurance scheme for unemployment in Britain were the trade unions. As the Board of Trade had noted, 'knowledge of the character, suitability, and industry of their members makes the trade unions the best to deal with "respectable men temporarily in distress owing to their inability to obtain employment"'.[7] The trade union movement had a proven record of providing assistance to its unemployed members. In his study of trade union provision, Beveridge classified this assistance in terms of 'tramping' and 'stationary' benefits. Many unions and societies provided some combination, but the emphasis was very much towards the stationary benefit as the century progressed.[8] These 'out of work' benefits were never available to more than a privileged minority of mostly skilled workers. Nevertheless, by 1908 there were 1059 unions – with 2 357 381 members – paying some sort of benefit to assist with travel, removal, or assistance.[9]

A second area to which policy-makers looked in devising the 1911 scheme consisted of a series of experiments with insurance schemes in continental Europe.[10] Several municipalities, such as Leipzig and Cologne, had provided subsidies to voluntary schemes of unemployment insurance, while in the Swiss canton of St. Gall there had been a failed attempt at a compulsory scheme. However, the most notable of these schemes was in the Belgian municipality of Ghent. What the social insurance literature came to describe as the 'Ghent system' involved encouraging trade union provision through public subsidies. It was the Ghent model which many experts on social insurance recommended for Britain,[11] as did both sides of the Royal Commission on the Poor Laws.

The 1911 Act did embody aspects of the Ghent model. It offered public subsidies to existing trade union schemes.[12] But by far its more significant and novel feature was that it also established a state-run scheme. This was cautious and narrow in its coverage, owing to its experimental nature. It covered some 2.25 million workers, mainly in shipbuilding, engineering, building, and construction – all trades which experienced neither chronic nor irregular unemployment, trades that were therefore deemed properly 'insurable'. A majority of those covered were skilled workers, and nearly all male. Despite its rather experimental status, the 1911 scheme established the format for unemployment insurance for many years to come: in contrast to the German social security system, contributions and payments were to be 'flat rate' and set at a rather miserly level so as not to encourage 'malingering';[13] the scheme was to be tripartite, with the state, employers, and employees all paying into the fund, and with representatives of the latter two groups playing a part in its management; and it was to be compulsory on the trades and sectors it targeted.[14]

The compulsory nature of the scheme made it vulnerable to criticisms that it was ill-suited to Britain's liberal and voluntaristic political culture. Yet two factors seem to have predisposed policy makers to go in this direction. The first was the widely recognized limitation of voluntary insurance. With the Ghent model 'there remained, in addition to those who might enjoy subsidised voluntary insurance, an uninsurable residue, a conglomeration of improvidents, who were often the most menaced, the most unhappy, the most dangerous from the point of view of a sound social order and a good organisation of the labour market'.[15] If the world of the insecure and seriously impoverished worker was to be brought within insurance coverage, then a voluntary scheme was inadequate to the task.

But second, there was Churchill's stated desire to involve employers in the governance of the unemployed on a systematic and permanent basis. 'Their responsibility is undoubted, their co-operation indispensable.'[16] As with workmen's compensation, this was in part about recognizing that the employers had a financial responsibility for unemployment, now that unemployment was officially perceived as a necessary and not an incidental feature of industrial life. But also by making unemployment insurance compulsory, the scheme enlisted the employer in its management and acquired an economy of administration that was beyond commercial and industrial assurance. Employers were 'enrolled', in the sense in which network theorists use that term, in governmental arrangements;[17] they were accorded a vital role, stamping insurance cards and verifying the truth of the unemployment of former employees. This was part of the genius of social insurance as one commentator saw it, 'it is this cheap collection of the pence which enables so much to be given for such small payment'.[18] The official centre of the administrative system may have been with the labour exchanges. But as a governmental assemblage, unemployment insurance was considerably more extensive and heterogeneous in its makeup, combining nominally 'public' and 'private' actors and arte-facts, and traversing the conventional boundary between 'state' and 'society'.[19]

Unemployment insurance began as merely one amongst a 'battery' of Edwardian policies for addressing a problem which was perceived to be multifaceted. If it was not initially perceived as a 'general or universal technique of welfare', this is nevertheless what it became by the middle of the century.[20] A consideration of the political and institutional dynamics by which state insurance expanded to cover a large majority of full-time industrial workers is beyond the remit of this chapter.[21] It is the fact of this dominance which is significant for this account of historical changes in the governance of unemployment. For insurance will shape the way unemployment is perceived, who is to count as unemployed, what kind of phenomenon it is. It does this, as will be shown in the following section, by governing unemployment in terms of 'risk'.

GOVERNING UNEMPLOYMENT AS RISK

A great deal of the political science and historical sociology literature on the inception of social insurance explores the social and political dynamics surrounding insurance schemes. Typically, social insurance systems have been theorized in terms of the factors and frameworks that best explain their evolution – the relative strength of labour movements,[22] the influence of well-organized and purposeful state bureaucrats,[23] but also the process of industrialization itself.[24] Such research has greatly enhanced our knowledge of the history of social insurance and welfare states more generally. It has been particularly important in pointing up differences between welfare states.

However, the research of François Ewald has demonstrated the promise of bringing a governmentality perspective to bear on the sub-ject.[25] What sets Ewald apart from other approaches is that he in-vestigates insurance as both a form of political imaginary and a political technology; he is therefore interested in the political and epistemological *effects* of insurance. This is significant for the purposes of the present study: bringing social insurance to bear upon the field of unemployment serves to institutionalize a *particular* kind of knowledge and treatment of the problem.[26] Let us see how.

Bound up with the practice of insurance is what Ewald terms the 'insurantial imaginary'. Within this 'imaginary' unemployment appears as an 'accident', a 'risk', which – just like death, sickness, or injury – affects a given population with a certain probability and inevitability. Insurance therefore embodies a sociological and statistical view of the world. Its application to the social field coincides, more or less, with the advent of labour departments and ministries within states which collect information and produce aggregate data about their workforces. Such data permits a social view of the hazards of employment. From the point of view of the individual, unemployment can be cataclysmic, a 'unique disaster'. However, '[i]n the life of a great organisation', as Beveridge put it, it is 'a phenomenon impressive and familiar'.[27] The insurance view of unemployment therefore affirms the sociological view of unemployment as a normal, inevitable, and in many ways necessary feature of industrial life. It stands at odds with the moralizing, fault-finding perspective which Chapter 1 equated with the nineteenth century's 'problem of the unemployed'.

But insurance is also 'an agreement to pay a certain sum of money as compensation against a loss which may or may not occur'. It is a specific mode of guarding against the damage which accidents pose 'to those whose property or person is attacked by them'.[28] Insurance treats any number of hazards according to its general formula, then: as threats to property. In his genealogy of insurance, Daniel Defert has shown how it is a 'generalizable technology'. While the practice of insurance was well established in the commercial world for many centuries, it is in the early nineteenth that it becomes applied to human life on a widespread basis, in the form of life assurance for the rich. By the middle of that century, as mutual societies start expanding amongst the aristocracy of labour in many European countries, insurance comes to gain a foothold in popular life.[29]

Claus Offe is right to see social security in terms of 'active proletarianization'.[30] If the proletariat is defined by the fact that the only property it owns is its labour-power, then social insurance represents the securing of that property against sickness, death, unemployment, and old age – the most common hazards which threaten its exercise.[31] As Giovanna Procacci has observed, there is never a general governance of problems; there is only government from a particular perspective, in terms of specific rationalities.[32] With unemployment insurance one finds unemployment governed in terms of a *liberal* social philosophy – as something which threatens the regular income, and therefore the self-sufficiency of the breadwinner and his household.

I have already noted that in placing unemployment on the same plane as birth, death, accidents, and all manner of other statistical regularities and 'social facts', social insurance breaks with the assumptions of the 'problem of the unemployed'. But it is not just the likes of the Charity Organisation Society who are out-flanked as the locus of explanation for this and other problems is shifted from human nature to social nature. Inasmuch as social insurance renders unemployment a natural, or perhaps a normal, feature of the social landscape, the view propounded by socialists like the Social Democratic Federation is also undermined – namely, of unemployment as an expression and instrument of capitalist class relations, and therefore a decidedly *political* phenomenon. Finally, there is a third political position antagonized by the insurance view of unemployment. While the Webbs were typical of many social experts in supporting the principle of voluntary insurance for unemployment, they were highly skeptical of those who would accord it a central role in social policy. As they saw it, social insurance was not a 'preventative' technique. It merely acted after the event. 'The unconditionality of all payments under unemployment insurance schemes constitutes a grave defect. The State gets nothing for its money in the way of conduct, and it may even encourage malingerers.'[33]

What links the moral reform, revolutionary socialist, and Fabian positions is a certain transcendentalism. Although they are dramatically different in terms of their methods and objects, each seeks a decisive and final resolution of the social question. Each is premised upon the possibility of a future state of social or human perfection. The method of insurance is quite different. It is above all pragmatic: its method is almost 'naturally' suited to the day-to-day *practicalities* of politics. As its advocates conceded, it does not eradicate the scourge of unemployment or sickness.[34] But neither does it preclude other measures directed towards that end. What it does offer, however, is an *immediate* improvement. As Churchill was to suggest, it deals with the here and now: 'Our concern is with the evil not with the causes, with the fact of unemployment not with the character of the unemployed.'[35] If twentieth-century socialist politics came to understand by 'reformism' the charting of a progressive political course between the *status quo* and revolution, then social insurance was an exemplary 'reformist' technology.

THE INVENTION OF 'INVOLUNTARY' UNEMPLOYMENT

In contrast with certain influential sociologists who aspire to found a narrative of modernity and modernization upon the concept of risk,[36] François Ewald, working in the tradition of Foucault, is wary about according it such an ontological status. Ewald posits that nothing is inherently a risk. Risk is instead a distinctive way of treating events. It is a 'principle of objectification'. The insurer actually produces risks – 'by making them visible and comprehensible as such in situations where the individual would ordinarily see only unpredictable hazards of his or her particular fate'.[37]

This argument is borne out by the example of the 1911 scheme. According to the expert view, 'unemployment or lack of employment is a more or less diffuse condition, which required careful definition'.[38] There were serious doubts as to whether it could be tested in the same way as other insurance risks. For it seemed that the truth of unemployment could not be located at the level of the body as it could with sickness. As one concerned official was to put it later: 'You can determine whether a man has typhoid fever ... by a doctor's certificate, but you cannot tell whether he worked on Monday and not on Tuesday.'[39] It was therefore necessary for the architects of this, the first compulsory and national unemployment insurance programme, carefully to define the risk of unemployment which was to be insured.

In this section I shall follow the main definitional, institutional, and technical procedures by which unemployment was rendered insurable, and governed in terms of risk. It is with the establishment and subsequent expansion of the unemployment insurance scheme (to a point where, by the 1930s, if it still excluded workers in clerical, retail, domestic service, and certain other areas, it did cover most employees in manufacturing) that we find one of the main dynamics and mediums by which a uniform definition of unemployment will be put in place on a national basis.

The definition of unemployment promoted by insurance is a very particular one. It is defined as a temporary, not protracted, interruption in a person's employment, attributable to impersonal and industrial factors.[40] In other words, insurance will only cover 'involuntary' unemployment. The history of a concept of 'involuntary' unemployment has been traced at the level of the history of economic ideas.[41] Here I want to suggest that an alternative history is conceivable, one that considers involuntary unemployment at the level of the administrative technologies which produce it as a manipulable space of government.

Before state unemployment insurance, there existed only a vague notion of who the unemployed were, and what their numbers might be. For instance, each of the trade unions administering out-of-work funds to their members had their own definitions of entitlement, and cultural assumptions as to what constituted unemployment. Beveridge – who researched these trade union funds extensively for the Board of Trade – recorded their diversity.[42] He found that, for example, the textile unions confined payments to their members who lost work through breakdowns in machinery; some painters unions only paid benefits in the winter months when work was scarce; and the London Society of Compositors allowed a fresh claim for benefits to start each year whereas others required a specific period to elapse between claims as a way of protecting themselves against 'unemployables'.[43] Given the absence of any uniform definition of unemployment within the trade union sphere, and the lack of one within the field of highly localized charitable and Poor Law practices, it is hardly surprising that in 1893 one finds the Board of Trade complaining: 'When statistics as to "unemployed" are called for, the difficulty is immediately encountered of how to define the work and give instructions to the clerks and collectors of the data who are to carry out the work.'[44]

So how did the advent of the 1911 scheme bring some regularity and consistency to definitions and assumptions about unemployment? And what power relations are involved in the production of a singular conception of unemployment? To answer this question it is necessary to follow the main divisions and exclusions which policy-makers applied to the field of the relief of the unemployed. Each of these was intended to delimit an insurable risk.

'Capable of Work'

The first set of exclusions that should be mentioned involves delimiting a series of risks which were considered to be properly suited to other systems of poor administration. One of the so-called statutory conditions for receiving unemployment benefits was that a claimant was 'capable of work'.[45] For example, those who lost work due to illness were not to be counted as unemployed, but as subjects of the health or workman's compensation schemes. There was 'no intention ... to make provision for other than able-bodied workpeople'.[46] As the Solicitor-General put it: 'It is a necessary condition for receiving unemployment benefit that the unemployed man should be "capable of work"; on the other hand, it is a necessary condition of the receipt of sickness benefit that the sick man should be "incapable of work".'[47]

If sickness insurance and workmen's compensation (introduced in 1897) reduced the number of the 'unemployed' to more manageable proportions by subtracting contexts for loss of work that were not properly 'industrial', then so did the old age pensions scheme introduced in 1908. As Churchill explained, this Act, 'far from being in conflict with a scheme of contributory insurance, is really its most helpful and potent ally ... It means that the whole field of insurance has become much more fruitful than it ever was before, that there is a new class of insurance business possible'.[48]

In this way, it is possible to place the advent of social insurance in the context of a wider historical and institutional development. It is part of the process by which the conceptualization and administration of poverty is specialized by means of a division of the population into discrete categories on the basis of an aetiology of the *causes* of their poverty: old age, sickness, disability, widowhood, unemployment, etc. Social insurance did not begin this process. This will to divide up the poor was consonant with the imperative of Victorian and Edwardian poverty research, fixated as it was with the proper 'classification' of its subjects. Moreover, the Poor Law had for some years been the setting for a not dissimilar kind of rationalization.[49] Yet it should also be noted that this division of the poor was not simply imposed by officialdom, but derives, albeit indirectly and awkwardly, from developments at a more micropolitical level. While this study has for the most part confined itself to official discourses and administrative practices relating to unemployment, it was observed in Chapter 1 that the unemployed have played an active role in constituting themselves as a distinct identity. Most visibly from the 1880s onwards, through the symbolism of their demonstrations and protests, and through political organization, as Flanagan has shown, 'the unemployed' constituted themselves as a political actor.[50]

Trade Disputes

The second type of exclusion effected by insurance rules is more explicitly political. The insurance regulations were framed to ensure that unemployment benefits would not be paid to workers actively involved in strikes against their employers, nor even to those who were made redundant by industrial disputes in which they were not par-ticipating. (This latter disqualification was discontinued in 1924.) 'It is ... unanimously held by students of the problem that benefits shall not be paid during labour conflicts.'[51] The converse of this was that job vacancies which arose as a result of industrial disputes were not to be counted by insurance officials as 'suitable employment' available to unemployed claimants. As A. I. Ogus has noted, 'official government policy has always been that the social insurance authorities should remain neutral in industrial relations'.[52] Such a position was a necessary condition if the representatives of employers and workers were to par-ticipate in, and give their consent to, the insurance scheme.

In this way, the insurance regulations again served to produce a more finite concept of unemployment than those that were customary within the labour movement. From the perspective of the trade union out-of-work schemes, it mattered little whether a worker was unem-ployed due to a downturn in the trade, or due to an organized dispute with an employer over wages or conditions. For the aim of this benefit was straightforward. As the Webbs pointed out, 'its most important function is to protect the Standard Rate of wages and other normal conditions of employment from being "eaten away", in bad times, by the competition of members driven by necessity to accept the employers' terms'.[53]

But from the perspective of the state, unemployment and strikes were to be clearly distinguished. From the end of the nineteenth century, and as the state extended its involvement in the social and industrial fields, these two problems were constituted and governed as separate concerns, as 'industrial relations' and 'unemployment'.

'Personal Causes'

In the process of making unemployment insurable, a third type of distinction was reinforced. The architects of the 1911 scheme sought to ensure that it would not cover the risk of losing employment through 'personal causes' – 'risks due to the wilful act of the workman', but also 'the personal risk attributable to exceptional deficiencies, physical, mental, or moral'.[54] If a phenomenon of 'involuntary' unemployment was being defined, then so was one of 'voluntary' unemployment. That unemployment could be voluntary was of course not a new idea. What was novel was the fact that the voluntary-personal becomes one factor in a wider field of causes and factors in unemployment, rather than being coextensive with it.

No doubt the likes of Llewellyn-Smith were motivated by financial considerations in excluding personal causes from the insurance scheme. But there were also moral arguments made: 'the personal risk of losing employment through bad work, irregular attendance, or drunken habits is one which it is absolutely necessary in the public interest to leave attached in all its forces to the individual workman'.[55]

But how would voluntary and the personal be distinguished from the involuntary in practice? A proportion of these 'personal' risks, it was envisaged, could be excluded by the regulations. As with the case of industrial disputes, rules could be framed to prevent or suspend bene-fits going to workers who became unemployed as a result of their own misconduct or through voluntarily leaving a position. Yet it was also recognized that, in reality, an individual's unemployment could rarely be neatly separated into voluntary and involuntary 'causes'.

> We can imagine the case of a carpenter who with equal truth might ascribe his unemployment to the competition of structural steel, to the general trade depression, to the severity of the winter, to local over-building, *or to the defects in his own training*.[56]

For this reason, it was decided that the scheme should have the 'automatic' safeguards of a maximum limit to the period for which benefits would be available to the claimant, and a minimum level of contributions which would be required before any claim could be made. 'Armed with this double weapon ... the operation of the scheme will automatically exclude the loafer.'[57]

This talk of 'loafers', with all its connotations of 'deserving' and 'undeserving', makes it tempting to fit the design and the motives of the insurance scheme into the trajectory of nineteenth-century social policy – to regard unemployment insurance as one more ingenious device dreamt up to discipline the poor. Clearly, there are powerful continuities in terms of the prejudices about the poor, and the disciplinary ambitions of authorities, which are invested in the insurance system. However, it is important to note that there are also novel aspects to the way in which the insurance system differentiates between applicants. We saw in Chapter 1 that as a mode of government, 'the problem of the unemployed' was about differentiating between individuals based on a knowledge of them as moral persons, i.e., in terms of their character. This is less the case with the insurance technique. Instead, it is governing eligibility for benefits in terms of what it defines as normal, insurable, involuntary unemployment – impersonal norms about unemployment and labour market behaviour which are derived from the observation of the industrial population.[58] Moreover, it is dividing between the eligible and the ineligible partly in reference to calculations of an internal and purely fiscal nature – maintaining the solvency of the insurance fund. Finally, insurance does not privilege a fixed conception of the good and the bad person or worker. As we have seen with the quote about the carpenter above, there is a recognition that deficiencies are not monopolized by distinct populations, be these the 'unemployables' or the 'residuum'. Instead, they are distributed, albeit unevenly, across the population.

The Acceptance of 'Suitable Employment'

There is one final aspect of the construction of involuntary unemployment which I want to consider. From the points I have made thus far it might be assumed that the definition of involuntary unemployment was shaped in very much a 'top-down' fashion, by public officials and the like. However, involuntary unemployment is not simply a contrivance of the insurance system. For it could also be considered a social and cultural practice and norm instituted by the labour movement. To be unemployed could mean several things. It could mean that such is the state of the labour market, a person cannot find *any* work. But much more likely, it means that they cannot find work *in their own occupation or trade*, under conditions to which they are accustomed. What trade union out-of-work schemes did was govern the latter situation: they made it possible for an unemployed person with a trade to 'hold out', to avoid having to take the first job that was offered. They embodied a sense of belonging to a trade.

This set of norms became inscribed in the state insurance scheme. The system afforded the worker what Ogus has called 'a "property-right" in his pre-unemployment earnings status'. It allowed the claimant a limited right to decline without punishment 'the offer of employment on terms less favourable than those which obtained in his usual occupation (thus recognizing the principle that the unemployed should not be forced to accept a lower standard of living than that to which they were accustomed)'.[59] Thus one can say that while the state scheme did come to dominate the field of income support, and it did impose national norms upon the practice of relief, this was not a one-way process. Elements of indigenous social practice and cultural and political norms were incorporated within official arrangements. Government is in this sense heterogeneous.[60]

Summary

I have argued that the rise of unemployment insurance entailed the generation of an official definition of unemployment as an insurable risk. This was a definition in which the concept was rationalized – evacuated of much of its former content, its cultural and social associations. Unemployment came to be defined in terms of impersonal and strictly economic forces which operate 'outside' the control of the individual. It was constituted as an *involuntary* condition. Social insurance can be associated with the view that although these forces cannot be controlled, at least their social consequences can be. It is only with the rise of Keynesianism (which I discuss in Chapter 5) that states acquire a means to act directly on the impersonal economic movements associated with involuntary unemployment itself. Indeed, by the middle of the century it is recognized that systems of social insurance are not viable *unless* they can be underpinned by technologies like Keynesianism or the National Health System which act on the economic or health *environment*.[61]

This attempt to plot the process by which a notion of involuntary unemployment is institutionalized within administrative practices is particularly salient today. For there is a paradox. On the one hand, it would seem that there has never existed a more impersonal and distant set of economic forces than those associated with the 'global economy'. We commonly hear how the day-to-day fortunes of factories, cities, and regions in different parts of the world are bound up with one another as never before. How could the unemployment of a region not be involuntary when it seems to be precipitated by the volatility of global financial markets, or the calculations of distant foreign investors?

Yet it transpires that involuntary unemployment is ceasing to be a central concept within expert reflection on contemporary unemployment, or for its management. This is certainly the case within mainstream economics. If Keynes had entrenched the concept of involuntary unemployment within economic theory, the trend amongst economists today is to treat unemployment as voluntary – as a 'choice' individuals make between work, family commitments, and social security benefits.[62] It is also the case with reforms to the income support system. Chapter 6 examines 'welfare-to-work' strategies. With their emphasis on mobilizing the jobseeker, reskilling them, and reinserting them in the labour market, their message is that the unemployed individual cannot 'hold out' for his or her job to become available again. They should no longer view their unemployment as something alien, something external which 'happens' to them. The onus is on changing oneself to remain employable, acquiring new skills, competing for jobs. The easy division between external and internal causes of unemployment, which was assumed with the invention of involuntary unemployment, is now in question.

THE SUBJECTS OF INSURANCE

One of the merits of governmentality research has been to develop our understanding of the relationship between the government of others and of the self, the intersection of politics and ethics, power and subjectivity. This theme resonates with Foucault's suggestion that we abandon our theories and models which place power as *exterior* to the subject in favour of a view which sees power as something which works *through* the subject.[63] Studies in governmentality have highlighted the various ways in which strategies of government presuppose and simultaneously seek to engender particular ethical predispositions, attributes, and capacities in their subjects; how practices of government and self-government intersect.[64]

In this final section I want to suggest how we might think the subject (in both senses of the word) of social insurance in such a way. Or to put it slightly differently, I want to know how we might subjectify our understandings of social insurance as a technique of governance. How might we understand the modalities of social insurance from a governmental-ethical perspective? This is an important exercise given the contemporary construction of social security within neoliberal and communitarian discourses. Neoliberals portray it as a device which inculcates passivity and welfare dependency in its subjects. I shall endeavour to show that contrary to this position, social insurance has always presupposed an *active* subject, albeit not active in the sense in which that term is used in current political debates.

Thrifty Subjects

A promising place to start might be with the theme of thrift and self-providence. Various strategies for governing poverty in the nineteenth century converged on the figure of the thrifty, self-reliant individual – political economists, charities, and assorted moral reformers extolled the virtues of thrift, urging the poor to discipline themselves against the temptations of immediate self-gratification, extolling men to become prudent providers for their families, to think about and save for the future, and their wives to become adept at household economy.

But there was also a more molecular, subterranean mobilization of thrift marked by the proliferation of a dense undergrowth comprising friendly societies, savings clubs, co-operatives, and other related institutions – a development which was viewed with a combination of approval and unease by the middle class.[65] In other words, thrift was not simply imposed from outside. It was also an indigenous, cultural, and social defence mechanism assembled, albeit haphazardly and unevenly, in the face of the dangers of industrial society. 'In both ideological and institutional terms, thrift was an *intrinsic* part of working-class history – an out-growth of working-class attitudes towards moral and social independence and stability, and not merely a habit thrust on them by other groups.'[66]

My argument here is that social insurance can be understood as a strategic intervention into this field, a calculated attempt to govern with the grain of these practices, dispositions, and attitudes towards self-provision, to multiply and extend them throughout society. As Llewellyn-Smith explained, unemployment insurance was not in opposition to the principles of self-reliance and thrift; it was not designed to remove, wholesale, the various risks which impinged upon the worker. 'For the community to guarantee employment to all irrespective of personal effort or efficiency would necessarily impair the national character and lower the national standard.'[67] Rather, like other social insurances, the aim of unemployment insurance was to engender a situation in which more and more workers would be in a situation where they could adopt the practice and ethos of the insuree: thinking and planning for the future. As we have seen, it did this by offering state subsidization to existing schemes, and by creating a scheme that was to cover hitherto uninsured areas of the labour market.

But beyond this, the various insurance schemes and social laws introduced at the turn of the century were to offer *hope*. By providing a framework, a bulwark, a basic foundation, social insurance was to activate the springs of self-reliance – in ways in which the negative, deterrent tactic of the Poor Law could not. 'It is a great mistake to suppose that thrift is caused only by fear', Churchill observed; 'it springs from hope as well as from fear; where there is no hope, be sure there will be no thrift.'[68]

Towards a *Social* Problematic of Thrift

All insurance is social in one sense since it realizes 'the social advantages of distribution of loss'; it substitutes 'social, co-operative provision for individual provision'.[69] What is distinctively 'social' about social insurance then? Social insurance embodies a properly sociological conception of the context and limits concerning the practice of thrift and insurance. Social insurance addresses itself towards a perverse state of affairs in which the sectors of society most in need of its protection are the least able to afford to pay a regular premium. Social insurance is, therefore, 'the policy of organized society to furnish that [insurance] protection to one part of the population, which some other part may need less, or, if needing, is able to purchase voluntarily through private insurance'.[70] It corresponds with the growth of a nascent sociological, and survey-based, knowledge of the poor, associated with the likes of Booth and Rowntree, which lent empirical strength to the argument that the failure of the poor to insure themselves was due not to a lack of foresight, but of income.

One could say that with social insurance there is a displacement of the thrifty subject from the moral discourse in which it is situated for most of the nineteenth century, and on to a social field. This is nicely illustrated by one of the earliest arguments for a compulsory insurance scheme. In a series of articles and speeches, Canon William Blackley championed the idea of 'national insurance'; the state was called on to establish a 'national benefit society' towards which all males and females, rich and poor, would be compelled to make contributions between the ages of eighteen and twenty-one. This fund would, he argued, provide for everyone in sickness and old age as 'a matter of right, not beggary'; 'everyone would have provided against destitution with his own money, and the misery, the disgrace, and the burden of our pauperism would be gone'.[71]

Now there are certain features of this scheme for 'compulsory providence' which were to find their way into the social insurance system – it was to be contribution based, contributions compulsory, and the scheme was to afford a certain 'right' to assistance. However, Blackley's was not a fully social technique, but in many ways still a moral one. His diagnosis of pauperism was still of a group of people who refused to acknowledge a moral and national duty of providing for themselves. The failure to save and provide for the future was explained as a moral one, not in terms of a social distribution of wealth or opportunity; 'the nation is an aggregate of individuals'.[72] Blackley's scheme was therefore designed as a mechanism that would simply enforce providence, one that would 'make the thriftless do their share'.[73]

We are now in a position to note that social insurance has a twofold significance for any account of the history of governing unemployment. I noted earlier how social insurance consolidates a fully sociological perception of the causes of unemployment, since within the insurantial imaginary unemployment comes to be seen as a normal, inevitable risk of industrial society, and not, primarily, a moral weakness on the part of the unemployed. A second observation can now be added. With social insurance for unemployment there is a recognition of the social and practical limits of insuring oneself against this risk. In short, the case for social – as opposed to voluntary – insurance comes to be accepted.

Subjects of Rights

Having discussed the way in which the operation of social insurance both presupposes a thrifty subject, and puts in place a mechanism for optimizing relations of thrift and self-provision, I now want to consider a second area in which ethical and governmental relations converge around social insurance. There is a powerful sense in which the subject of the state unemployment insurance scheme is a liberal, rights-bearing *individual*. For unemployment insurance reconstructs the field of the relief of the unemployed in terms of various techniques and principles which it imports from the judicial sphere: benefit payments are to be regarded as a 'right'; administrative practice is to be guided by national regulations; and there is to be a system of courts and tribunals where appeals and grievances arising out of the claiming process are to be heard – a system of administrative justice which will accumulate its own body of case law.[74]

In actual fact, it would be better to regard this sphere of administrative justice as *quasi*-judicial. Mindful of the way in which the law courts had become enmeshed in the workings of the workmen's compensation system of 1897, making the compensation process lengthy, complex, and expensive, the architects of the social insurance scheme had been adamant that insurance practices should be regulated outside the judicial sphere. As Lord Scarman would later reflect, 'the social insurance legislation (and social security generally) was not conceived as being part of the "ordinary law of the land"; it pertained to "administration"'.[75]

Regardless of the rather uncomfortable relation which the administration of the social insurance scheme may have had to the legal system, there is still a sense in which the structure of the insurance system encourages a specific mode of individuality in its subject. A governmentality perspective is sensitive to this point, perhaps more than others, because of the way that it does not regard the individual as pregiven, a fixed locus of agency or a centred identity. Instead, it insists that we see individuality not just as culturally and historically specific, but always the effect and the correlate of specific technologies. I shall develop the point that social insurance is one such technology of individuation more fully by comparing it once more with the trade union out-of-work schemes.

The trade union schemes had a fairly weak conception of the individual as a bearer of rights against the community. As Sidney and Beatrice Webb remarked, 'the Out of Work benefit is not valued exclusively, or even mainly, for its protection of the individual against casualties'.[76] Its purpose is not the regulation of the welfare of the recipient *qua* individual. Instead, this benefit exists in the collective interests of the trade and those who earn their livelihood from it. It fulfils this purpose by preventing the erosion of the standard rate of wages in the trade. The subject benefits from the fund, but mainly as an active member of the collectivity.

Perhaps one of the most striking exemplifications of the fact that trade union mutual practices do not privilege a liberal, individualized subject of rights is with the lack of any legal claim which the member can make on the fund, despite contributing to it.[77] Insurance against unemployment was not, of course, the only service which unions offered for their members. In competition with the friendly society and the industrial assurance company, the more established trade union also provided a range of 'friendly' benefits. Members would typically contribute to a fund which included sick pay, superannuation allowances, and 'burial money'. Yet for most unions there was no separate reserve for these payments; neither was there any contractual guarantee that funds would actually be available to the individual in old age or sickness. For the membership always reserved the right to commit all its funds, if necessary, to the task of maintaining members out of work, and/or conducting a major strike. Once again, the collective interests of the trade took precedence.

For these reasons, unions were sometimes accused of being actuarially unsound by public officials. However, more perceptive observers, such as the Webbs[78] and the Chief Registrar of the Friendly Societies, defended them against this accusation.[79] The union funds were not run on actuarial lines, but this did not mean they were financially unsound. When funds were low, the unions could always poll their members and levy a new charge. Or they could raise the contribution level. Trade unions possessed a resource not available to commercial insurers – the solidarity of their membership. This allowed them to organize security in a different way.

It should be clear how actuarial practices – employed in commercial insurance, and to some extent under social insurance – have individualizing effects. 'Actuarialism methods represent individuals in terms of risk. The idea designates the rules according to which costs are to be shared out. The risk-premium relationship is one of proportionality.'[80] Actuarialism makes it possible to offer a predetermined payment in exchange for set regular contributions. It uses probability calculations to institutionalize security, in the form of a guaranteed payment, in an individualized, contractualized basis. Trade unionism, on the other hand, stands for a less-individualized form of security, one which can count on the repeated mobilization and the solidarity of the membership.

In juxtaposing trade union and state insurance like this it is not my intention to suggest a simple opposition. The out-of-work schemes may not have promoted liberal individuality. But seen within the larger field and the history of governing poverty and the unemployed there is still a sense in which they contribute to a strategy of governing unemployment, as it were, through persons. Compare the out of work payment with the practice favoured by highly immobile trades such as coal mining or textiles. Here there was a practice of 'short-working'. If social insurance acts on the temporality of the wage, short-working is about 'the elasticity of working hours'. It is a tactic which spreads loss over 'the whole body of men instead of being concentrated, by complete dismissal, upon a few'.[81] This tactic lessened considerably the possibility of an individual or group of persons emerging as the bearers, symbols, or possibly the causes of whatever shortfall in work arose. The contemporary equivalent of this tactic is of course political arguments and legislative interventions to regulate working time in the expectation that this will spread employment. I noted in Chapter 2 that this strand was suppressed with the rise of the insurance strategy, for various reasons. With it, perhaps, went the possibility of a far less individualized treatment of unemployment.

Towards a Genealogy of 'The Claimant'

There is one final point I wish to make concerning insurance and its subject of rights. Whereas the Poor Law stood for a harsh, inquisitorial, and undignified treatment of the poor, unemployment insurance constructs the relief of its subjects in terms of entitlement and, eventually, a sense of *social citizenship*. It governs them as legitimate 'claimants'. This fact is by now well established.

What is perhaps less studied is the fact that there is a practical dimension to the construction of this 'claimant' persona. The space of the claimant was not merely opened from above by an Act of Parliament, and the establishment of the insurance system. Nor is it simply the reflection of the growing strength of the labour movement at the end of the century. These were important conditions of possibility for framing the administration of the poor in terms of rights. However, the making up of the claimant also entailed the more molecular, pedagogical, and practical work of organizations like the National Unemployed Workers Movement (NUWM).[82] At issue here is the more mundane work of schooling people in the practicalities of how to operationalize one's 'rights' – *how* to claim, *how* to answer the questions of the labour exchange officials, *how* to conduct oneself in the context of an appeal to the tribunals. As one NUWM pamphlet explained to its reader: 'The right to UI benefits depends on many highly technical details. This pamphlet will help you in some of your difficulties and show you when it is necessary to seek the advice of experts.'[83]

There were doubtless other repositories of counter-expertise offering advice to the claimant about the insurance system besides the NUWM, other forerunners of today's claimants' unions and welfare rights groups. But the NUWM is an interesting example not just because, as a communist movement, it demonstrates that the claimant was constructed through oppositional discourses and practices as well as official ones. For it also demonstrates that the construction of the claimant served different purposes: the NUWM provided advice to claimants not as an end in itself (as, say, a public advice bureau might), but specifically, as a basis for recruiting potential members to its greater political cause.

This figure, the claimant, deserves a genealogy of its own to which I can only gesture here. This would explore not just the alignments between tactics of opposition, and of rule, but also the misalignments and unravellings – what Deleuze and Guattari call 'lines of flight'.[84] The following official complaint is worth giving in full since it illustrates nicely that if the generation of an official definition of unemployment intensified the regulation of the poor in the sense that I have been arguing, it also opened up the possibility of new forms of subversive personal re-invention on the part of those same subjects.

> In pre-war days the dock labourer who had done four full days work and 'played' on the fifth day would not have been looked on or referred to as 'unemployed'. Textile operatives during a spell of short-time working would not have described themselves as 'unemployed' or 'out of work'; they spoke of themselves as 'playing to-day', or 'stood off for a week'. The young woman who helped in a shop on Fridays, Saturdays, and sale days, and stayed at home during the remainder of the time would not have thought of herself as 'unemployed' when she was at home and would probably have regarded any such suggestion as offensive. The married woman whose husband was in steady work and who, while ready to respond to an urgent call from a former employer, was not an active

candidate for work, would have been described by no one as unemployed. To-day all such persons, if they maintain a claim to benefit, and have acquired the habit of 'lodging their books' and maintaining registration when not actually working are counted during that time among 'the unemployed'. In the gross total of 'insured persons unemployed' they may not loom very large; but they are certainly an inflation of the numbers of 'unemployed' according to the pre-war conception of what constitutes unemployment.[85]

This genealogy of the claimant would also, without doubt, find that the present is marked by mounting suspicion regarding the legitimacy of the claimant. It would show that today public norms and policies are moving towards a position where it is no longer legitimate to merely claim benefits. Recipients must be seen to be *earning* these payments, whether through the undertaking of retraining, work experience, or jobseeking activities. This question is taken up in the final chapter.

Social Subjects and 'Society' Effects

In concluding this section it is necessary to enter a caveat with regard to the previous argument about social insurance and its liberal subject of rights. This is, of course, that we would do better to see this subject as one pole within a relationship; social insurance also presupposes and deploys a social subject. Benefit payments might be constructed as an individual 'right' of the claimant. But they are also framed by a social rationality. Just as the trade union can be understood as securing its own existence through its out-of-work benefits, then social insurance offers the state a similar possibility. The benefit payment 'is given because [the individual] is a member of the social community whose interests are to secure the efficiency of every one of its members'.[86] Social insurance is in this sense a badge of the social citizen. It marks the passage by which the worker becomes a full member of society, industrial work a service and a duty to the nation in the same way as fighting, and unemployment a burden borne on behalf of society. Indeed, campaigns for the inception of social insurance schemes frequently made this analogy between industrial and national service. Social insurance was to be a means of honouring the 'soldier of industry' who has suffered for the well-being of the nation in the same way as we honour 'the soldier who has served or suffered on his country's battlefield'.[87] Similar claims were made by women's organizations on behalf of women's claims to social citizenship; with varying degrees of success, they sought to construct motherhood as a form of service to the nation.[88]

The example of unemployment insurance has been used to illustrate an argument which is by now familiar to Foucaultian sociologies – that we should see the individual as multiply composed, the effect of a proliferation of discontinuous technologies. I have traced some of the ways in which modes of invidiuality are 'made up'. However, it is possible to use the case of unemployment insurance to make a similar anti-essentialist argument about another foundation of the social sciences, *society*. One could analyse the relationship of social insurance to both the objectification and the subjectification of society. The process of objectification is well demonstrated by the fact that the unemployment insurance system was to produce data about the labour market, the working patterns of the population and much else besides. As one observer anticipated, 'the working of Unemployment Insurance will provide the nation with such information upon the subject of unem-ployment as it has never before possessed'.[89] In this and other ways, the insurance system contributes to the formation of the social as a visible and governable domain.

But there is a subjectification process also. Unemployment insurance does not make society a subject of government in the way that the technologies of mass communication, public opinion, and the universal franchise do; it does not purport to give society a means of expression, a voice. But by establishing a relationship between the person receiving benefits and the entire insurance population – which is now the regular workforce rather than a single trade or sector as it was for the trade union out of work funds – it could be said to give society an interest and a stake in the government of the unemployed, in ways that did not previously exist. This point is well illustrated in the inter-war years. In the chapter which follows we will see that if the unemployed truly fall under a *national* spotlight at this time, it is perhaps not unrelated to the fact that it can now be argued that it is society, as a collective subject, which is now – through the unemployment insurance fund – paying for their support.

CHAPTER 4

GOVERNING *THROUGH* THE LONG-TERM UNEMPLOYED: UNEMPLOYMENT BETWEEN THE WARS

During the inter-war years the centre of gravity of the employment problem, as far as official perceptions are concerned, shifted from casual employment to 'long-term unemployment'.[1] Most of the literature on this period takes as self-evident the existence of a group identifiable as the 'long-term unemployed'. While there can be no disputing the fact that millions of people had direct and indirect experience of the devastating effects of prolonged joblessness and poverty during this time, this chapter cautions against accepting the validity of this relatively new categorization of the unemployed at face value. Instead, it argues that the social consequences of mass unemployment were in fact managed, partly at least, in terms of a division of the unemployed into a 'normal' and a 'chronic' population. While this division of the unemployed population was not without its precedents, it came to serve new political functions during the inter-war years.

The first section shows how the 'long-term unemployed' were, in a sense, invented as a way of perpetuating the fiction that there is such a thing as 'normal unemployment' (whose construction I discussed in Chapter 3), and that it can be governed by social insurance. The chapter then goes on to examine some of the perceptual grids which were deployed to give meaning to the long-term unemployed: inter-war social psychologies, sociologies, ethnographies, and social surveys of the unemployed are all discussed as intellectual technologies which were used to make long-term unemployment interpretable. It will be observed that they construct the long unemployed as a population 'in need' and as suffering from a process of 'demoralization'.

The last part of the chapter considers the relevance of long-term unemployment for a genealogy of the governance of unemployment and a history of the present. It traces the way in which a technology of 'unemployment assistance' was fashioned to provide support for the long-term unemployed. Unemployment assistance represents a form of governance somewhere between social insurance and the Poor Law. Its significance resides with the way in which it makes 'need' into an manageable domain, and the basis for a political relation between the individual and the state.

MASS UNEMPLOYMENT AND THE CRISIS OF SOCIAL INSURANCE

Because of the changing ways in which unemployment is recorded, it is difficult accurately to compare levels of unemployment between the wars with other periods.[2] Nonetheless, most historians concur that levels of unemployment were generally higher in the inter-war period than they were before 1914. There was a brief industrial boom following the end of the war, but this collapsed in 1920. Official unemployment then shot to 2 171 000 in 1921. Conditions gradually improved after 1922, but worsened substantially with the international recession of 1929–32. Throughout the inter-war period, recorded unemployment never fell below one million workers; in relation to the official workforce, the percentage unemployed was rarely less than ten per cent of the official workforce.[3] As it had done in 1914, it took mobilization for war to solve this persistent unemployment problem.

The pattern and incidence of unemployment changed significantly from the pre-1914 period. Inter-war unemployment was characterized by its concentration in the industrial sectors, which had led Britain's industrial progress in the previous century, namely coal, cotton, wool textiles, shipbuilding, and iron- and steel-making. These were export-orientated sectors which found the terms of international competition following the First World War particularly harsh. The regions and areas in which these industries were concentrated – Scotland, northern England, South Wales and Northern Ireland – were therefore the worst affected. Shipbuilding towns like Barrow suffered insured unemployment rates of nearly fifty per cent compared with a national average of just over twelve per cent.[4] Images of such places have subsequently shaped the way we imagine mass unemployment.

The so-called 'depressed areas' bore the brunt of registered unemployment. However, London, the south, and the midlands – previously the geographic centre of the unemployment problem – enjoyed fairly widespread prosperity at this time, thanks in part to the fact that these areas became centres for the 'new' industries like electronics and consumer durables. These industries were less exposed to the volatile international economy. They also utilized new mass production techniques.[5] If the inter-war period saw the first signs of 'Fordist' *mass* production in the UK, *mass* unemployment was to be concentrated in pre-Fordist sectors.[6]

Mass unemployment was, of course, in no way a problem confined to Britain between the wars.[7] What was peculiar to Britain was the way in which unemployment policy was almost singularly focused upon the issue of cash payments to the unemployed.[8] In Sweden and the United States, for example, programmes of public works featured prominently (and famously, in the case of the US 'New Deal') in measures intended to alleviate unemployment. This was not the case in Britain, where public works were tried on only a small scale. In Britain, the politics of inter-war unemployment centred upon 'the dole'.[9]

For this reason, I need to give some account of the complicated structure of the unemployment relief system between the wars since its restructuring was closely tied up with the social and political salience which came to attach to the long-term unemployed identity.[10] For most of the inter-war years public support for the unemployed was structured in terms of a two-tier system.

The least-stigmatizing and most valued form of relief was 'covenanted' or 'standard' unemployment insurance benefit. This was the direct descendant of the experimental 1911 scheme. It was provided by right to workers in insured trades who fulfilled its conditions The original scheme had covered 2.25 million, almost entirely male, workers in seven trades. By 1920 the insurance scheme had been expanded to cover some twelve million workers. Various considerations prompted this expansion. The Treasury had for some time been keen to expand the insurance system in the hope that by encompassing more regular trades its financial soundness would be improved.[11] But unemployment insurance was also universalized as a way of transferring recipients of non-contributory 'out-of-work donations' (OWD) into a contributory scheme. OWDs had been granted to demobilized troops and civilians without work at the end of the First World War.[12] But overriding these concerns was a more general one: the expansion of the insurance system was the state's response to popular expectations about better social provisions engendered by the population's experience of war.

The lower tier of the system was based on a series of 'discretionary' benefits targeted at those who did not qualify for insurance benefits under the original conditions.[13] Such payments were known colloquially as 'the dole'. The dole was in fact subject to considerable mutation, especially during the 1920s, taking the form of 'uncovenanted', 'extended', 'transitional', or 'non-standard' payments.[14] As was noted in Chapter 3, insurance benefits were designed to assist 'regular' workers who, it was assumed, would be unemployed only for short spells. The insurance system was to be protected from the 'malingerer' by the rule that no one could claim benefits for more than twenty-six weeks in any year. It was also to be safeguarded by a 'one-in-six' rule that made one week's benefit available for six weeks of contributions into the fund.

The various non-standard benefits made insurance payments available to workers who no longer qualified for support under the original rules and assumptions of the insurance system. As such, there was a relaxation of the eligibility requirements. Benefits were made available to workers whose unemployment was persistent as well as to individuals who had made only a few contributions into the fund. Why was this? Basically, it was because the only other form of support available to workers who had exhausted their claim to insurance benefits was the Poor Law. As Lloyd George put it to the Unemployment Committee of the Cabinet in 1921: 'No Government could hope to face the opprobrium which would fall upon it if extreme measures had to be taken against starving men who had fought for their country and were driven to violent courses by the desperation of their position.'[15]

For the present purpose of an attempt to trace the emergence of the long-term unemployed as a new problem category, these nonstandard benefits are significant for several reasons. First, they represented a *de facto* expansion of the definition of the central state's responsibility for the support of the unemployed. This was now 'to maintain all those who are out of work through no fault of their own so long as they remain out of work'.[16] Membership of the 'industrial army' rather than the insurance scheme was coming to be the criterion for the receipt of benefits.[17]

However, this relaxation of strict insurance principles in the administration of benefits contributed to a financial crisis for the insurance fund.[18] Various committees and inquiries were held in the latter half of the 1920s at which representatives from industry and state officials discussed ways in which the benefit system could be rationalized, and the solvency of the insurance fund restored. But these concerns only came to a head at the end of the 1920s when the international economic situation worsened. What Tomlinson characterizes as the 'growing agitation against the burden of government expenditure'[19] culminated in 1931 with the publication of the Report of the Committee on National Expenditure. This called for severe cuts in social spending. The Labour Government of the time was not prepared to make such cuts; the task fell to the National coalition government that replaced it in 1931.[20]

The National government moved quickly to restore strict eligibility criteria to the insurance scheme. The policy of the 1920s, of incrementally and expediently expanding the insurance system to manage mass unemployment, was therefore curtailed.[21] In the 1930s, the idea that the 'long-term unemployed' were not suitable subjects for unemployment insurance – even though their former industrial credentials were not in doubt – would serve as rationalization for the restoration of unemployment insurance, and its restriction to the 'normal' unemployed.

THE INVENTION OF 'LONG-TERM' UNEMPLOYMENT

We are now in a position to discuss long-term unemployment more fully. One of the main arguments of this chapter is that the recognition of a problem of long-term unemployment in the 1930s cannot adequately be treated as a straightforward response to empirical changes in the nature or distribution of unemployment. Official statistics certainly reveal growing numbers of people experiencing painful spells of prolonged unemployment by this time.[22] But it was not inevitable that public and social scientific attention would come to define a new problem-group, the long-term unemployed. The argument that is developed here is that the division of the unemployed into normal/long-term becomes salient because it provides a support for programmes seeking to cut public spending. This is nicely illustrated by the debate that took place around the Royal Commission on Unemployment Insurance, between 1930 and 1932. This inquiry had been appointed by the Labour Government in 1930 'to make recommendations with regard to the scope of the Unemployment Insurance Scheme and the means by which it might be made solvent and self-supporting, and to make arrangements for the able-bodied unemployed outside the scheme'.[23]

The Royal Commission on Unemployment Insurance and the Discovery of 'Chronic' Unemployment

In its recommendations for the future of the insurance scheme, the Majority Report of the Royal Commission called for a return to insurance principles, with a separate system of means-tested relief payments to be provided for applicants who failed to satisfy insurance criteria. The Minority Report took a contrary position. More sympathetic to the arguments of organized labour, the Minority Commissioners called for the scrapping of insurance. They concluded that 'mutual insurance is a quite unsuitable method by which to meet a risk so heavy and incalculable as unemployment'.[24] Instead of insurance, they recommended a system of unconditional 'compensation for loss of unemployment', fully funded by the state. According to one historian, this proposal was destined to be rejected 'not least because of its prohibitive cost'.[25] However, it is worth considering the case made by the Minority Commissioners. For they actually contest the assumptions about unemployment and insurance which came to be hegemonic, and which we tend to take as self-evident.

The Majority had drawn attention to a relatively new phenomenon: 'chronic' unemployment. Available evidence seemed to point to the fact that the very nature of unemployment was changing by the end of the 1920s. Official research implied that mass unemployment was no longer fully comprehensible as a serious but nevertheless temporary aftershock of the First World War. For instance, in a 1928 report on the 'depressed regions' the Industrial Transference Board had found that there was 'a surplus of unemployed labour in certain industrial districts, particularly those where certain export industries were concentrated, and that this was not a temporary phase'.[26] As the Majority Report saw things:

> The unemployment from which the great majority suffer is occasional in character, occurring in a life of more or less regular employment; only a small minority of the population suffer from chronic unemployment, but their unemployment accounts for a large part of all unemployment.[27]

On this reckoning, it was chronic unemployment that was chiefly responsible for the breakdown of the insurance system. Their new typology of unemployment suggested the answer – confine insurance to occasional unemployment and devise some method of conditional assistance for the victims of chronic unemployment.

However, the Minority Report rejected the usefulness or salience of this typology. It admitted that there existed a population of continuously unemployed, concentrated in certain areas and industries. But these 'do not amount to more than 100 000 of the total number of the unemployed' at the start of the 1930s.[28] At the other end of the scale was a considerable proportion of the insured population 'who are continuously employed and never draw benefit at all'. And in between these two extremes lay the majority of cases whose circumstances might be described as 'normal'. They suffer from 'intermittent unemployment' which 'lasts a short period when times are good and a long period when times are bad'.[29]

So the Majority Report sought to manage mass unemployment in terms of a distinction between chronic and normal unemployment which they mapped onto two distinct classes, two groups which were to be separated by administrative devices. But for the Minority the salient distinction was less between classes of person, *but between good and bad times*. Instead of insurance, what was needed was 'a scheme which will meet both the needs of more favourable times when unemployment is low and the needs of abnormal periods like the present'.[30] What we find, then, are conflicting definitions or mobilizations of 'the normal' in relation to the field of unemployment; one takes a social, the other, a temporal axis.

The point the Minority Report was at pains to make was that the division of the unemployed which the Majority proposed was basically unsound.

> The clerical worker who loses his employment through reduction in staff, or the factory worker 'stood off' because of shortage of orders, or the shop assistant because of slackness of trade – these in good times would tend to get back to work in a short period before they had exhausted their benefit. Because times are bad their search is prolonged and they pass to transitional payment. *They cannot be described as a different type of unemployed.*[31]

This is the crux of the Minority Report argument. The division of the unemployed into two separate classes, which the Majority Report proposed, was quite arbitrary. Whether assessed in terms of skill, employment records, or physical condition, the bulk of those claimants who had exhausted their claim to insurance benefits were not markedly different from those who had not.

This was the dilemma which the Majority acknowledged: 'it is not possible to draw a hard and fast line between the different elements in the problem of unemployment'.[32] They tried to overcome this tension by claiming that they were not, in fact, differentiating between moral types, between the deserving and the undeserving, as earlier approaches to the unemployed had. 'The differentiation we make is not between individuals but between different types of unemployment.'[33]

But if this division of the unemployed – between an insurance and a relief class, between the occasionally and the long-term unemployed – had been exposed as somewhat arbitrary and artificial by the Minority Report, and contested by the political activities of the unemployed themselves, it would nevertheless come to appear more natural and self-evident as the 1930s progressed. The argument of the next section is that social scientific and other types of investigation of the 'long unemployed' in the 1930s played a significant role in this naturalization process. For the implication of their theories about the psychological 'demoralization' which afflicted those who underwent long periods without work was precisely that the long-term unemployed *were* different from the other unemployed. In this way they provide a theoretical rationale for a different type of administrative treatment.

My argument is therefore that we should not see the investigation of the long-term unemployed as an inquiry into a preconstituted reality or group. Social scientists did not simply find long-term unemployment, with all its deleterious social and psychological consequences, somehow already there. Instead, social science was instrumental in constructing long-term unemployment as a special type of unemployment, as a particular object and subject of governance.

KNOWLEDGES OF LONG-TERM UNEMPLOYMENT

Thus far we have seen how a problem-space of 'chronic' unemployment is first marked out as the constitutive 'outside' of 'normal' unemployment, and that the crisis of the administration system at the end of the 1920s provided the particular conditions under which this problem was raised. We can turn now to the matter of how a positive knowledge of the so-called 'long unemployed' is produced.

New Forms of Inquiry: Probing the 'Minds and Feelings' of the Unemployed

For most of the 1920s it is probably fair to say that the dominant representation of unemployment is a statistical one. In previous chapters we saw how the advent of labour exchanges and unemployment insurance serves to standardize unemployment. As a result it becomes possible to quantify unemployment, to discuss it in terms of durations, distributions, volumes, and masses, and to give it a geometry. In the 1930s, however, a new perception of unemployment will take shape alongside the statistical view.

The sociological and socio-psychological inquiries considered in this section offer themselves as an alternative to the 'objective', statistical representation of unemployment. They claim to deal with a hitherto neglected 'subjective' dimension. What is important about these studies for the purposes of this chapter is not whether they are accurate or ideological when judged by current sociological criteria. They are of interest here for what they say about the organization of knowledge about unemployment between the wars, and the way organized knowledge interplayed with administrative practices. This division between the 'objective' and the 'subjective' is an epistemological distinction internal to discourse on unemployment, yet one which continues to organize it to this day. By interrogating the status of this distinction, the nature of this study can be seen more clearly. To analyse unemployment at the level of discourse means that rather than asking, 'What is the *meaning* of unemployment?' we ask, 'How does unemployment come to have meaning?' These studies of the subjective dimension are then one of the ways in which unemployment acquires meaning through discourse. They illustrate how it is that between the wars 'unemployment came to assume a human face'.[34]

The 1930s saw a sociological and socio-psychological dimension of long-term unemployment opened up. Its investigators are quite explicit that theirs is a very different form of analysing unemployment; everywhere the distinction between the unemployment *object* and the unemployed *subject* is to the fore. The author of *Unemployed Man*, a pioneering study in this field, contrasts his 'more particular and human study' with 'that kind of statistical analysis of the industrial and personal circumstances of unemployed persons which has been made by the Ministry of Labour'.[35] Likewise, the Archbishop of York introduces the most in-depth study of the long-term unemployed, the Pilgrim Trust's *Men without Work*, as 'a new approach to the problems created by unemployment ... one which ... gets much closer to the real difficulties than a purely economic approach'.[36] While the compilers of the *Memoirs of the Unemployed* point out: 'How little, indeed, do we yet know of what unemployment means, not in terms of economic loss, but in terms of human experience.' Hence their aim is 'to give a clothing of typical human experience to the statistical skeleton so clearly defined in the figures of the Ministry's investigation'.[37] After all, 'no human being finds it easy to regard himself as a statistical unit'.[38]

How do these studies intend to get at their unemployed subjects, their 'minds and feelings' as well as 'those "shadows behind the queues", the women and children at home'?[39] A range of investigative devices were pressed into service – and in some cases pioneered – to uncover the 'experience' of long-term unemployment. One recurring technique is what we might call *living amongst the unemployed*. This is what E. Wight Bakke, an American social scientist, did in Greenwich. Bakke took lodgings with a working-class family in order to 'share their life in so far as it was possible' so as 'to get as complete a picture of the whole life background and foreground of the man out of a job'.[40]

Someone who became famous for living amongst the unemployed and other 'down-and-outs' was George Orwell. In *The Road to Wigan Pier* he recounts the time he spent in one poor northern boarding-house. He professes it to be 'a kind of duty to see and smell such places now and again, especially smell them, lest you should forget that they exist; though perhaps it is better not to stay there too long'.[41] There are clearly echoes of the slum writing of the 1880s and 1890s in this 'dole literature'.[42]

One of the best known of the social studies of the unemployed elevated living amongst the unemployed to the status of a 'method'. In their 'sociography' of the unemployed of Marienthal (a small industrial town in Austria), Jahoda, Lazarsfeld, and Zeisel describe what they call 'immersion' (*sich einleben*): the social scientist was to live amongst the community in order 'to gain such close contact with the population ... [as to] learn the smallest details of their daily life'.[43]

Another aspect of this will to know unemployment subjectively was its bid to capture the voice of the unemployed. The long unemployed are enjoined to speak by this new type of investigation – in interviews, but also in autobiographies like the *Memoirs of the Unemployed*, which were first collected for the BBC's *The Listener*. Here the claim is to 'represent the authentic voice of the unemployed authors – the first occasion on which this voice has been heard in the long discussion of unemployment that has dragged on for so many years'.[44] Not that this voice was unprompted: each participant in the study was asked to reflect on specific aspects of their unemployment. For example:

> They should describe their struggle against misfortune from their last dismissal until today. They should state when and how they lost their last job, and what assistance they or the members of their family have received or are receiving in the way of unemployment and other relief, trade union benefit, charity, etc.[45]

One respondent noted in passing: 'We do not show any of the signs of long unemployment.'[46] This remark is very telling. It illustrates how this literature manages to make 'long unemployment' discursive. Through the medium of these investigations, long unemployment becomes a 'social' condition, something (self-) identifiable in terms of certain 'signs'. But what were these signs?

To answer this question we need to turn to the first of the two axes of inquiry constituted by this inter-war social investigation of the unemployed, that of 'morale'. The second of these will be 'need'. While other aspects of the existence of the unemployed were also scrutinized (e.g., a concern with their 'physique'), these two are prominent in identifications of the unemployed. In the final section of the chapter I shall examine the techniques which were developed in the 1930s to govern need and morale

'De-Moralization'

The 'signs' of long unemployment were made legible with considerable help from the emerging field of social psychology, an expertise and a specialist knowledge whose interest in the problems of economic life tended to intensify in the early decades of this century.[47] Following studies like Marienthal it became common to speak of the unemployed subject and his/her family in terms of their 'motivation', 'attitude', and more generally the state of their 'mental health'. The matter on which most of these inquiries concurred was that the long unemployed were subject to a process of 'demoralization': 'unemployed men are not simply units of employability who can, through the medium of the dole, be put into cold storage and taken out immediately they are needed. While they are in cold storage, things are liable to happen to them.'[48]

Peter Miller has shown that the terms used to understand the demoralization of the unemployed – these 'things that are liable to happen to them' – draw extensively on, and in turn complement, the psychiatry of the subject at work.[49] This psychiatry, which develops between the wars, reveals how work is instrumental in sustaining and promoting the worker's 'mental health'. Conversely an absence of work, e.g., through protracted unemployment, will be detrimental to mental health.

Thus the form in which the demoralization of the unemployed subject is specified is in terms of a series of lacunae associated with a state of non-working: the breaking of the social bonds formed in the workplace, a loss of structure to the day, a loss of self-respect and status connected with working and earning, an absence of the physical and mental stimuli provided by work. These factors are seen to produce a host of psychiatric disorders in the subject, including anxiety, stress, and depression. They can also result in feelings of anger, bitterness, and isolation. Such problems are also seen to have reverberations for marital and familial life.

Most accounts agreed that this deterioration of the unemployed man's mental health occurred in stages. For Beales and Lambert the unemployed man's reaction to his condition underwent a 'rough progression' from initial 'optimism' to 'pessimism' and ultimately 'fatalism'.[50] Bakke discerned a similar tendency, which he called 'adjustment'.[51] For the Pilgrim Trust this process of demoralization was manifested in three types of unemployed men: those who thought only about regaining employment; those who sought employment, but more out of habit than conviction; and those who considered unemployment their normal state and would have difficulty accepting employment were it available.[52] Ultimately the unemployed would acquiesce in their situation; the existence of 'unemployed communities' made life bearable albeit 'switched down to a lower economic plane'.[53] Orwell saw this as 'proof of their essential good sense ... Instead of raging against their destiny they [unemployed communities] have made things tolerable by lowering their standards'.[54]

These studies evidence little concern with the problem of the unemployed woman.[55] She does not appear in Bakke's investigation, while only one of the twenty-five memoirs presented by Beales and Lambert is written by an unemployed woman. However, *Men without Work* is interested in the effects of unemployment on women as workers and as wives, but suggests that 'the problem of the unemployed woman cannot be separated from the question of the function of the woman in national life'![56] The absence of a consensus upon the desirability of married women's employment must to some extent account for the reluctance of investigators to explore their unemployment. Where the Pilgrim Trust did examine married women with a long tradition of employment in textiles, they concluded that they were less prone to the demoralization and apathy which inevitably afflicted their male counterparts.[57] Unlike her husband, a woman was seen to have other sources of status and investment than paid work, namely domestic work; consequently she 'may become unemployable less slowly'.[58]

How does this demoralization process which is identified between the wars compare with the demoralization which studies of the poor and of city life described in the latter half of the nineteenth century? It seems that inter-war demoralization lacks the cataclysmic overtones which Nikolas Rose senses in the earlier concept. For instance, 'in [Charles] Booth's work one can see emerging a new conception of demoralization, as a cumulative process with long-term effects upon the quality of the population as a whole'.[59] By the 1930s the process has become more strictly defined in the terminology of social psychology and psychiatry, and is located within the psychic interior of the unemployed individual.

Like most social science research today, these investigations of the social dimension of unemployment addressed topical political questions. One of these – which has echoes in current discussions of 'the underclass' – concerned the future 'employability' of those who had spent long periods without work. The Pilgrim Trust inquiry sought to establish whether there had developed a 'hard core' of 'unemployables' who are left behind in the dole queues once the economy revived in the mid-1930s. This was certainly Beveridge's suspicion as he spoke of the 'legacy' of the 'great depression' being a 'mass of long-period unemployment – more than 350 000 men and women in insured trades'.[60] The long unemployed were seen as a 'hard core', 'the most serious element in the problem of unemployment today'.[61] Economic recovery was underway, yet it seemed as though the labour market stubbornly refused to 'reabsorb' those who had been out of work for long periods.

The Pilgrim Trust sought to establish to what extent 'personal' factors could account for this 'hard core'. 'Long unemployment ... is one of those problems where cause and effect are inextricably mixed – where, for instance, long unemployment may itself make a man unemployable'.[62] In other words, they suggest that demoralization is a possible *cause* of unemployment.

In previous chapters we saw how a definitely economic explanation of unemployment is formulated. While this did not signal the death of moral or personal explanations, it did accord the latter a much reduced role in comprehending the unemployed. The discovery of 'unemployment' placed moral factors in context. When the Pilgrim Trust point out that with the rise of long-term unemployment 'a *social* problem of the first order had arisen'[63] they are reasserting the social-moral against the economic pole in explanations of unemployment – not at a general level, but certainly for specific populations and situations. In other words they are using the unemployed to explain unemployment. At the same time they are demonstrating that there is no easy, linear progression from moral-social to economic explanations, from 'individualistic' explanations to 'structural' ones. For there are politically and historically determined reversals as well.[64]

Theories of 'demoralization' doubtless accorded with the very real and terrible sense of despair and deprivation which individuals, families, and 'unemployed communities' underwent. But they also fulfilled a political need – a fact which probably accounts for their salience in the 1930s. We need to recall the problems facing the inter-war system of relief which we reviewed at the start of the chapter. The problem for administrators was to provide a grounds beyond financial expediency for what was a fairly arbitrary division of the unemployed population between 'insurance' and 'relief'. Social-psychology and sociology provided such a ground. As Bakke observed: 'The unemployed person changes as the period of unemployment is prolonged. After twenty-six weeks of unemployment he is not the same sort of case as he was the day after he came out of employment.'[65]

If 'he is not the same sort of case that he was', then obviously his case could justify a different form of administration from insurance. I shall show in the final section that the demoralization of the long unemployed subject will offer a rationale for the much more intensive form of regulation, designated by 'unemployment assistance', which targets this category.

But on the other hand long unemployed men and women are nevertheless ex-workers, and still to be regarded as 'workpeople' or 'potential workers'; 'it is a point of fundamental policy that its [Unemployment Assistance Board] applicants should be regarded as forming part of the ordinary supply of labour in all their contacts with official machinery'.[66] In this way the long unemployed man and woman occupy a somewhat ambiguous position within administrative discourse: somewhere between the subject of social insurance and the subject of the Poor Law. Theirs is a condition which patently requires cash assistance, yet one for which 'continuous money payments in idleness are a manifestly inadequate provision'.[67] The unemployed man 'is not going to have the same freedom in saying what sort of life he will have' – but at the same time he is not going to be, and for political reasons cannot be treated as, a pauper.

In the final section of the chapter we will see how unemployment assistance is developed as a response to the political and social status of the long-term unemployed. As a technique of governance between insurance and poor relief, and charged with promoting the 'welfare' of its population, we will see that it occasions something of a departure in techniques of governance. Quite ironically, the problem around which this technique formed was to wither up; by 1942, with the war economy in full tilt, the International Labour Organization stated that

> one important conclusion can be drawn from the past, namely, that 'unemployability' has not been an objective concept: its definition has varied with economic circumstances ... it has been demonstrated, according to the Ministry of Labour, that unemployables are non-existent unless they are really physically or mentally incapable of work of any kind.[68]

While 'demoralization' and 'unemployability' will be revealed to be much more relative and temporary in their nature, the technologies they will give rise to are perhaps more enduring. As unemployment assistance mutates into 'national assistance' and ultimately 'supplementary benefits', other populations 'in need' besides the unemployed are found. The scope of 'assistance' will necessarily broaden.

The Social Survey Movement: Measuring 'Need'

The inter-war years saw the long unemployed scrutinized and analysed in terms of other discursive grids besides the socio-psychological. For instance there were investigations of the effects of long-term unemployment on public health, including a debate (which persists to this day) as to the consequences of unemployment for sickness and mortality rates.[69] Links were also sought between unemployment and crime.[70] We can speculate that it is because of its fixed and very regional nature (i.e., unemployment is no longer a 'fairly rapidly moving stream') that it has become amenable to these forms of analysis. That is, unemployment has become concentrated on distinct communities, populations, subjects which can now be described as 'wholly unemployed'. In this way it will yield stable objects and control cases for the purposes of scientific investigation.

The inter-war years also saw a large number of mostly private social survey based investigations of the extent of poverty amongst the working class. The 'social survey movement' was not concerned specifically with the problem of long-term unemployment. Its initial aim was to establish more generally whether progress had been made concerning poverty overall.[71] However, the movement was to deepen and broaden empirical understandings of the link between poverty and unemployment.

It was noted in Chapter 1 that Charles Booth provided the most systematic and extensive account of the link between lack of employment and poverty of his time. Yet Booth's conception of poverty was impressionistic.[72] His poverty maps and surveys were based on visual observations made by visitors to the homes of the poor and working classes. These observations were made by School Board Inspectors whom Booth enlisted to work on his survey. What was remarkable about Booth was that he systematized and greatly enlarged the scale of this type of observation of poverty.

The social survey movement utilizes a different conception of poverty, one which renders it visible and quantifiable as 'household need'. B. S. Rowntree was the pioneer of this type of survey, though the principle can be seen in the work which the Royal Statistical Society did on 'workmen's budgets'.[73] I want to touch briefly on Rowntree's method, since it typifies the kind of hard, quantifiable, and standardized conception of poverty as 'need' which the form of government designated by 'social assistance' will operationalize. In the last section of this chapter we will see that when the long unemployed become the responsibility of the Unemployment Assistance Board they will constitute the first major testing ground for a programme of governing 'need' on a standardized and nationally uniform basis.

The space in which it is possible to conceive a government of 'need' and thereby poverty is first opened up at the start of the century with Seebohm Rowntree's survey of York: *Poverty, A Study of Town Life* (first published 1901). As Karel Williams has shown, one of Rowntree's principal aims there was to formulate a definition of something he called 'primary poverty': the condition of those 'families whose total earnings are insufficient to obtain the minimum necessaries for the maintenance of merely physical efficiency'.[74]

> Yet Rowntree was 'not simply proposing a definition of a new kind of poverty'; the definition was associated with a new investigation and measurement of poverty. The 10 per cent in primary poverty figure [for York] was obtained by bringing together two separate calculations, the earnings calculation and the minimal expenditure calculation.[75]

The latter calculation could be attempted thanks in part to developments in Edwardian nutritional theory. Such developments held out the possibility of specifying minimum nutritional standards for the maintenance of 'physical efficiency' in the human body. The former calculation could be made on the basis of a knowledge of local wage rates. In this way Rowntree sought to found a scientific measure of 'poverty', which was to be made visible as the inadequacy of a house-hold's income in relation to its minimal necessary expenditures.

Of course, Rowntree would not arrive at an essentially 'objective' calculation of minimum necessary expenditure. *Poverty* 'zigzagged wildly and incoherently between natural and cultural poles in its specification of minimum necessary expenditure' so that its primary poverty line 'was arbitrary and could be moved upwards and downwards according to taste'.[76] What is significant, however, is that Rowntree established a framework for an empirical knowledge of poverty which has the household budget at its heart.

Except for the fact that it will incorporate certain technical breakthroughs in sampling technique, the survey approach remained basically the same for the inter-war years. A. L. Bowley had pioneered statistical sampling during the war and this innovation greatly extended the scope of the survey approach, lifting it out of the confines of a single town. As a consequence it became possible to produce knowledge about poverty in a comparative framework as Bowley did with his *Livelihood and Poverty* (1915), as well as at the level of the nation.[77]

It is important to note that this empirical conception of poverty embodied in the social survey movement is not a general knowledge of poverty. For it is linked to a liberal problematic. It takes as its norm the *self-supporting* household. Poverty is therefore rendered as a deviation from this norm, the extent to which (for reasons that may be 'behavioural' or 'structural') the household's income fails to match its expenses.[78]

'UNEMPLOYMENT ASSISTANCE': A TECHNOLOGY OF 'WELFARE'

Thus far I have traced how the cognitive apparatuses and intellectual machinery of sociology, social psychology, and the social survey move-ment produced specific knowledges about the long-term unemployed in the 1930s. I have outlined two lines of inquiry concerning the long-term unemployed subject, one concerning the state of their 'morale', the other rendering them as subjects 'in need'. In this final section I turn to the question of how the long-term unemployed became the objects of new forms of administrative and governmental practice, and the relationship between such practices and the knowledges and con-cerns that have just been noted.

The Advent of Unemployment Assistance

At the outset of this chapter I observed that it was the crisis of the unemployment insurance system in the late 1920s which shaped the way that the issue of prolonged unemployment was to figure within the political agenda. In 1931 the newly formed National government, in one of its first steps, set out to make the insurance scheme solvent again. It did this by applying strict new eligibility requirements for the receipt of insurance benefit. This had the immediate effect of removing some 800 000 people from the insurance scheme (which had at that time been paying benefits of one sort or another to almost 3 million unemployed). This raised the question: what provision was to be made for the long-term and frequently unemployed who were no longer to be supported by the insurance system?

This question was answered in the 1930s by a series of experiments in providing non-insurance based relief (or 'assistance' as it became officially designated) to the long-term unemployed. Basically this took two forms: the Public Assistance Committees (PACs) and, after 1934, the Unemployment Assistance Board (UAB).[79]

From 1931 to 1934 assistance for the long-term unemployed took the form of 'transitional payments' (TPs) which were administered by local PACs. TPs were paid at the same rate as insurance benefit, but were subject to a household means test. The PACs had been formed by consolidating the vast number of Poor Law Unions into a regional structure in 1929, at which point they took over the Unions' former responsibilities for the poor.

This way of relieving the unemployed was fraught with difficulties. The unemployed associated the PACs with the Poor Law and all of its stigma. The application of the household means test took PAC officers into the homes of applicants and this was generally regarded by working people as an invasion of the home. The fact that it was the household which was tested was perceived to be particularly unjust: it meant that distant relatives or non-relatives could be made responsible for the support of the unemployed individual as well as immediate family.

In creating the PACs, the government had sought to fashion a form of social administration which would be more insulated from social pressures than the Poor Law had been in its later years. However, the PACs proved similarly vulnerable to political protest and pressure. As a result, there appeared great variations in the stringency with which the means test was applied. In areas like Rotherham, Durham, and Glamorgan, where sympathy for the unemployed was well insti-tutionalized, the means test was all but abolished.

The UAB seems to have been set up in 1934 as a response to the failure of the PACs. Unlike the PACs, which were regional, the UAB was a national organization. As Briggs and Deacon have pointed out, it was designed to take relief out of politics by insulating the administrative system from local influences.[80] However, it was not immune from protest either. In attempting to bring its own, less-generous relief payments into operation, it was forced into a famous reversal, the so-called 'standstill' measure. This gave the unemployed the right to collect relief payments from the UAB at the former higher rate given by the PACs. Despite this setback, the UAB remained in operation until the war, and later became a more general relief agency, the National Assistance Board.

Unemployment Assistance and Government

The tendency within social history and public policy literatures has been to see these events in class-analytical terms. Successive government reforms concentrated and bureaucratized the unemployment assistance system in response to popular pressures and struggles that had won various concessions out of the Poor Law.[81] This perspective is invaluable since it demonstrates how institutional forms are never designed in a political vacuum. Their form has to be seen in relation to a field of social and political forces. The following remarks about unemployment assistance are therefore intended to complement, not contradict, existing accounts.

Clearly, the rise of unemployment assistance implied the standard-ization and nationalization of the relief of poverty. According to its first annual report, the UAB 'would not be justified, as a central department administering central funds, in proceeding on any other principle than that of equality of treatment for households in similar circumstances, wherever they lived'.[82] One observer heralded it as 'one of the major social experiments of the century' since it was quite unprecedented – 'a nation-wide relief agency administering needs payments according to uniform scales'.[83] In this sense, the UAB brought the practice of assisting the non-insured poor and unemployed into line with insurance practices which, since 1911, had also been organized on a national basis. If statistical and surveying breakthroughs were making it possible to 'see' poverty at a national level, then developments in administrative practice were following.

However, we still need to ask: what sorts of governmental tech-nologies made it possible to organize unemployment assistance on a national basis? Conventional and radical social policy approaches tend to take the availability of administrative forms for granted. Here we need to move away from an 'internalist' perspective and consider developments in other fields of administration. My suggestion is that the emergence of the public corporation as a new, transposable model for public administration was not unrelated to the changes which occurred within the field of poverty management.

The Public Corporation

Between the wars, the public corporation – of which the British Broad-casting Company and the Central Electricity Board were prototypes – was heralded as 'a new and unique administrative form'.[84] Its pre-decessor was obviously the municipal corporation, which can be traced back to the experiments in municipal socialism conducted by the London County Council at the turn of the century, and ultimately back to Joseph Chamberlain's Birmingham in the 1860s. Its contemporary was the large business corporation which first made a serious impres-sion on the economic field between the wars. Indeed, it is observed at this time that 'there is a paramount need for the study both of Industrial Administration and Public Administration with a view to the discovery of a common territory, or perhaps more accurately with a view to the enlargement of the admitted common territory'.[85]

The public corporation is seen as a semi-autonomous body organized and run like a large business but forbidden from drawing profits from its services. It is to be unlike the government department staffed by civil servants and headed by a Minister answerable to Parliament. The public corporation is run by a board which, although publicly appointed, is endowed with a large degree of autonomy in regard to its policy and execution: for the 'national political system is ill adapted to commercial administration'.[86] In this way the public corporation will promise 'a greater degree of economic or business efficiency in the operation of the service than might be achieved by what until recently have been regarded as the normal methods of managing a business owned and operated by the state'.[87]

Public corporations like the BBC and the UAB are political tech-nologies which, as already observed for social insurance in Chapter 3, make it possible to actualize concepts of citizenship and national community. Although unemployment is much higher in the 'depressed areas', although the costs of broadcasting to the Highlander are greater than to the city dweller, these services are to be uniformly provided and financed not by local rates or tariffs but for the most part by taxes; receiving and paying for these services in this way is an index of the citizen's membership of and obligations to the national community. With the advent of the public corporation, principles of uniform and impersonal treatment, which had long been features of the citizen's legal rights, can be extended into the field of social administration, and to social rights.

The Means Test and Governance through 'Need'

There are other ways in which the advent of unemployment assistance is significant for a history of the governance of unemployment and poverty, besides this national effect which it produces within the social field. By making the means test central to its routine practices unemployment assistance institutionalizes what I am calling 'governance through need' on an official basis. When the Unemployment Assistance Board explains that for the person who had exhausted their claim on the insurance scheme 'it was difficult to see upon what principle other than that of "need" [unemployment] assistance could be given',[88] the sense in which it employs 'need' is as a moral claim – one that is made on the state/community by those who have become destitute through no fault of their own. However, for 'need' to become a basis for assistance, it will have to be translated from this political-moral register into an administrative one. That is, it will have to be made operable as a concept and a relieving practice. This was to be the function of the Means Test.

We saw in the previous section how an empirical conception of poverty was advanced by Rowntree and taken up by the inter-war 'social survey movement'. Drawing on this particular way of 'seeing' poverty, the UAB was able to treat the 'needs' of its applicants as a knowable and administrable domain. 'Need' was simply the calculable deficit of a household's resources in relation to its 'normal' needs; assistance was to compensate for this deficit. In this way the Means Test produced 'need' as a governable object.

The UAB's Means Test led to an escalation and intensification of supervision and surveillance within the unemployment relief system.[89] The UAB was, of course, by no means the only agency engaged in the surveillance of the unemployed. As we saw in Chapter 3, the advent of unemployment insurance gave the state a certain amount of leverage over the individual. To remain eligible for benefits, workers had to comply with various norms regarding such things as their working patterns, their reasons for quitting employment, and the regularity with which they looked for work when unemployed. For the most part these conventions were limited to the sphere of work.

However, with Unemployment Assistance, 'need' becomes the object and site of regulation and assessment. With the Means Test, virtually the whole field of the applicant's social existence and that of his or her household is opened up to official scrutiny. Various social commentaries on the 1930s note how the long-term unemployed and their families loathed and often feared the Relieving Officers of the PACs and then the UAB, who were authorized to inspect their homes and possessions. These officials were instrumental in the management and normalization of inter-war poverty. For they applied the uniform assistance scales which set out the 'normal needs' of households of varying compositions – for food, rent, clothing, and certain 'sundries'.

Part of the Relieving Officer's job was to exercise 'discretion': 'It was an essential part of the Regulations that they should contain adequate provision for the exercise of what is called "discretion", that is, for the modification of the standard scale and rules to fit the circumstances of an individual case.'[90]

Wherever needs diverge from the 'normal case' they have the potential to become special objects of inquiry. The case of rent is illustrative, since it was expected that this more than any other need would show marked variations by region. Wherever a household's rent was significantly higher than the 'notional rent' contained in the scales, it became an object of argumentation: was the claimant paying this rent out of necessity? Had they considered subletting, or bargaining with the landlord/lady, or ultimately, a change of residence? The sanction which could always be invoked was that existing rent would cease to be fully covered as a need.

The UAB was certainly not the first official body to govern the poor in terms of some conception of their needs. The infamous Speenhamland system, named after the village in Berkshire where it was introduced in 1795, saw the Poor Law paying supplements to the wages of the poor. These subsidies were based on the cost of bread and the size of the family of the applicant.[91] Neither was the UAB the first authority to send its representatives into the homes of the poor and destitute. This had been a practice of certain aspects of Poor Law relief. Various local authorities like the School Board had their own inspectors. And this had also been an aim of Victorian and Edwardian charitable visitors. What was novel about the UAB was not only the way that such practices were made systematic, routine, and national in their scope, but also the fact that since long-term unemployment made so many 'respectable' working families destitute, it greatly extended the scope of this form of social administration.

The last point I want to make concerning governance through need is that it serves to modify the political relations within the social field between the individual-claimant and the state. With social insurance, the citizen-claimant is governed according to a logic of 'entitlement'. This is a binarizing practice: individuals and populations are either entitled or not.[92] Originally entitlement was decided by the individual's contribution record. However, as already noted, by the 1920s a whole battery of tests were deployed to make this categorization possible once the original 'insurance' criteria of the administration system became unworkable. The 'genuinely seeking work' test was one of the most infamous of these. But it is interesting to note how the early means test was also used for the same purpose: various social services and certain non-standard forms of unemployment benefit were either granted or withheld depending upon proof of the applicant's 'need'.[93] One is either needy or not.

By the time of the UAB's means test in the mid 1930s a different political relation around the notion of need can be discerned. The function of the UAB means test is less one of disqualifying the ineligible applicant, more one of quantifying the precise amount of assistance due to the claimant on the basis of a calculation of their needs. It will be able to grant differing amounts of cash where previously the courts of referees and employment committees which operated it could only grant or withhold the fixed rate.[94] In this way need will be opened up as a finely graded and empirically graduated social and economic condition. This process corresponds with the extension of the scope of the state's responsibility for the welfare of society: the shift to a position which sees need as a normal condition pertaining to large numbers of the population.

Unemployment Assistance and 'Morale'

Finally, in light of the earlier discussion of 'demoralization', I should briefly note how 'morale' begins to be seen as an object of governance with regard to the long-term unemployed. Part of the UAB's remit was to make provisions for maintaining the morale of the unemployed. One way it did this was by liaising with the unemployed club movement which grew up in the 1930s. The club movement was centred in the voluntary sector and was led by philanthropists.[95] It sought to organize occupational centres for the unemployed, where they could socialize, but also stay active by doing handiwork, sport, boot-mending, etc. The club movement professed to counter the isolation and inactivity which could be associated with prolonged unemployment. But there is also a sense in which they were supposed to provide an alternative community to the 'unhealthy' unemployed communities which social observers thought had grown up around cinemas, betting offices, and other places where unemployed people congregated.

A second way in which morale began to be seen as a manipulable set of relations was in terms of the investigative resources which the UAB possessed. There can be little doubt that when the Means Test was first made central to the administration of unemployment relief in 1931, it was primarily as a way of curbing public expenditure in this area. By the late 1930s, the investigatory apparatus which had grown around it was coming to be perceived by senior public officials in new ways. Not just as a means in the pursuit of narrow, fiscal objectives, but, more positively, as a technology for the promotion of morale and welfare.

> Do you know that every one of the 600 000 men and 400 000 women [on the UAB register] is visited, in his or her home, once every four weeks, by

an Unemployment Assistance Officer? Not called up to be stood in a queue and questioned at a table, but visited at home ... It has never until to-day been possible to see each unemployed person as a separate and distinctive case needing special aid. It has still less been possible to treat each one as such. The nature and method of the UAB has made that for the first time possible.[96]

This is a good instance of the way in which governmental technologies are sometimes redeployed, their purposes reimagined as they become harnessed to new political objectives and changing conceptions of the role of the state and its relation to the citizen.

As a result of the depression during the inter-war years, many people experienced prolonged periods of unemployment, and with it great suffering and distress. This does not in itself explain why a group that is recognizable as the 'long unemployed' is vested with so much social and political significance at this time. This chapter has argued that to understand this event, we need to look at other developments. The crisis of the insurance system is crucial here. The management of inter-war unemployment involved as one of its major aspects the invention of a new population and social identity – the long-term unemployed. This category allowed prolonged unemployment to be managed while at the same time holding on to the reconstituted insurance system as a way of governing the 'normal' unemployed. We can conclude that society's problem of prolonged unemployment and industrial depression was governed, in part, *through* the 'long unemployed'.

Long-term unemployment was a temporary phenomenon. With mobilization for war in the 1940s, unemployment disappeared. However, it has a legacy. Out of society's confrontation with this issue in the 1930s, new ways of understanding and acting on individuals and populations took shape. This is the case, for instance, with the practice of unemployment assistance. This develops as a way of governing individuals in that grey area between social insurance and Poor Law, persons who lack a contractual, 'earnt' right to public support, but who, in an age of mass democracy, cannot be treated as paupers. Unemployment is therefore a space of invention: like other problem-sites, it gives rise to ways of governing which are mobile and flexible enough to be taken up in other contexts.

CHAPTER 5

UNEMPLOYMENT AND ITS SPACES

So far this book has confined itself to the formation of modern employment policy and early conceptions of unemployment. In this and the next chapter the theme will be transformations in the government of unemployment over the last fifty years or so. There are several conceptual frameworks one could use to place the development of employment policy this century in a wider political and economic context. For instance, it is not uncommon to find changes in policies for the labour market, and many other aspects of public policy besides, discussed in terms of the rise and fall of the 'post-war settlement' – a politically institutionalized consensus, centred on the state, between the class forces of capital and labour.[1] Also commonplace have been discussions highlighting a shift in the ideological underpinnings of such policies: from Keynesianism to monetarism or neo-liberalism,[2] while certain scholars have drawn our attention to more fundamental, organizational transformations at the level of political economy. A whole host of developments within the field of employment policy – ranging from workfare to training, and deregulation to self-employment – are said to be connected with a shift in socio-economic logics, as post-Fordist forms of organization supplant those familiar to Fordism, and as states respond to the challenge of globalization.[3]

This chapter will connect, albeit obliquely, with some of the territory charted by the literature cited above. However, its ambitions are somewhat different. It does not offer the reader a comprehensive overview or theory of policy changes in the post-war period. Instead, it endeavours to open up a new angle of perception on this territory. It proposes to analyse changes in employment policy in terms of *a history of its spaces.*

Before proceeding, perhaps I should clarify what I mean by 'space'. This chapter does not address the spatiality of unemployment in the way that a political economist or economic geographer might, that is, in terms of an account of the uneven development of the economy and the social and economic structures which determine a given distribution of economic activity.[4] Neither does it treat space as reducible to legal and administrative boundaries. Instead, the chapter is concerned with the way in which different governmentalities privilege particular imagined spaces as the settings for particular forms of ethical relations, economic processes, or social dynamics. These imagined spaces can then function as valorizations for political reforms and proposals to reorganize the institutional framework of public policies. The premise of the chapter is therefore that one can identify different imagined geographies or architectures of unemployment. For example, for the Victorians the question of poverty and irregular employment was intimately bound up with the shambolic and promiscuous space of the slum: it was on this scale that some of the most powerful moral and social processes contributing to the transmission of disease, and of pernicious social habits, were believed to operate.

If previous and subsequent chapters highlight the differing ways in which unemployment is posed as a problem within different governmentalities, this chapter emphasizes the different spaces which unemployment is imagined to occupy. It emphasizes the shifting imagined geographies of unemployment which are presupposed by Keynesianism, post-Fordism, and other theories of social and economic life, and by such symbolic figures as the 'inner city'. The aim is to denaturalize the spatial assumptions of programmes of government.[5]

To this end, the first section of the chapter offers an account of some of the ways in which unemployment was constructed as a *national* problem. It suggests that Keynesianism is exemplary as a policy rationale and technique which seeks to place the governance of unemployment on a fully national basis. But if Keynesianism exemplifies what it is to govern unemployment within a national frame, the rest of the chapter concerns more recent programmes and policies which seek to get at unemployment in terms of other levels and scales. Hence in the second section it is suggested that with the rise of various measures of 'local economic development' and the like, it is possible to identify measures which seek to govern unemployment through localities. The final section considers certain debates about the social and economic problems of the European Union. In their haste to criticize or propose new public policies for unemployment in Europe, most scholars seem to have missed a very interesting development – that the debates in which they engage presuppose the existence of, and help to construct, a

European object of unemployment which is irreducible to the employment problems of the constituent member states. It seems that unemployment is now also being conceptualized and governed as a problem which is located in a *supranational* space.

THE NATION AS A SETTING FOR THE GOVERNMENT OF UNEMPLOYMENT

Writers in different areas of the social sciences are presently bringing our attention to a peculiar feature of our concepts and theories about social life. It is that for some time, they have been state-centric.[6] The social sciences took it for granted that societies were national societies, economies were national economies, their borders circumscribed and coincidental with the territorial boundaries of the nation-state. The territorial state has been treated as though it were a 'container' of society and its problems. What was in fact an historical contingency was considered a social necessity. For as John Agnew has pointed out: 'The nation state, based on a circumscribed territory, involved the creation of a unified and homogeneous space in which the various aspects of social practice – culture, knowledge, education, employment – were rationalized and homogenized.'[7]

Unemployment is clearly another aspect of social practice that has been constructed as national. For instance, the long-established convention within political and economic analysis of comparing unemployment rates between countries suggests that it is a national property, a phenomenon somehow located *inside* nation-states. However, I want to suggest there are at least two ways in which one could deconstruct this assumption and lessen the hold which 'the national' has on our thinking.

First, we can imagine a history of unemployment in terms of the political-geographical scales on which it has been conceptualized and addressed. This would doubtless show that unemployment has been the subject of shifting and competing spatializations. To some extent this study has already alluded to such a history. In earlier chapters it was noted that for the late nineteenth century unemployment was quite palpably regarded as an urban problem, centred on towns, docks, slums, and other disorganized and chaotic spaces. If social thought and investigation became preoccupied with the disturbing prospect of the physical degeneration of the population at this time (see Chapter 1), then this process had its own imagined geography in which the town was like a swamp into which the poorer classes were sinking.[8] We have also seen that during the interwar years there emerged a perception of unemployment as a regional problem; 'depressed areas' like the North-

East were identified as being in need of special 'assistance'.[9] Later in this chapter we will trace the re-emergence of a paradigm of urban unemployment in the 1970s. In these and no doubt many other ways, it is possible to reveal other spatializations of unemployment, and to suggest that although the national has been the dominant construction, it is by no means the only one.

But as well as tracing the changing imagined geographies of unemployment, one could also unsettle assumptions that it is self-evidently a national phenomenon by analysing employment policy at the level of its political technologies. One could demonstrate that key governmental technologies have actively *constructed* unemployment as a national object of regulation. Again, this theme was tangential to discussions in earlier chapters. For example, it was observed that the labour exchange system opens up a new perspective on the labour market: it allows it to be 'seen' abstractly as a national entity. Similarly, the technology of social insurance places the government of unemployment on a national basis. It spreads the risks associated with redundancy across a *national* population, rather than that of a specific trade, sector, or locality. It enables a gradual break to be made with the highly localized practice and ethos of the Poor Law. A similar significance could be attached to Unemployment Assistance, an invention which featured in the previous chapter.

However, so far in this study little has been said concerning what is perhaps the major political and institutional innovation in terms of rendering unemployment as a fully national object – the advent of 'Keynesian' economic management in the 1940s. That will be the task here.

Unemployment and the National Economy

It is a commonplace that with his *General Theory*, Keynes posed a serious challenge to the dominant conception of unemployment within economic theory.[10] Neoclassical economists maintained that the economy would nearly always automatically tend towards full employment; this was its normal state. Persistent unemployment was therefore explained as a deviation from this norm, in terms of exogenous and contingent factors – such as collective bargaining and social protection systems which prevented the 'efficient' adjustment of labour supply to demand.

Keynes argued to the contrary. Unemployment was actually a normal feature of the way the economic system actually operates: 'the evidence indicates that full, or even approximately full employment is a rare and short-lived occurrence'.[11] Unemployment was endogenous to the economy. What explanation did Keynes give for this? To put it very briefly, he reasoned that in mature capitalist systems like Britain and the USA, the social organization of consumption and investment was such that aggregate demand in the economy tended to fall short of the level that would be required to keep the economy operating at full employment. On this basis he recommended a new and permanent role for the state in relation to economic life – as a manager of the economy. While his *General Theory* did not offer any technical blueprints, its message was quite unequivocal: the state was to play a central role in the maintenance of full employment through the calculated and counter-cyclical deployment of public spending, taxation, and monetary policies.

As Cutler, Williams, and Williams have suggested, concepts like 'state interventionism' are too blunt for the purpose of assessing Keynes' political rationality. Keynes was, like Beveridge, an advocate and an architect of 'liberal collectivism'.[12] He maintained that if the essential liberal principles of private property and personal liberty were success-fully to confront the challenges of socialism and fascism, and to survive the problems besetting pre-Second World War capitalism, there would need to be a *strategic* collectivization of certain aspects of social life. To prevent the socialization of the means of production sought by some socialists, Keynes advocated *the socialization of aggregate demand*. To lump Keynes under the heading of 'state interventionism' is therefore to oversimplify matters. He advocated a quite limited, and specifically liberal form of intervention – one calculated to sustain capitalism through the minimum necessary amount of socialization.

But what impact did Keynes' arguments have on actual policies? Studies of economic policy-making have shown that the relationship between economic thought and the practice of economic policy in the 1940s is a complicated matter. It is certainly more than a question of Keynes' ideas simply 'winning out' over neo-classical orthodoxies as earlier, idealist studies of the rise of Keynesianism implied.[13] To capture some of this complexity, some commentators have focused on the political and institutional conditions, especially within the policy-making apparatus, which favoured the adoption of 'Keynesian' ideas at this time. Margaret Weir, for example, highlights the creation of the Economic Section within the War Cabinet: 'leading Keynesians were able to use it as a base from which to influence the Treasury from the top down'.[14]

Other writers have placed an emphasis on the technical and logistical capabilities which had to be in place for Keynesian policies to become viable. For example, successful Keynesian policies required the prior development of an apparatus of national income accounts which could measure levels of economic activity. They also required the central state to be able to adjust levels of public spending flexibly in response to economic conditions – something which could not be done in a political system where local authorities have considerable fiscal autonomy.[15]

Finally, it has been suggested that the conversion of key economic policy-making centres within the British state to Keynesian principles should be seen in relation to prevailing *economic*, and not just political or institutional circumstances. Hence Jim Tomlinson has pointed out that the Treasury gave initial support for Keynesian budgetary techniques during the Second World War not as a means to combat unemployment, the traditional Keynesian target, but inflation, which was seen to be a major risk for the war economy. Similarly, Keynesian thinking could be affirmed by the Treasury in the 1950s and early 1960s when domestic and international economic prospects were favourable and the political costs of adopting a policy of 'fine-tuning' the economy were minimal. But the fact that a Keynesian response was not forthcoming when it was really needed – that is, when mass unemployment struck again in the 1970s – indicates that political support within the policy apparatus had been highly conditional.[16]

Having addressed the matter of how the policy-making system became converted to Keynesian ideas and principles, we can now turn to a question which is much more central to the concerns of this chapter, and of the study as a whole. What interests me here is how this Keynesian moment will strengthen the governmental perception of unemployment as a *national* problem. There are several interesting points to be made in this respect.

First, with the rise of Keynesianism, there is a notable change in the very constitution of the object of unemployment, in terms of how it is embedded in assemblages of power/knowledge relations. If unemployment had been largely governed as an object of social administration until the 1940s, the advent of Keynesianism saw it territorialized in a new way: within the emerging field of macroeconomic policy.[17] This does not supplant the social administration machine, but rather, takes shape alongside it. Henceforth, it is no longer just social policy experts who will routinely discuss it and seek its truth, but economists and others who will develop their own specialist knowledges about, and around, unemployment.

The rise of econometrics played a notable part in configuring unemployment in terms of a set of quantifiable economic relations, operating on a national scale.[18] Econometrics has been defined as 'every application of mathematics or of statistical methods to the study of economic phenomena'.[19] While precedents for the twinning of economic thought and statistical analysis have been found as early as the sixteenth century in the work of Political Arithmeticians such as

William Petty and Gregory King, it is in the 1930s and 1940s that econometrics becomes institutionalized as a practice and a branch of economics. It is at this time that the Econometrics Society is founded, along with the Cowles Commission in the United States, and the Department of Applied Economics at Cambridge University. Econometrics also became important within the economic policy-making system following the Second World War. It could be readily aligned with the new, Keynesian practices of economic management to which the UK government had become committed in its bid to engineer full employment in the economy (see below).[20] For econometrics facilitated the building of macroeconometric models of national economies, and the development of an allied technique of short-term economic 'forecasting'. Economic modelling and forecasting were pursued in government departments as well as within universities and research institutions like the National Institute of Economic and Social Research. Between 1945 and 1974, forecasting featured as part of the weaponry of the government in its bid to 'fine-tune' the economy to maintain high levels of employment and economic performance.[21]

It is in terms of this complex of institutions, government objectives, econometric experts, and modelling and forecasting techniques that we can see unemployment becoming located within a new series. In Chapter 3 it was noted how unemployment acquired a certain meaning once it became an object of social insurance; it appears as another 'accident' set within the series death, illness, fire, theft. Here we can note that as it becomes a concern of macroeconomic policy, it enters into a different kind of series: unemployment becomes another *economic* indicator alongside the inflation rate, the balance of payments, the annual rate of national product and so on. At the level of statistical models of the economy, but also within public understandings, the unemployment rate will become a privileged index of the health of the national economy. Hence, during the post-war period the perception is of unemployment as a phenomenon somehow located *inside* nation-states, an impression that is only enhanced as fledgling international organizations adopt the unemployment rate as one of their many axes for comparing the performance of different national economies.[22]

There is a second point which, for the purposes of a history of the government of unemployment, needs to be emphasized about the Keynesian turn within economic policy. If the Second World War was decisive in forging a political and social consensus around the need for, and obligation of, the state to take a much more central and positive role in the management of social and economic affairs, the availability of Keynesian fiscal and budgetary techniques meant that this objective could be made governable in a way that was compatible with core liberal principles.[23] It meant, quite crucially, that for the first time 'full employment' could be declared as a positive and proper objective of public policy.[24] Armed with the technique of economic management, and buoyed by the way in which the British economy achieved (by its own modest standards) highly impressive rates of economic growth during the 1950s and early 1960s, it seemed to policy-makers and politicians that the riddle of unemployment had been 'solved': the state had the power to dictate the employment level but without unduly compromising liberalism. This political perception was duly consolidated with the discovery within economics of the 'Phillips curve', which suggested that there existed an inverse relation, and therefore a policy trade-off, between wage inflation and unemployment. The Phillips curve 'seemed to suggest that policy-makers faced unlimited options: they could pick any level of unemployment and the price would be just a bit more inflation'.[25]

Third, and finally concerning Keynesianism and its consequences for the government of unemployment, we should observe that with the advent of this new form of economic policy there is a depersonalization of the government of unemployment. With Keynesianism, unemployment is governed without any need to interrogate the moral or social status of the unemployed, without the need to reform persons.[26] For it governs *through* the national economy: it constructs the latter as a manipulable object which can be managed in such a way as to obviate prolonged unemployment. It identifies unemployment as a *sui generis* property of the national economy. We saw in previous chapters that even social insurance – which seeks to decentre the juridical and moral subject within the governance of unemployment and poverty – still governs through persons. It still requires a knowledge of the bearer of unemployment which it uses to assess claims and so on. Keynesianism acts solely at the level of economic relations. It finally breaks what had seemed a natural link – that the governance of unemployment must at the same time involve the government of the unemployed.[27]

Unemployment after Keynesianism: Still a National Problematic?

Reflecting on the 1970s, one senior economic policy-maker has declared it 'a decade of tumult, doubt and discontent' in which inflation reached staggering dimensions, wages outstripped prices, and unemployment rose from 600 000 at the start of the decade to 1.5 million by its end. These turbulent economic conditions, and the political anxiety which they provoked, saw a profound alteration in the political status of unemployment. Despite its magnitude it 'ceased to be the touchstone of policy as the need to control inflation took precedence over the earlier aim of full employment'.[28]

If Keynesianism was a decisive – although not by any means the only – governmental intervention in terms of figuring unemployment as a national problem, did the demise of Keynesianism in the 1970s and 1980s spell a weakening of this national frame? Explanations abound of monetarist and supply-side doctrines popularized by the 'New Right' within politics in order to undermine the Keynesian consensus in the 1970s.[29] But what is less often remarked about these neo-liberal doctrines is that they do not challenge Keynesianism in one important sense. They do not contest this idea that unemployment is a problem of *national* economies.[30] They simply locate it in a different region of the economy. The supply-side theory of unemployment held that it was foremost a 'structural' and not, as the Keynesians assumed, a 'cyclical' problem.[31] It was better performance on the 'supply' rather than the 'demand' side of the economy which was at issue.[32] According to this view, each economy has a 'natural rate' of unemployment which is determined by a complex interplay of supply-side factors, including the structure of labour markets, tax and benefit regimes, training and education systems, the research and innovation capacity of firms, and many other things besides. Hence the locus of intervention is shifted from the active management of aggregate demand, to the myriad factors which influence the supply of labour. But the territory remains that of the national economy.

Globalization, Competitiveness, Jobs

Like the Keynesians whom they criticized, monetarist economists like Milton Friedman saw the economy as a more or less self-contained machine, coextensive with the boundaries of the nation-state.[33] Supply-side policies were affirmed on the grounds that they would effect a lasting improvement in the performance of the domestic economy, largely by improving the *internal* relations between its component parts. However, over the last 15 years or so, thinking about the supply-side has become connected with a significantly changed image of economic life, one that emphasizes its global proportions. 'Ours is an open trading economy', asserted a 1985 Conservative White Paper on employment.[34] 'This means competing with other countries in initiative, in quality and design, in marketing and service, and in prices and costs. If we do not give good value for money our products will not sell abroad, nor even at home.' The White Paper concludes that of the many 'penalties' facing nations which fail in this global challenge, 'the worst … is unemployment'.

During the 1990s this new understanding of the economic system has been developed further by academic and journalistic commentary as well. States and other economic actors are imagined as nodes in a global network or space of economic flows – a space in which capital, goods, information, and so on, move rapidly and almost effortlessly across borders.[35] At the same time that this global order, with its unbound financial markets, has emasculated the conduct of national macro-economic policy, it has placed a premium on strategic supply-side policies. A country's infrastructure, its education system, its financial structure, its cities, its tax system – these become just so many of the variables which will govern a nation's 'capacity' to 'adapt to change' and respond to the 'challenge' of competition in the global world.

Now it is not my objective to assess the accuracy of this 'globalized' conception of economic order.[36] What interests me here is simply the fact that, as a key element within the governmentalities of the left and right, it shapes the way in which the problem of unemployment is now posed. The reform of a nation's supply-side 'infrastructure', its labour market and education and training institutions, these are no longer measures which are simply to improve the internal coherence and per-formance of a 'domestic' economy. They are presented as improve-ments to the 'competitiveness' of the nation, measures which will boost the 'job-creation' powers of the economy in relation to its competitors. For instance, greater labour market flexibility, or workforce 'skills' are frequently emphasized as critical resources in 'attracting' jobs which now, rather like other factors of production, are imagined as flows. This logic was certainly underpinning the rhetoric of the last Conservative government whenever it described Britain as the 'enterprise centre of Europe'. Britain was imagined as some sort of giant enterprise zone poised to attract the mobile investment and jobs which found continental Europe, with its sclerotic labour markets and red tape, less attractive.[37]

We can conclude this section with the observation that the nation has not been a natural ground for employment policies, but a frame that has been constructed by different theories and policies. As such, the particular function it has played within governmentalities has not been unchanging. Keynesian policies governed unemployment by acting on what they took to be a self-contained, national economic system. Today there is a sense that job-creation is not exclusively endogenous to national economies, but involves a game of competition to create and attract jobs in the context of a global economic environment. The equation of unemployment and international rivalry is certainly not unprecedented. We saw in Chapter 2 that it is implicit in the discourse of Tariff Reform at the turn of the century. But its articulation today is somewhat different. For one thing, most of today's exponents of the competitiveness agenda are not economic protectionists but keen advocates of a liberalized world trading and production regime. But also, Tariff Reform failed to dominate the political agenda. At present, the same could hardly be said of competitiveness.

UNEMPLOYMENT: A PROBLEM OF LOCALITIES?

If employment policy, like most public policies, was plainly national in its organization and logic for much of the post-war period, the situation is less straightforward today. While the national continues as a crucial frame of reference for employment policy, albeit in new ways as we have seen, a mere glance at the recent history of urban and employment policy reveals that the locality is now accorded a vital and strategic significance within the governance of unemployment. The last twenty years or so have seen a proliferation of local economic development and enterprise strategies, co-ordinated by formal and 'informal' agents of local government.[38] The message of Urban Development Corporations, City Challenge projects, and the myriad other agencies and 'partnerships' through which the subnational is promoted, is that nowadays the prospects for social cohesion and job-creation depend considerably on the fortunes of specifically *local* or *urban economies*. Furthermore, if the consensus, as I argued above, is that henceforth nations must 'compete' for jobs in a global economy, the capacity to do this successfully is seen to depend on structures that are local:

> Britain's competitiveness ... depends on the productivity of its human and capital resources. This at root depends on the capacity of its businesses and the people who manage and work in them. That capacity is primarily a local requirement. Hence [our] focus on enterprise and training as a process of local capacity building ... It is chiefly in local contexts that the battle to develop improved capacity to respond to the global challenge will be lost or won.[39]

The strategic significance of the regional and the urban is different from what it was in the post-war period. Within the political rationalities and tactics of rule which were dominant then, the region was merely an administrative sub-unit of the national, connected with 'the chopping-up of problems into manageable areas'.[40] Regional policy served a variety of purposes, but predominant were the objectives of redistributing manufacturing activity across the national space (e.g., through public subsidies for relocating firms) so as to promote a national standard of social justice, counteract 'overheating' in the more active parts of the economy, and prevent the emergence of concentrated pockets of unemployment.

At present, the local/regional is much more than a mechanism for passively administering and transmitting national plans. Rather, it has become a privileged space, condensing a series of positive values, and itself a site of agency. For instance, as one White Paper on employment insisted,

> it is at local level [*sic*] where individuals and institutions most directly share a sense of community and can best shape a common purpose. It is where young people and adults learn the skills they need for working life and it is where business develops.[41]

In political terms, the local is privileged because it is the space of the affiliations of partnership and community, of participation, self-governance, and particularity. In economic terms, the local is important because, as different theories of post-Fordism and post-industrialism explain, it is a space of economic dynamism and innovation, a space of association and networking between firms and other organizations which is conducive to flexibility.[42] Change has also occurred in philosophies of public administration: many of the administrative machines reviewed in this study, such as unemployment insurance and assistance, were invested with the belief that they would govern more effectively by being national. In certain key respects it seems that today the reverse is true: local specificities are to be recognized (see, for example, the discussion below of the rationality of the Employment Zone).

Research within political economy has provided a powerful set of explanations for this new political and intellectual emphasis on the local/regional. One factor which has been mentioned is the role that regional political-administrative elites have played in advancing a regional agenda within politics.[43] Added to this, and beginning in the late 1980s, was a series of improvements to the 'structural funds' available to disadvantaged and less developed areas within the European Union.[44] This development provided a powerful impetus for political authorities to define their social and economic concerns in a regionalist language, and to develop regional development strategies.

But the rise of the region has also been explained in terms of global factors. For instance, the notion of 'glocalization' has been proposed to highlight the fact that political and economic processes of globalization and localization seem to occur simultaneously and perhaps dialectically.[45] It has also been suggested that while the national remains an important forum for political struggle, there has nevertheless been a 'hollowing out' of the nation-state.[46] Political authority has been ceded upwards towards multilateral bodies like the European Union in a bid to grapple with economic forces (most notably financial markets) which now escape and overwhelm national authorities. But there has also been a strengthening, albeit highly unevenly, of local and regional actors, which, in many cases, have successfully forged alliances with power structures which bypass nation-states. Examples of these are the development of interregional networks of governance in Europe, and the case of regional 'states' like California and Hong Kong which now compete with nation-states in the global economy.[48]

But if we have now some sense of how and why the local/regional has been accorded a new significance and strategic set of roles within governmentalities, we have not yet considered the implications of this development for the government of unemployment.

Governing through the Local Economy

It is a core assumption of the various development strategies and plans which have tackled the urban dimension of unemployment over the last twenty years or so that the creation of jobs, skills, enterprise, and prosperity are all to be encouraged by the 'regeneration' and 'revitalization' of specifically 'local' or 'urban economies'. The great majority of academic experts and practitioners of local and urban development take the existence of the local/regional economy for granted; in this way they contribute to its naturalization. But it is also possible to see the local economy in discursive terms.[49] That is, we can regard the local economy as the effect, as much as the target and foundation, of governmental programmes and strategies.

As Deakin and Edwards have shown in their insightful work on the connection between the 'enterprise culture' and urban renewal, one of the first sites where the social problems of the city come to be figured in terms of the deficiencies of a specifically urban economy is with the 1977 White Paper, *Policy for the Inner Cities*. The dominant perspective on urban problems at this time was the essentially welfarist paradigm of 'urban deprivation'. This saw the 'inner city problem' in terms of a population on whom various disadvantages and inequalities were concentrated, including poverty, poor health, endemic unemployment, mental disorders, and overcrowding. Urban deprivation was also a racialized paradigm.[50] For it drew on fears of a strong connection between the concentration of inner-city hardship and unemployment in ethnic minority groups, and the risk of rising crime, disaffection, and social and civil disorder. In sum, the urban deprivation paradigm called urgently for better and, in particular, targeted provision for these 'special needs'. Such needs were to be met by initiatives like the Urban Programme, the Community Development Projects, and Educational Priority Areas.

The significance of the 1977 White Paper was that it placed the question of the 'inner city' *economy* firmly on the political agenda, and at the heart of the various troubling social phenomena which seemed to be bedevilling the city – not least its physical neglect, its paucity of community spirit, and morale. The document underlined 'the erosion of the inner area economy and the shortage of private investment which might assist the process of regeneration'.[51] It identified a striking collapse of manufacturing employment in particular in urban areas, and the migration of middle-class and skilled working-class people into the suburbs and outlying regions. Accordingly, a set of key economic variables were identified as pivotal to the future prosperity of urban communities; variables, such as the skills-base of the population, small business activity, transport and communication infrastructure, which continue to set the parameters for policy practice to this day.

It is possible to interpret the politics of urban policy and the assorted projects for regeneration and renewal since the White Paper as a series of arguments and practical experiments about how best to deploy this urban economy.

The right loudly heralded the market as the instrument that would revive the urban economy. Major centre-led initiatives, such as the Urban Development Corporations and the Enterprise Zones, were to harness the enterprise and dynamism of the private sector to drive the regeneration process. A distinctive feature of these and other initiatives was a strong reliance on the redevelopment of derelict land and property, and their guiding assumption that economic regeneration would have 'trickle down' effects on the local community, in terms of jobs and economic activity.[52] Businesspeople were to be given a leading role in the management of many of these new quasi-public bodies which sprang up within the urban development field. The Training and Enterprise Councils were exemplary in this respect. Whereas industrial training had previously been administered on a tripartite basis, incorporating business and labour representatives, the councils were to be locally organized and business-led and run on a managerial basis.[53] Moreover, *Policy for the Inner Cities* had foreseen a leading role for local authorities in co-ordinating and catalysing the regeneration process. However, one of the hallmarks of Conservative urban policy was its determination to effect local regeneration almost without local authorities, which were deemed obstructive and out-moded in their approach.

But if the right came to regard the city as a key strategic battlefield in its campaign to refashion social life and public policy in the image of the market, then so did a fraction of the left see it as a point of departure for new experiments in socialism. For the 'new urban left', the urban was to be the setting for a series of initiatives which, it was hoped, would 'prefigure' a new socialist politics – a politics which would challenge not only the harsh policies of Thatcherism, but also the centralism and bureaucratism of the Labour party, as well as conventional conceptions of the role of local government.[54]

In terms of its approach to economic policy, this new local socialism was to be 'decentralised, accountable to local communities and sensitive to local needs'.[55] With its strong connections to Labour-controlled municipal government in large areas including Greater London, the West Midlands, and Sheffield, the new urban left was able to undertake a series of initiatives aimed at reviving the urban economy, and tackling the employment crisis of the early 1980s. One of the ways it sought to do this was framed in terms of 'restructuring capital'. This placed the emphasis on the development of the local economy not by orthodox measures (e.g., using public funds to lure outside investment), but through the nurturing of indigenous firms and sectors. A key initiative in this respect were the Enterprise Boards, such as the one set up by the Greater London Council, which aimed to utilize local authority pension funds to make strategic investments in the local economy. Notable also was the 'sector strategy', which sought to strengthen the lateral linkages between relevant interests like firms, employers organizations, local government, training, and education.[56]

The sector strategy is interesting because it exemplifies the point made earlier about the 'constructedness' of the local economy. Along with the skills audit, the strategic plan, and the periodic local labour market assessments commissioned by local development agencies, the sector strategy does not simply find its local economy already there.[57] Instead, these and other technologies actively construct local spaces as the containers of their own economies and local labour-markets – by measuring these spaces in terms of their internal economic properties and processes, by endowing them with an endogenous capacity for growth, and by assessing their institutions (schools, roads, local governments) in terms of the contribution they are to make to a future which is imagined in economic terms. It is not just economic theories like 'flexible accumulation' and 'post-Fordism' which lend the notion of a local economy credibility and make it salient within governmental strategies. It is also these technologies which render it a visible and governable entity. Therefore they stand in a similar relation to the local economy as did the labour bureau, discussed in Chapter 2, to the national economy.

According to Harding and Garside, the election of the Conservatives for a third term in 1987 marked something of a watershed for local economic policies.[58] Central government had been at odds with the approach taken by many Labour local governments, and through its own policies had gradually centralized control over the field of urban development. Faced with the prospect of further diminution of their influence, many of the radical Labour authorities reluctantly adopted a 'new pragmatism'. This stance continues to set the terms of

policy-practice regarding local economic development and employment initiatives today. Some of the key features of this new pragmatism
are therefore worth noting:

- the recognition that the private sector is the motor of regeneration;
- an acceptance that local authorities have a role to play in local
  development – but only as one 'player' in what has become a
  crowded field of private and parastatal developments agencies, enterprise offices, training providers, place marketers and the like;[59] and
- an agreement that the basic task of local development is making the
  locality capable of meeting the challenges of global forces – mainly
  by optimizing its 'organizational capacity', and improving the performance and co-ordination of its institutions in the training,
  innovation, communication, culture, and other fields.[60]

Finally, it is necessary to make an important qualification regarding
these remarks on the place of the locality within the governance of
unemployment. For an obvious criticism is that this is not a genuine
localism. For one thing Britain's local and regional authorities lack the
sort of autonomy which their counterparts enjoy in federal states
like Germany; many of the major initiatives to regenerate the city or
the region have been centrally controlled and implemented. But in
addition, the extent to which many local authorities and regeneration
agencies have the power to make a significant impact on the fortunes of
their struggling urban or regional economies might also be doubted
given the globalization of significant industrial sectors.[61]

Such criticisms are obviously valid. However, the extent to which real
political authority has been devolved from the centre, or the ability of a
given local authority to shape its economic future – these are probably
questions which can only be answered empirically. What I have been
concerned with in this section is not the distribution of power understood
in a realist sense, but rather with the changing ways in which political
authorities have imagined their task, and changes in the way that the
problems to be governed are defined. We have seen that it is possible to
understand recent developments in the government of unemployment in
terms of the *invention* of the local economy. This is an event that has
brought new types of authority and expertise (e.g., economic development officers, training agents) to bear upon the (formerly) social territory. It has also meant new ways of theorizing and measuring the problems
facing communities (e.g., as locales suffering from inadequate skills).

Employment Zones

While the idea of the local economy continues to function as an *a priori*
of strategies for tackling unemployment for the political left and right,

it is by no means the only way in which the geography of governance is being realigned around the local. I want to conclude this section on governing through localities by considering a very recent policy initiative, the Employment Zone (EZ). Not only will this provide an example of the present government's 'welfare to work' approach to unemployment (which is discussed more fully in the next chapter). It will also allow me to make the point that the local is not reducible to a fixed or given physical space. It serves different functions within different programmes of government. The EZ finds a new use for the locality.

The idea behind the EZ is that it will be a designated political-administrative area where institutional innovations in the governance of the unemployed are to be fostered. Cities and regions with acute labour-market problems, such as Liverpool and Glasgow, have been given EZ status. The EZ is another technology of partnership: it enjoins such actors as local authorities, business organizations, and third-sector bodies to co-operate and to submit proposals to the state for innovative schemes. These schemes are to take advantage of the extra funding available to the EZs, but also the fact that certain rules normally governing the administration of employment and social security policy may be relaxed inside the EZ. (An example of such 'red tape' obstructing innovation in social policy would be the official separation of funding for the unemployed into the discrete fields of 'benefits', 'training', and 'employment creation'.) In this way, it is hoped that the EZs will be experimental spaces for the development of 'prototypes' of new public-private forms for governing unemployment.

If the device of the Enterprise Zone was about harnessing the supposed dynamism of the business entrepreneur to the regeneration of the city, then the Employment Zone has one eye on the 'social entrepreneur'. Employment experts are mindful of the successes which third-sector organizations like Glasgow Works and the Wise Group have had in winning the motivation and commitment of the long-term unemployed, and in returning the latter to the labour-market. These organizations have established what they call 'intermediate labour-markets' where the long-term unemployed can gain training, and work experience doing useful jobs in the community for a 'real' wage.[62] Unemployed people are thought to be more motivated and committed to such projects since they lack the stigma and other negative connotations bred by a succession of ineffective state 'schemes'. We might understand the EZ as an attempt to align such promising and indigenous lines of social entrepreneurship as this with official objectives.

To conclude, the Employment Zone says several things about the present tendency towards governing through localities which this section has been highlighting. First, it provides us with another example of the local being deployed as a site of innovation and creativity, this time in opposition to the bureaucratism of the (national) benefit and regulation regime. For it will 'harness the creative potential of local communities to find new paths into employment'.[63] The local is some-how closer to communities, individuals, experience, and initiative; whereas the social state is distant and cumbersome. But second, the case of the EZ illustrates that the deployment of the local is con-stantly shifting. In this instance, it seems to represent a new plane of (de-)administrative space, a micro-world where the sectors of 'training', 'benefits', and 'job-creation' – previously divided by regulatory con-ventions – are reunified.

UNEMPLOYMENT AND SUPRANATIONAL SPACES: EUROPE'S JOBS CRISIS

It was noted in the first section that it was conventional to regard unemployment, like inflation or poverty, as something located within nation-states, the property of a national economy or national society. However, just as the primacy of this national frame is being undermined by the tendency identified as government though the locality, it is also possible to identify a tendency which frames the problem at a supra-national, European level.

Previously, to speak of 'unemployment in Europe' meant unemploy-ment as it occurred within the nation-states comprising that region. This is still often the sense of debates about European unemployment.[64] However, in this final section, I want to explore the sense in which the outlines, if not the full substance, of a different discourse are taking shape – that of *European* unemployment. Within a number of fairly recent high-level policy documents, as well as within journalistic com-mentary, it is common to find unemployment discussed in terms of a comparison of 'Europe' and 'America', as though there was a distinctly European form of unemployment.[65]

From the point of view of political economy, we would expect that the creation of a single European market – a process accelerated by the Single European Act of 1988 – would give rise to a specifically European dimension to unemployment. As the economies of Europe have become more closely integrated by trade and investment linkages, it is only to be expected that unemployment would increasingly be determined by factors 'outside' a given national economy. However, a more state-centric, institutionalist perspective would predict the identi-fication of a European problem for a different reason. Researchers working in this tradition have drawn our attention to the role that enterprising social scientists, civil servants, and state-building politicians played at the turn of the century. For it was then that their efforts helped to force unemployment and other social issues onto the policy agenda.[66] A similar process is perhaps happening with the consolidation of the European Commission as a key player in social and economic issues in recent times. Grahame Thompson notes that the Commission 'rediscovered' unemployment in the early 1990s, a moment marked by the Edinburgh summit in 1992. Until this point, its attentions had been diverted with the project of completing the single market.[67]

Fruitful as an inquiry along either of the above lines might be, given the limitations of space and the general orientation of this study it is solely as a discursive phenomenon that I shall be discussing this 'Europeanization' of the unemployment question. I am mainly interested in *problematizations* of European unemployment. Hence, this section briefly identifies three different debates, each of which presupposes some connection between processes and institutions of European integration, and unemployment. These are about the job consequences of European Monetary Union, the possibility of Euro-Keynesianism, and the competitiveness of Europe as a regional economic power. Each has the discursive effect of refiguring conceptions of unemployment at the level of political and economic relations now imagined to be inter- and supranational, i.e., more than the sum of the separate member-states.

Economic and Monetary Union

Like any policy, that of Economic and Monetary Union (EMU) has been underpinned by a variety of political justifications. Amongst the most prominent of these are that: EMU represents the logical, final, and irrevocable step towards the completion of a single European market and economy; it will further the process of political union; and that it will provide a stable and secure framework for the newly unified Germany.[68] EU members have not entered into EMU fundamentally as a means to ameliorate the region's employment situation. Nevertheless, proponents of EMU have argued for it as a neo-classical solution to the jobs crisis. The assumption is that, although there may be short-term 'adjustment' problems associated with the harmonization of national monetary policies, in the medium term 'if monetary union leads to more stable monetary and fiscal policies, lower real interest rates should boost jobs'.[69] As John Eatwell has pointed out, an optimistic, if implicit, assumption surrounds the Maastricht Treaty (which set the framework for EMU), 'that monetary stability is all that is required for full employment to be restored'.[70]

However, critics of EMU fear that it will exacerbate employment problems. The strict convergence criteria which EMU demands of signatory member states – for example, that they cut public spending in order to reduce their budget deficits to no more than three per cent of GDP – will push the jobless figures up. Furthermore, it is predicted that the European Monetary System will have an inherently anti-inflationary monetary and fiscal stance, strongly determined as it is by German monetary principles, and that this will lock Europe into a deflationary situation; 'the system bodes ill for European employment'.[71]

It is not the essential accuracy of these two positions and the predictions they make that is at issue here. What is significant about this argument, for our purposes, is that, despite the fact that these two camps disagree over the consequences of monetary union for employment, they agree that there is some sort of important connection. In other words, we have our first example of a debate which interrogates specifically European causes of unemployment, in this case the process of European institution- and market-building. Moreover, the debate itself can be seen to be a surface for empirical work which will seek to define and quantify the specifically European sources of unemployment. For instance, the proposition that EMU will only be effective if the various member states are closely integrated economically has encouraged the development of econometric models to identify the extent to which unemployment is caused by 'domestic' (e.g., German unification) or 'pan-European' sources.[72] The 'pan-European' emerges as a new object of analysis within discourses about unemployment, just as the local or national economy has done previously.

Euro-Keynesianism

The perspective on European unemployment embodied in the Maastricht Treaty is a neo-classical one. It assumes that the market will provide an 'automatic' solution. Far less influential in political or institutional terms, yet nevertheless significant for our purposes, is a different line of reasoning which interprets Europe's difficulties in Keynesian terms. A number of commentators have called for economic strategies which would deploy the European Union as an instrument for actively co-ordinating not just monetary but fiscal policies at a European level to stimulate reflation.[73]

Yet serious doubts have been raised over the ability of the EU to pursue a 'domestic' reflationary programme. For instance, Eatwell points out that although the EU countries are integrated to the extent they form a 'quasi-closed economy', each has important trading relations with non-EU economies. This fact alone would make co-ordinated fiscal expansion difficult on a purely EU-wide basis. For this, and other reasons, Eatwell argues that policy co-ordination needs to be organized at a more global level, e.g., at the level of the G7.[74]

Again, it is not the economics, or the features of specific proposals, that should concern us here. Rather, it is the fact that in debates about the possibility of reviving Keynesian policies in a more globalized economy, we find further proposals which would territorialize unemployment in new ways. Hence, Eatwell predicts that something more than another Bretton Woods system is required. Bretton Woods was the international agreement in effect from the end of the Second World War until 1973 which sought to make economic management policies viable in the different national contexts. It was 'a fixed exchange rate system ... buttressed by strict capital controls and by active trade policies', largely consistent with the interests of the then dominant economic power, the United States.[75] Basically, Bretton Woods stabilized the international situation so that national governments could be left alone, as it were, to proceed with domestic economic policies. But, we are told, this is no longer possible in a global economy. What these Keynesians envisage are new organizations that will co-ordinate national policies on an ongoing basis. 'The present, largely ceremonial, summits of the G7 would need to be replaced with meetings which actually dealt with substantive issues. A permanent secretariat should be created with the skills and authority to manage the international payments system.'[76] In other words, the governance of unemployment would be conducted in terms of a new field or assemblage of 'international policy co-ordination'.

Job Creation: 'Europe *v*. America'

Our third and final instance of Europe becoming a *sui generis* level and object (and indeed subject) of strategies for tackling unemployment is with the European Commission's own proposals for addressing what it sees as a major jobs crisis. A key statement in this respect is the 1993 'Delors' White Paper on competitiveness.[77] While it acknowledges the existence of a Keynesian component in unemployment, the overriding emphasis of this document is that Europe has a 'structural' problem. Its central argument is that to address its jobs crisis, Europe needs greater flexibility and competitiveness in its social and economic arrangements. To this end, the White Paper sets out a number of, by now, familiar measures which are to improve the competitiveness of Europe as a regional actor. These include the reorganization of 'employment systems' to make them more supportive of job-creation processes, investment in training and education, improvement of the Community's research and innovation systems and related measures to adapt Europe to the coming 'information society', and the development of 'trans-European infrastructure networks'.

The White Paper illustrates nicely how one of the key arguments surrounding employment policy in recent years – namely between a broadly 'social' position, and a neo-liberal side which emphasizes 'deregulation' – also takes a powerful geographical dimension, one that has been prompted by comparisons between the recent job-creation records of Europe and the United States. The White Paper draws on another imagined geography of unemployment. Only this time, the space is inter-continental. 'America' condenses a series of signifiers which include: deregulation, entrepreneurship, opportunity, innovation, job-creation. Europe, on the other hand, stands for 'eurosclerosis', rigidity, tradition, regulation, unemployment. As we saw, in recent years the UK has sought to position itself within this discursive matrix as the 'enterprise centre of Europe', opposed to the 'European model', and closer to the US one.

In finishing this section there are two things I want to note about this opposition of Europe and America around the question of unemployment. The first is that it is of course not monolithic; there are resistances. For instance, a number of important commentaries have drawn attention to the social and political costs of the American 'jobs miracle'. The quality of many of the jobs created by the US economy is in doubt, it being alleged that they are preponderantly low-paying, short-term, insecure, and menial in nature. Whereas Europe might have its unemployed, America has its 'working poor'.[78] Perhaps more damning is the questioning of US statistics regarding the long-term unemployed: it has been suggested that to get a truer reflection of the extent of unemployment in America it is necessary to factor in the large numbers of 'long-term incarcerated' under its severe criminal justice regime, a population which draws disproportionately on young black urban males.[79]

The second point to note is that in all of this there is a redramatization of the discussion of unemployment. Unemployment is certainly not being associated with the degeneration of the population, as it was at the turn of the century (although fears about the condition of the 'underclass' are rife). And perhaps it is no longer equated with the threat of revolution, as it has been at various moments. However, the fact that the debate is being framed in terms of comparisons between America and Europe, and treated as a question of distinctive societal and cultural models, is nevertheless significant. Employment questions are no longer merely questions of public policy; they call into question distinct ways of life. As *The Economist* put it, characterizing the European perspective: 'What sensible Parisian or Roman office worker would envy his job-insecure counterpart in crime-ridden Washington, DC, or the exhausted *sarariman* making his daily two-hour commute to central Tokyo?'[80] It is not just the culture of the unemployed – which, we have seen, has periodically been an issue within discourses on unemployment – that is at stake here. It is culture in a much wider sense – national, and even continental cultures of work, lifestyle, social values, are being brought into question.

The social sciences are presently at a point where they are reassessing many of their spatial and geographical assumptions. This is certainly the case as far as the study of the state and governance institutions in OECD countries is concerned. Explanatory models which assumed that societies or economies were somehow bounded by nation-states, and that states were like billiard balls in their interactions with one another, have come under challenge. The processes by which states appear to be devolving aspects of political authority 'upwards' in the form of regional trading agreements, currency agreements, and other forms of inter-national accord (e.g., around justice issues), but also the phenomenon of the strengthening of sub-national, regional authorities in many countries, and also the 'privatization' of large swathes of the public sector – these are just a few of the trends which have led certain observers to speak of processes of 'hollowing out' and 'denational-ization' with regard to the state,[81] or to develop new theoretical models in terms of concepts like 'multilevel governance'[82] and 'multilevel politics'.[83]

This chapter has not addressed institutional changes in the state in this context. But using the example of frameworks of employment policy, it has charted a territory that is in some ways tangential to this field of study. For we have seen that it is possible and fruitful to interrogate the spatial and geographical assumptions which underpin the construction of social problems. In this way, the chapter is sig-nificant for a genealogy of the social. For it highlights the fact that the social was, for much of its history, assumed to be a national space of government. Today, the outlines are becoming perceptible of other spaces in terms of which problems of social justice, social inequality, social division can be acted on.

CHAPTER 6

GOVERNING DIVIDED SOCIETIES: THE NEW DEAL

The first four chapters in this book have dealt largely with some of the problematizations out of which the modern conception of unemployment and unemployment policy arose. The previous chapter introduced a range of more contemporary concerns, albeit largely from the perspective of the different spatializations of the unemployment question presupposed by various governmental programmes and strategies. In this final, substantive chapter I want to complement my historical focus with a case study of a very recent initiative within unemployment policy – the Labour Government's New Deal for the unemployed. Labour has presented this as '[t]he largest assault on structural unemployment ever undertaken in this country'.[1]

It would be misleading, however, to suggest that this chapter was somehow bringing our discussion of unemployment 'up to date'. For this study does not pretend to be a comprehensive history of unemployment policy. Rather, it should be read as a series of strategic encounters with historical materials, engagements which are intended to sharpen our comprehension of the present. One of the central tasks of this book has been to enhance our understanding of what it means to govern unemployment from a 'social' perspective. The contribution of this chapter is to assess whether the approach to the unemployed which is currently fashionable with governments, an approach variously described as 'workfare' or 'welfare-to-work', and which the New Deal seems to exemplify, can still be considered a form of *social* governance.

The chapter begins with a brief description and contextualization of the New Deal. The sections which then follow are organized around a series of analytical axes. These seek to assess the New Deal in terms of the political task it has been accorded, namely: the 'integration' of society; the novel forms of political rationality which inform it, especially communitarian logics; and how we might understand it in terms of strategies of security.

AN OVERVIEW OF THE 'NEW DEAL'

For the 'New' Labour Government, elected to office in 1997, the New Deal represents its major commitment to provide a 'first step on the employment ladder' for young people with little or no experience of work, and long-term unemployed adults. It is also to offer support to a number of other groups who, in the current terminology, have previously been 'excluded from the labour market', such as lone parents, people with disabilities, partners of the unemployed, and older workers. Each of these target populations have their own, specially tailored 'New Deals'. These different New Deals are intended to run, initially, for four years. They are funded by a 'one-off' 'windfall tax' on the 'excess profits' of newly-privatized utilities. This has raised £3.5 billion.

It is the New Deal for young people (NDYP), in many ways the flagship and the prototype of the programme, that I will concentrate on here. NDYP is targeted at all young persons aged between eighteen and twenty-five who are unemployed for more than six months. Originally, this was estimated at 250 000 individuals. NDYP is co-ordinated by the Employment Service, the institutional descendant of the public labour exchange system. One of the key elements of the New Deal, and the features which are held to mark its novelty, is an initial 'Gateway' period. This consists of a series of 'one-on-one' meetings between the 'jobseeker' and his or her Personal Adviser. During the Gateway, the jobseeker is to receive intensive counselling and careers advice. Those who are identified as 'job ready' are to be assisted in finding 'non-subsidized jobs'. However, in cases where 'the jobseeker needs more help to improve their employability and become job ready' the personal adviser, or advisers in other 'partner organizations', will direct the jobseeker towards the New Deal's four main options, the principal 'opportunities' it has on offer.[2]

The main 'option' is a job with an employer. Through a series of government consultations and a high-profile marketing campaign, employers have been exhorted to recognize their 'social responsibilities' and provide 'opportunities' for the young unemployed. But their main incentive is the £60 per week subsidy which is available for up to six months towards 'the cost of employing the young person'. The remaining options are six-month spells of: work with a voluntary sector organization; work with the Environmental Task Force; and for those without basic qualifications, full-time education or training (although provision is also to be made for part-time training under the other options).

This New Deal, and its counterparts, are being presented by the Government as central components of its wider 'welfare-to-work' strategy. The New Deal is to link up with a number of interventions, including the Employment Zones initiative (see Chapter 5), the new minimum wage, the provision of a range of 'working benefits' (of which the US-style working families tax credit is a key development), and the introduction of certain improvements and new subsidies concerning child care. In combination, these measures are, in the words of the Chancellor of the Exchequer, about 'ensuring work pays more than benefits and raising the rewards from work ... because, in future, work will pay, those with an offer of work can have no excuse for staying at home on benefits'.[3]

Because of its novelty, scholarly work is only just emerging on the New Deal.[4] However, a significant body of research does exist on the movement within the social and employment policy fields towards 'workfare' and 'welfare-to-work', a trend of which the New Deal seems to be part.[5] This research has identified a number of salient features of workfare schemes. Workfare programmes have been invested with an assortment of objectives, including combating 'welfare dependency', improving the work ethic of the poor, boosting the self-esteem of the unemployed, reducing public expenditure on benefits, raising the skills levels and motivation of the workforce, countering benefits fraud, and renewing society's support for the principle of income support. As Desmond King has pointed out, a central aspect of workfare is the principle of 'conditionality' – the idea that the receipt of benefits should have attached certain conditions, 'responsibilities' such as actively looking for work, and retraining. Of the western nations, the US has probably been in the vanguard of the workfare movement, but other anglophonic countries like Australia and Canada have also been receptive to its principles. In Britain, a major step towards workfare was taken when the Conservatives introduced the Jobseekers Allowance in 1996.[6]

Workfare has been subject to varying theoretical interpretations. For instance, Desmond King has stressed the political, ideological, and institutional context shaping the implementation of such schemes. He highlights the influence that 'New Right' ideas about the obligations – as opposed to the rights – of citizenship had on the move towards 'work-welfare' in the US and the UK.[7] We will take up this matter later. But King also contends that if 'work-welfare' represents a quite general response of states to the unemployment crisis, then the institutional structure of the state, and earlier policy legacies, nevertheless mean that these reforms will take a unique trajectory in different countries.

However, there have also been attempts to provide a more socio-structural account of the rise of welfare to work programmes. The work of Bob Jessop is exemplary here. Jessop has coined the term 'Schumpeterian workfare state' (SWS) in order to highlight what he sees as key tendencies in the emergence of a new form of state under advanced capitalism. If the 'Keynesian welfare state' was, in the broadest sense, functional to the post-war regime of Fordist capitalism, then the SWS might be thought of as the political and policy apparatus that correlates with capitalist accumulation under post-Fordist and globalized conditions. Under the SWS, 'domestic full employment is de-prioritised in favour of international competitiveness and redistributive welfare rights take second place to a productivist re-ordering of social policy'.[8]

In taking a governmentality perspective on welfare-to-work, and the New Deal in particular, I will not be providing an account of the structural or institutional *causes* of these policy developments. My objective is somewhat different. With the main part of this chapter I want to interrogate the New Deal in terms of its significance for a history of the government of unemployment. This entails asking such questions as: what novel forms of understanding of social problems like inequality does it draw upon; what new methods of acting on these problems does it utilize; how does it provide a new kind of diagram for involving social actors? It is to the first of these questions that we now turn.

UNEMPLOYMENT AND SOCIAL DIVISION

There was a definite social and political context for public policies for unemployment in the aftermath of the Second World War. T. H. Marshall captured this in his famous essay on social citizenship when he made the point that welfare societies were to be *integral* societies, fully *national* communities. He was clear that there would remain various forms of social stratification. However, through some combination of income redistribution, mass education, and risk reduction, the welfare state was to reduce greatly the salience of class divisions. Marshall envisaged 'a population which is now treated ... as though it were one class'.[9]

The context for the New Deal is in many ways the perception that this once 'whole' national society has become fractured. The background to the New Deal is therefore a set of fears and concerns that Britain – perhaps more than many western countries – has become a 'divided society'. The evidence for this social fracture abounds in surveys and reports.[10] Unemployment, because of the way it has become so concentrated on particular populations and areas, is therefore increasingly bound up with the larger problem of the divided society. The task accorded to the New Deal, and similar initiatives, is nothing short of reversing this process of fracture. It is to respond to 'a deep desire in Britain that we should be one nation; a society in which we care for one another, take responsibility for one another and act on the recognition that the exclusion of some blights us all'.[11]

To grasp more fully how the New Deal is to intersect with the social question, defined in this way, it is necessary to consider in greater detail how this process of exclusion has been explained in expert discourses. Not surprisingly, there are a number of competing explanations. Certain commentators emphasize a cultural and political dynamic. For instance J. K. Galbraith identifies a 'culture of contentment' on the part of a somewhat selfish 'middle-class' majority.[12] Their stake in maintaining the *status quo* has been successfully nurtured by neo-conservative politicians – who have engaged in political crusades against progressive income taxation and 'welfare' – to the detriment of an increasingly disenfranchised and impoverished minority.

Other observers take a more structural perspective, focusing on the forces of economic globalization. In the era of 'economic nationalism' society was bound together by the fact that national economies were integrated mechanisms; everyone benefited from economic growth. But today we inhabit a global order in which 'the centrifugal forces of the global economy ... tear at the ties binding citizens together – bestowing ever greater wealth on the most skilled and insightful, while consigning the less skilled to a declining standard of living'.[13]

If these narratives are typical of the way in which the trend towards social division has been understood, there are also discourses which have focused more closely on the subjects, and victims, of social division. It is to concepts of 'the underclass' and 'social exclusion' that I want to turn to since they lie closer to the administration of the social field.

The Underclass

It is perhaps the convention to see a certain tension or even opposition between narratives couched in terms of 'the underclass' and those which favour the language of 'social exclusion'. The notion of an underclass is most commonly associated with conservative debates in the United States about urban poverty.[14] However, as Loic Wacquant argues, UK politicians, police officials, media commentators, and others have been particularly receptive to US debates about the underclass, and the thrust of their logic which is to reconstitute social issues as problems of 'urban disorder' and 'security'.

Usually 'the underclass' invokes a specific sector of society, an almost pathological community, cut off from the wider world by virtue of its asocial values and habits. The underclass represents a milieu in which a dangerous culture of drugs, violence, unemployment, single mother-hood and welfare dependency, all intersect and reproduce; a world in which mainstream values concerning work, marriage and personal responsibility are seriously lacking.

Social Exclusion

Because of its moralistic overtones, pejorative connotations and highly-racist associations, many commentators on poverty – especially in western Europe where there is a stronger social-democratic presence within politics – prefer the language of social exclusion to that of the underclass. Indeed, social exclusion is fast becoming officialized within the field of social administration. Labour has set up a Social Exclusion Unit, while the European Commission has established its own 'observatories' dedicated to its study. Countless congresses and books have taken up the theme.[15] Whereas the underclass concept is accused of 'blaming the victim', the notion of social exclusion allows for a fuller 'structural' explanation of the phenomenon of the divided society. As Pete Alcock puts it:

> Encapsulated in the term social exclusion is the problem of the inter-play between the social and economic forces which are marginalising large groups of people who are more or less permanently outside of the labour force (including, but hardly exclusively, many lone parents) and the experience of this process by those who are the primary victims of it. It is a problem of class polarisation, of economic inactivity and dis-appearing opportunities, of demographic and cultural upheaval, and of pressure to adapt social policy to meet the rapidly changing circumstances of people whose past expectations, and hopes, no longer meet their current needs.[16]

Without doubt, these two concepts do embody very real and salient political differences in their approach to poverty and social policy. This is especially the case wherever social exclusion is mobilized as a means of presenting poverty as a process which denies citizenship to the poor.[17] But it is also important to note that there are significant ways in which these paradigms converge, or, more accurately, produce overlapping and therefore reinforcing discursive effects.[18] It is possible to give two examples in this respect.

Strategies of 'Conceptual Containment': Localizing the Poor

Lydia Morris has suggested that public debates about the underclass can be seen as 'an exercise in conceptual containment'. 'Rather than revise our understanding of social organization to accommodate a number of rather complex changes, some explanation is sought which leaves the social world as we understand it more or less intact.'[19] The notion of the underclass does this by localizing the causes of mass unemployment in the cultural and social dynamics of a pathological sub-population. In this way it protects the wider social system from the criticism that it is dysfunctional.

However, I would want to side with Ruth Levitas, who has indicated how the notion of social exclusion also produces certain 'containment' effects. Levitas contends that social exclusion discourse 'presents "society" as experiencing a rising standard of living by defining those who have not done so, who have become poorer, as "excluded from" society, as "outside" it'.[20] In other words, it normalizes society by redefining and narrowing its boundaries to the 'contented' majority. Society is not the problem; society can look after itself. Any serious discussion of societal pathologies (e.g., society's endemic productivism, consumerism, culture of over-working, boom–bust cycles) is suppressed. The excluded are not a sign then of a systemic problem within society. The problem is serious, but manageable: society is not inclusive enough. Unlike the underclass theorists, researchers in this field do not seek to 'blame the victims'. Instead, they focus on the 'barriers' that are excluding the poor.

Social exclusion renders the problem of poverty as a manageable domain by constructing it in the form of a series of marginal populations (single parents, street-sleepers, the long-term unemployed – in sum, the excluded), and the barriers and processes which serve to marginalize these groups (poverty 'traps', run-down council estates, 'failing' schools).[21] It localizes the poor. In this way, the target for remedial action is displaced. Political intervention is no longer aimed at the level of the social system, as it was for the welfare state, whether we understand by this the structure of social inequality, the relationship between employers and workers, the distribution of income, the properties of the national economic system, the distribution of work or employment opportunities, each considered as structures.[22]

We are now in a position in this discussion where we can begin to grasp the significance of the New Deal. Its versatility lies with its ability to draw both on the underclass paradigm and the social exclusion one. In the former it finds a justification for its strict, paternalistic stance. The young unemployed have been wrongly socialized, schooled in a culture of welfare dependency, apathy, and dependency. Like any good parent, the state must administer a firm but fair hand. The Government is keen to reiterate that the New Deal offers the four options, or 'opportunities' outlined in the first section. However: 'With these new opportunities for young people come new responsibilities. There will be no fifth option – to stay at home on the full benefit . . . Benefit will be cut if young people refuse to take up the opportunities.'[23] Seizing one's 'opportunities' has become an obligation of citizenship.

> Such a tough discipline is necessary to demonstrate the seriousness of the government's efforts and break the culture of hopelessness, idleness, and cynicism which a concentration of hard-core unemployment has bred throughout Britain where a generation has been brought up on the dole. Young people, when asked, support these principles. To them it is not 'workfare'. It *is* fair, and it offers work.[24]

But the New Deal also depends on the localization of the social problem which is effected by social exclusion. It is to be a 'gateway' or a 'pathway' back into society for people who are 'trapped'. Like many other recent social policy measures, such as the education action zones, employment zones and health zones, the New Deals for Lone Parents or Older Workers, or the plethora of targeted urban initiatives mentioned in Chapter 5 – it is targeted directly at the margins. It is therefore unlike such technologies as social insurance and Keynesian economic management, which act at the level of the social system, manipulating society-wide variables of income, risk, economic demand, etc. The New Deal merely corrects for a deficit of opportunities. Because of the way the problem is defined, the New Deal can aspire to address unemployment without disturbing society. It is because unemployment has been defined as a problem of the margins and not the centre that the New Deal – a programme which does not in any measurable way challenge the prevailing social or economic order – can be heralded as 'revolutionary', as a bid to forge 'one nation' out of the social wreckage of the divided society.

Social Integration through Paid Employment

There is a second way in which the underclass and social exclusion paradigms overlap in their redefinition of the social problem. For both the social fracture is coterminous with a division between a working and a non-working society. For observers of the underclass, this is expressed in highly moralistic terms: a generation is identified which fails to acknowledge that work is a social obligation and a responsibility. For theorists of social exclusion, the emphasis is placed upon social factors. Inadequate work skills, institutional and market disincentives, family structures, bad public transport – these and many other things are highlighted as preventing the excluded from taking work. Yet both sides in this debate can align with a programme like the New Deal because it offers to improve the skills, employability, motivations, and prospects of its subjects. What does not seem to be in question is the assumption of the New Deal that integration into society and the labour-market are one and the same thing. As Levitas has observed, a striking consequence of this singular emphasis on paid work as *the* factor of social cohesion is that it ignores the fact that other forms of activity – i.e., much of the unpaid domestic work performed by women – are socially valuable.[25]

But is the New Deal's emphasis on reintegration through work really that novel? After all, didn't the Beveridge model of social policy also seek to make labour-market participation central? Didn't Beveridge in his recommendations for social security advise that there should be strict eligibility requirements and flat-rate benefit payments, set at a low level relative to wages, precisely to ensure that the incentive to stay in regular employment was maintained.[26] This is true. Yet the difference between the New Deal and the Beveridge model is that with the former re-integration into the labour market is held up as the optimal outcome for *all* adults. 'Work is at the heart of our reform programme. For those able to undertake it, paid work is the surest route out of poverty ... The new welfare state should help and encourage people of working age to work where they are capable of doing so.'[27]

To put it differently, Beveridge-style welfare states were based on the political and cultural assumption that most workers were adult males.[28] The range of different New Deals noted in the first section suggests that now *we are all potential workers*. Integration (or reintegration) into paid work is the proper path not just for the unemployed, but for a range of identities previously constituted and provided for as the 'non-employed' – mothers, students, people with disabilities, the partners of the unemployed. The New Deal has taken on board the OECD's idea of the 'active society': 'realization of the full human potential of the population involves the employment not only of the unemployed, but of all those who wish to participate – whether working full-time, part-time, or in casual employment'.[29]

We can conclude from this that a different model of social integration is presupposed by the New Deal. The welfare society assumed a restricted definition of the workforce premised on the socio-cultural identity of the adult male breadwinner. It assumed, and helped to naturalize, a gendered division of responsibilities, with paid employment being concentrated on adult men while caring and other domestic duties were the preserve of women. One way this was actualized was in Beveridge's proposal for different 'insurance classes', which were to reflect 'the different ways of life of different sections of the community'.[30] 'Employees' and 'others gainfully occupied' were obviously part of the workforce, but 'those rendering vital unpaid service as housewives', 'those past earning' and 'those not yet of age to earn' were accorded a formal position outside the workforce. *Social* security therefore assumed and encouraged bonds of solidarity and income redistribution between these different earning and non-earning sectors. It fostered lines of mutuality linking men and women, rich and poor, young and old, employed and unemployed. Under the social, society exists as an *order of interdependence*. But with the New Deal the emphasis is on promoting *independence*, which it makes synonymous with individuals in paid work.

We will return to the model of security associated with the New Deal in a later section. But at this point I want to turn to the question of the political rationality of the New Deal. This, I will argue against some observers, is not reducible to neo-liberalism.

THE TURN TOWARDS COMMUNITY?

In the discussions that have surrounded the New Deal, one theme which remains constant and to the fore is that of responsibility.

> Too many people in Britain have slipped through the labour market ... We have a responsibility to offer people decent employment or training opportunities and these will be available under the New Deal. But it is a two way deal. In return people must take responsibility for their own development and their part of the bargain will be to make a positive contribution to society.[31]

To appreciate more fully the significance and the exact nature of this appeal to 'responsibilities', it is necessary to consider a recent mutation in the political rationalities surrounding social policy, namely the rise of certain communitarian arguments. It is by now well noted that in its attempt to steer a path between the neo-liberalism of the previous Conservative regimes, and the statism of 'Old' Labour, the present Labour Government has drawn, albeit selectively, on communitarian themes. The American communitarian, Amitai Etzioni, is frequently cited as an intellectual influence of several leading members of the Government, including the Prime Minister.[32]

No doubt, some would argue that Labour's adoption of the language of community is largely superficial – a smokescreen which obscures its actual commitment to right-wing, neo-liberal policies. In many cases this might be the case. However, Nikolas Rose has suggested that we take the language of community more seriously: there may be more to it than mere rhetoric, ideology, or even political philosophy. For contemporary political rationalities and strategies, community seems to constitute an alternative to 'the social' – 'a new territory for the administration of individual and collective existence, a new plane or surface upon which the micro-moral relations among persons are conceptualized and administered'.[33]

This point can be illustrated if we compare communitarian with neo-liberal political programmes. There are certainly ways in which they overlap. First, they are both defined in terms of their critique of statist governance. For instance, they agree that despite its genuine intentions, the welfare state has spawned a culture of dependency which is a serious element of the social problem. Second, they both propose diagrams for governing in terms of the mobilization of, and alignment with, the regulated choices, responsibilities, and aspirations of individuals. And third, they both rely heavily on the mobilization of self-regulating, 'non-political' mechanisms to pursue these ends – 'non-political' in the sense of being considered as beyond the state and the formal arenas of politics.

In the case of neo-liberals, this non-political mechanism is of course the market. It would be misleading to imply too much coherence or overall rationality in the manner in which the labour market was deregulated, social security benefits tightened, or trade union laws reformed under the Conservatives. These measures were often pushed through on an *ad hoc* basis in response to local and contingent political concerns and pressures. Nevertheless, by the mid-1980s these and other measures were being presented as components of a relatively coherent and systematic neo-liberal approach to unemployment. As several Conservative White Papers argued, high levels of employment would only be achieved by removing the various obstacles to enterprise which cluttered labour and product markets.

However, with communitarian logics, the 'non-political' mechanism in question consists of an appeal to the bonds of community, to the responsibilities and allegiances we have as members of communities, to the ethical responsibilities we have to ourselves and to others. This realm of ethical relations is not reducible to the market, but neither does it displace the market.[34] For the communitarian position is that markets can only operate properly when they are embedded in social relations of trust, reciprocity, community, etc. Communitarianism therefore connects up with related arguments about socio-economics and social capitalism.

But if neo-liberalism stakes the government of unemployment on the idea of the self-regulating market, and welfarism the strategic management of the socio-economic, how exactly does communitarianism propose to manage unemployment? One answer it gives to this question is a renewal of the social contract. On the one hand it attempts to retrieve the principle of collective action and support for the unemployed, a principle that had been badly tarnished under the Conservatives. It reasserts a commitment on the part of the community, the nation, to provide new opportunities for the unemployed. The New Deal is pivotal in this regard. Yet, there is a 'trade off'. The unemployed must earn this support. They must exercise personal responsibility: actively looking for work, acquiring skills, improving one's employability, not defrauding the taxpayer (living off benefits is deemed to be 'corrosive of our attempt to build a sense of community') – these become ways in which they earn the community's continued support.

It would be misleading to overstate the novelty of the communitarian emphasis on the responsibilities of the unemployed. Throughout this book we have seen that most forms of assistance have had their conditions. For instance, social insurance required that the claimant be a regular worker, genuinely unemployed. Moreover, it assumed the claimant would exercise the duty of thrift and would possess savings to supplement his or her income from benefits. For people claiming non-insurance benefits, the conditions were stricter. So what is different with a programme like the New Deal?

A clue is provided by Nikolas Rose. In contrasting government in terms of the social with that of community, he points out that under the former, one's responsibilities were always set in the context of a wider 'social order of determination'.[35] In the case of the unemployed, this meant that, although the subject had a duty to be a regular worker, look for work, save for rainy days, etc., this was always tempered by the recognition that unemployment was predominantly a *social* problem – industrial, cyclical, regional in nature. It was acknowledged that the scope for the individual to make a difference to his or her fate was closely determined by 'material' circumstances.

But with government through community, this social order of determination is only weakly entrenched within political debate. For communitarian logics, programmes like the New Deal are important not primarily as socio-economic interventions, but as arenas where the unemployed can demonstrate their ethical worth to society, where they can earn society's respect. The New Deal is also important for the perception which New Labour wants society to have of itself – as a caring, moral collectivity. The New Deal is not aimed exclusively at a social system understood in socio-economic terms, but also at society understood in terms of its moral structure. To some extent, then, the New Deal is shielded from the criticism that training and jobseeking schemes are somewhat limited in tackling persistent unemployment because they do little to affect the aggregate supply of jobs: it is about the ethical as much as the economic.

EMPLOYERS AND THE NEW DEAL: UNEMPLOYMENT AND 'CORPORATE SOCIAL RESPONSIBILITY'

We have already noted how communitarianism formulates the task of social reform in terms of a moral crusade to 'regenerate' society. By this it means getting various social actors to take up their social respon-sibilities – individuals, families, neighbourhoods, voluntary groups. But this also includes business. One of the more notable features of the New Deal, and a development which is significant for genealogical studies of social governance, is the way in which it seeks to involve business in 'a new partnership with the Government and young people, to attack the waste of unemployment'.[36] Anticipating the New Deal, a senior member of the Labour Government called for a 'concerted drive' to get com-panies to extend their 'corporate social responsibility activities' to help the long-term unemployed.[37] Accordingly, the implementation of the New Deal has been accompanied by a high-profile 'national crusade', employing TV and print media, and various government consultations and presentations to businesspeople, appealing to them to 'sign up' to the New Deal and 'pledge' jobs for the unemployed. 'Getting the young unemployed back to work is not something that Government can deliver on its own. It needs the support of everyone, especially employers.'[38] The Chancellor has urged 'every business to play its part in this national crusade to equip this country for the future by taking on young unemployed men and women'.[39] The roll call of participants has even become something of a benchmark of the success of the New Deal.

I want to suggest that this appeal to business is more than rhetorical. For there is an emergent paradigm of social action and intervention associated with the notion of 'corporate social responsibility', which, it seems, resonates with some of the communitarian themes we described in the previous section. By briefly exploring this notion of corporate social responsibility I shall be scrutinizing a highly significant aspect of contemporary governmental relations, namely new ways in which business is being positioned in relation to social questions.

The last decade or so has seen the popularization in the UK and North America of such concepts as 'corporate citizenship', 'the new corporate philanthropy', and 'corporate social responsibility'.[40] At the same time, there is a growing number of networks and institutes, such as the UK Social Investment Forum[41] and the Boston College Centre for Corporate Community Relations.[42] The US Department of Labor has its own Corporate Citizenship Center. These have been formed to debate and propagate principles of corporate citizenship amongst businesspeople and the public. Some of the issues being brought together beneath these rubrics include: ethical investment; human rights in the context of global trading and production activities; employee development and participation; and community relations.

It is the community development aspect of corporate citizenship which interests me here. One of the most prominent organizations in this respect in the UK is Business in the Community (BITC). Its chairperson, Sir Peter Davis, has been appointed to head a 'task force', whose mission is to win the support of the business community to the New Deal. According to its 'mission statement', BITC's aim is '[t]o support the social and economic regeneration of communities by raising the quality and extent of business involvement and by making that involvement a natural part of successful business practice'.[43] To this end, it co-ordinates a range of activities which include:

- the Percent Club, a group of companies who make commitments to 'invest in their communities' at least half a per cent of their annual UK profits;
- Cause Related Marketing, which links companies and their products to particular 'causes' (e.g., the supermarket Tesco's and its Computers for Schools campaign); and
- a series of economic regeneration initiatives which seek to bring 'business skills and expertise to community enterprise, small business development and local partnerships'.

In addition, BITC illustrates how this fairly loosely configured sphere of community involvement is being turned into a calculable field of government, supporting its own forms of expertise. BITC has been active in devising a set of 'principles of corporate community investment'. These comprise various measurements, benchmarks, indicators, notions of 'best practice' so that firms will be able to 'manage and evaluate their investment in the communities in which they operate'.[44] In other words, community involvement on the part of business is to be rendered a more calculable, rational activity – a set of techniques. In this way, the objective of aligning it with the main areas of the firm's commercial activities is facilitated.

It is not my task here to explore how this paradigm of corporate social responsibility might differ from the much older ones of 'business ethics' or 'business philanthropy', nor to work out in any detail what factors might account for its contemporary salience. At least two developments seem significant, however. First, it is perhaps a response to the scrutiny that has been brought to bear on the activities of large global companies by consumer groups, environmental activists, and human rights organizations. It reflects a heightened sensitivity on the part of companies towards questions of 'corporate image'. Several companies have stated that these community-related activities are not really 'philanthropy' since they are really strategic investments in the future of the business. But second, it seems to reflect the breakdown of the old regulatory frameworks (e.g., corporatism) and the decline of welfarism which defined business's relationship to the social. In debates about corporate responsibility and citizenship, I would suggest, we find ongoing attempts to formulate new principles and techniques for action. Rather than develop these two themes, I shall confine myself to the question of the significance of corporate social responsibility themes in terms of the history of the government of unemployment.

An important point to note is that under the New Deal, business is appealed to as a community which has responsibilities and commitments towards the wider community, to the nation (for Etzioni, the 'community of communities'). Unemployment comes to be defined as a 'blight', a 'waste', something potentially avoidable – rather like a problem of the environment which we are all encouraged to feel some sort of ethical responsibility to address. Indeed, this fits with Etzioni's definition of the communitarian movement; its members 'are dedicated to working with our fellow citizens to bring about the changes in values, habits and public policies that will allow us to do for society what the environmental movement seeks to do for nature: to safeguard and enhance our future'.[45] Just as the unemployed are to do their bit in this crusade against unemployment, then so should employers and other communities (e.g., schools, the professions).

Contrast this with the position that was accorded to business under the post-war welfare state. There, we have a social paradigm: the understanding that a certain level of unemployment was a necessary and unavoidable feature of industrial life. Beveridge called it the 'necessary margin of idleness'. As such, business was assumed to have a very specific and statutory responsibility towards the support of the unemployed. Since it profited from unemployment, it was statutorily bound to support the unemployed, most notably through national insurance contributions.

Under the New Deal, as with the unemployed, the appeal to business is as a moral rather than as a social subject. Business is enjoined to lend its involvement as a good corporate citizen – not because there might just be a link between flexible employment stategies, global outsourcing, downsizing, and social problems of unemployment and social exclusion.

The Windfall Tax

The question of how the New Deal is funded is interesting in this respect. Almost from the inception of the New Deal, Labour maintained that the programme would be funded by a one-off 'windfall levy'. This is on formerly public companies which have made 'excessive profits' following privatization.[46] In one respect, this decision has relatively straightforward political motivations: the windfall levy allowed Labour to raise the funding for a major innovation in social policy, but without exposing itself to damaging criticism that it was, like 'Old' Labour,

135

a party of 'tax and spend', a party of big government. The privatized utilities were an easy target because public and media hostility towards so-called 'fat cat' directors had already done the job of discrediting them as reputable capitalists.

But the message that the windfall levy sends only serves to confirm the point that the relationship of employers to the New Deal is more a moral than a social one. Unlike the social insurance contribution, the Windfall Tax is not based on a positive or social argument, neither is it permanent or universal in its coverage of the financial and industrial field. It is not tied to a view of unemployment as a systematic problem. Instead, it is rationalized on negative grounds – it is levied on a one-off basis as punishment against certain errant companies who made 'excess' profits. The implication is that only the 'bad' business, which offends community standards, will be taxed in this way; the 'good' have nothing to worry about. Finally, the fact that the Windfall Tax is a one-off measure reinforces the view that the long-term unemployment of young people and others is somehow anomalous. There are certain echoes here of the late nineteenth century, when mayors opened funds for the relief of the unemployed: the understanding was that a particularly severe winter, or some crisis in trade, had led to a collapse in work.[47] A fund was needed to tide over the unfortunate. In a sense, the Windfall Tax both draws on, and contributes to, the construction of severe unemployment and social exclusion as anomalies or pathologies – be they of individuals and their communities (underclass theories) or institutions. What it is not is a product of the larger system.

STRATEGIES OF SECURITY

In our discussion of the New Deal we have considered it in terms of its association with current problematizations of social division, and we have analysed it in relation to discourses of community, and what it means to govern through community. In this final section I want to interrogate the New Deal in terms of a third axis: what is its significance for a genealogy of security? In Chapters 2, 3, and 4 I analysed some key moments in the emergence of a strategy of social security. We can assess the New Deal in terms of its difference from this strategy on at least two dimensions – at the level of its engagement with the individual and with the population.

Active Subjects of Security

A history of problematizations of long-term unemployment would show that official perceptions as to the social risks of exclusion from work are certainly not immutable. By comparing discourses on the long-term unemployed today, and in the 1930s, for instance, it is possible to get an idea as to how problematizations have changed. Then, as we saw in Chapter 4, protracted exclusion from work was linked to concerns about the physiological, psychological, social, and moral welfare of the 'unemployed man'. Unemployment led not just to the atrophy of physique and the withering of manual skills. It also undermined a person's self-worth, it tore apart the delicate web of social and status ties which social-psychologists had identified as surrounding the worker, it placed the unemployed at considerable risk of 'demoralization'. In this way we can understand why the unemployed club movement generated considerable interest amongst social observers and unemployment experts, as well as some degree of public funding. Beyond the national assistance system which had been set up to manage the income of the unemployed household, the club movement offered a mechanism for sustaining the 'morale' of the unemployed and their communities.

The debates which surround the question of protracted unemployment today have many continuities with the past. Work continues to be invested as a powerful mechanism of socialization, integration, and self-esteem. As the underclass thesis demonstrates, the loss of work still provokes racialized fears about growing amorality, vice, and lawlessness, and raises the spectre of a 'lost generation'. However, there is at least one aspect of contemporary debates which was not present in the 1930s.

Today, there is a widespread assumption that through paid work, individuals are, or should be, building up a bank of marketable skills, maintaining their 'employability'. The image of work we get from discourses about the 'learning organization', the 'flexible firm', and so forth is as the setting for a new kind of transaction around knowledge, one that will supplement the wage relation. The workplace, we are told, must become a place of learning. Promoting people's potential will no longer come from social security, but by developing their skills.[48] Successful businesses must harness and invest in the skills and talents of their 'most valuable assets', their employees, if they are to prosper in the rapidly mutating and highly competitive information economies of the next century. In turn, individuals take from work not just a wage, a status, or social connections, but the opportunity to keep acquiring new skills. On this basis, a new type of risk comes to be associated with unemployment: it produces individuals who lack the necessary skills to compete for jobs. Furthermore, these are not just work skills, but the skills of jobseeking. For in the precarious world of temporary or short-term employment, 'jobseeking' has become a crucial competence and field of administration in its own right.

What mark, if any, has this new view of work, and consequently of the sort of risk which unemployment poses for the individual, made on the New Deal? A considerable one, I would argue. We argued before that the New Deal interpellates a moral subject, an individual who takes responsibility for themselves, but who also acknowledges obligations to society. But it also presupposes, and seeks to nurture, an enterprising, active subject; like the learning organization, the New Deal will 'utilize their [the unemployed] talents and energy and equip them with the skills to compete for future jobs'.[50] This 'skills' and 'employability' argument becomes an additional reason, then, for making participation on one of the four New Deal options compulsory.

The social security system under the welfare state was based upon a conception of security as income maintenance. As Chapter 3 noted, this is most evident with social insurance, a technology which governs the risk of interruption to the labourer's ability to sell continually his or her labour-power. It secures the individual as an *employee*. Income maintenance of course remains a feature of the New Deal. However, inasmuch as the New Deal seeks to improve the skills of the individual, their ability to present and market themselves, there is an emergent sense in which it can be said to govern the individual as a *self-employee*. The model is one in which each unemployed individual is to become a micro-business, a human enterprise which must become adept at winning a series of employment contracts.

Practices of the Self

We have established that the New Deal addresses itself to an active subject. But we can go further than this. Instructive here is Mitchell Dean's research into the Australian Government's attempts to reform its income support system for the unemployed. The objective was to introduce principles of what the OECD terms 'active labour-market policy': to shift the emphasis from 'passive' mechanisms of income maintenance to 'active' ones of improving the jobseeking, motivation, and skills of the unemployed. These principles are now acknowledged as valid by most western governments, especially the UK.

But what Dean highlights as particularly interesting about these reforms is their will to 'engage "clients" in their own government by demanding their complicity in ... practices of self-shaping, self-cultivation and self-presentation'.[51] He illustrates this point by analysing these 'active' reforms at a technical rather than a purely rhetorical level. They have as their correlates certain 'technologies' or 'practices of the self'. He mentions the 'Newstart Agreement', a contract drawn up between the employment service and the unemployed individual through which the latter 'agrees' a course of action and a set of measures for addressing his or her unemployment. But there is also the Job Search Workbook, containing advice on preparing a résumé, writing applications, telephoning employers, and attending interviews. The effect of these and other technologies is to figure the individual as an active manager, although guided by the employment service personnel, in the government of his or her unemployment. The enhancement of employability becomes a personal project. If Keynesianism represents a zenith in terms of strategies for the macro-management of unemployment, these 'active' programmes stand for a proliferation of countless individualized micro-managements.[52] This is not to suggest for a moment that unemployed people did not manage their unemployment in the past, whether in terms of household budgets or any other survival tactics. The point is that, now, the personal strategy has become an instrument of government: official authorities require the individual to govern themselves in terms of a personal strategy.

The administration of long-term unemployment in the UK has seen similar technological innovations as these, most notably with the introduction of the Jobseekers Allowance in 1996. Here I shall just mention certain innovations in practices of the self that are specific to the New Deal. In the first section we noted that a centrepiece of the New Deal is its Gateway, a 'path' through which the unemployed 'choose' one of the four options.

> Throughout the Gateway and options, New Deal will provide young people with more choices than ever before. The overriding aim is to secure their active and committed participation in selecting one of those choices which they believe to be in their own best interests.[53]

The Gateway represents a particular tactic by which governmental authorities are seeking to access that most prized factor – the commitment of the unemployed. By reconstituting the experience of the employment service as though it were a mortgage broker or a travel agent, wherein the unemployed person is figured as a 'client', and the staff as 'personal advisors', it strives to produce what we might call an 'ownership effect'. Because you 'choose' the product, it is somehow closer to you; it becomes 'personal', a reflection of your individuality. Leaving aside the question of how it is actually experienced by unemployed people, what the Gateway seems to aspire to do is to overturn the perception attached to previous 'schemes' – that they are imposed by an external authority on the recalcitrant individual.[54]

The programmatic rationality of the New Deal is isomorphic with changes across a number of social fields. From pensions to housing, from education to healthcare, we find a similar pattern: the positioning of the subject as a consumer-client, the turn towards the market as a mechanism of governance which promotes choice, a new role for expertise which 'advises' the consumer, and so on. However, there is an important caveat to be made in all of this. It would be fallacious to push the comparison between these fields and the management of unemployment too far. In short, there are likely to remain big differences between the experience of getting a mortgage and using the employment service. Old stigmas and prejudices remain. Most forms of consumption are not backed up with the sort of sanctions which the employment service can mobilize against the errant jobseeker. Perhaps the distinction which Dean draws, in analysing this new centrality of practices of self within programmes of government, is useful. This is between 'governmental self-formation' and 'ethical self-formation'. While the distinction can never be absolute, the former designates the way governmental authorities seek to shape selves; the latter is more about how individuals shape themselves from within. The balance between these poles will vary across different social sites. It seems fair to assume that the accent will remain with the former as far as the government of unemployment is concerned.

Population

We have seen that as a practice of security the New Deal engages an active and enterprising individual. But it has another pole: it can also be discussed as an intervention at the level of the social body. In order to understand it more fully in this respect, it is necessary briefly to consider its relation to former regimes of social security.

Jacques Donzelot points out that one of the defining features of the welfare state and of Keynesianism as a programme of government is the following. It 'makes it possible to forge a link between the economic and the social which, in principle, entails no subordination of one to the other since it proposes to link them together by a *circular mechanism*'.[55] The nature of this mechanism is encapsulated by the double task accorded to social security payments. Not only were these expressions of social entitlement and right on the part of the unemployed or the aged. They were also a means of acting on and boosting the purchasing power of the poorer elements of the population, thereby stimulating aggregate consumer demand within the economy and preventing the vicious economic spiral into unemployment.

The trick which Keynesianism seemed to pull off was to make the social and the economic not only generally compatible, but necessary to one another. For orthodox political economy this had not been the case. It is true that many employers had long been aware of the positive contribution which social policies could make to the efficiency of their workforces,[56] and Fabian socialists and other advocates of 'national efficiency' had argued a similar point. However, Keynesianism entrenched the case for extensive publicly funded social policies by highlighting their positive *macroeconomic* effects; social spending could be good for the economy.

The New Deal, like most other initiatives within social security in recent years, does not share this assumption of a circular mechanism between the social and the economic. Like other instances of 'work-fare', it is termed 'productivist' because it has been designed in response to arguments that the welfare state had become *dis*-economical. Productivist social policy is rationalized by arguments that it is to enhance the *competitiveness* of businesses and nations in an increasingly global marketplace.[57] Where the 'old' welfare state offers only 'passive' support to its subjects, the New Deal is to be 'active', helping to integrate them into the world of work, giving them the skills to compete for jobs. Where social security is criticized for discouraging employment – whether by burdening employers with excessive labour costs or by catching the claimant within a series of poverty and unemployment 'traps' – the New Deal is to be employment-centred.

We can get a better sense of the new types of security practices for which the New Deal stands if we consider its relation to the wider social security system. If the New Deal is the lynchpin of the government's 'welfare-to-work' strategy, then the reform of the taxation and benefits payments system is heralded as 'stage two'. The Government is currently introducing a programme of 'working benefits'. These have been given the job of 'ensuring work pays more than benefits and raising the rewards from work'.[58] They include the adoption of an American-style system of working families' tax credits which can be paid through the 'pay packet' rather than in the form of a benefit cheque (a device which is, among other things, designed to remove the 'stigma' of welfare); a guarantee that the income of families with at least one full-time earner shall not fall below £180 per week, and that the same family will not pay income tax unless it earns more than £220 per week; and the long-term aim of introducing a ten pence tax rate for low-earners.[59] In addition, a minimum wage is to be introduced for the first time.

What is interesting about these reforms is that they point to a changed rationality for the system of income support. In other words, it is possible to see how technologies from previous regimes of governance are not always scrapped, but can also be redeployed in accordance with new political objectives. For the primary focus of income support seems to be shifting from income maintenance to the management of work incentives; and from the maintenance of aggregate demand within the economy to the promotion of participation in the labour market on a society-wide basis. 'The tax and benefit systems need to make sure it is in people's interests to work.'[60] A similar thing can be said for the introduction of the minimum wage: this is also based on an argument about making unskilled work more attractive to the individual, whereas the architects of the welfare state had proposed the notion of a minimum standard of income and welfare on social grounds, i.e., as a basic entitlement.

The fear that unemployment and other benefits were problematic because they sap the will to work is of course not a recent one. Such concerns are arguably as old as the Poor Law itself. However, under the welfare state, under strategies of social governance, these concerns were mitigated or outweighed by the various other positive desires which were invested in the social security system, including the amelioration of poverty, the redistribution of income, the compensation for social risk, the recognition of social citizenship, and the maintenance of consumer demand within the economy. Today as many of these other arguments are in retreat, the connection between income support and labour market behaviour is coming to the fore, and with it, the possibility of deploying the income support system in more positive ways in the management of work incentives.

One conclusion to be drawn from this chapter is prompted by this last observation. The government's welfare-to-work programme presupposes that its subject is a rational economic actor who will respond to market incentives. It seeks to act on an individual located in a field of economic rewards and incentives. Yet we saw that in many ways the New Deal imagines a different territory, a space of community, of ethical relations and mutual responsibilities. It seeks to mobilize the unemployed, as well as other 'communities' such as business, in the name of their social responsibilities. Clearly, then, there is no one-to-one relationship between policies and political rationalities. We should not assume that a communitarian logic is somehow displacing the more market-orientated neo-liberal logic. Instead, they seem to coexist and intertwine around the same programmes. If there is, as many observers have noted, a waning of the figure of the social citizen within governmental strategies, it is not being supplanted in any direct fashion. This chapter has highlighted the plurality and inconsistency of the New Deal – it embodies assumptions about the unemployed as moral subjects, enterprising subjects, and as possible subjects for a paternalistic form of government.

A second point which can be drawn from this chapter concerns the merits of taking a genealogical perspective in tracing the construction of unemployment. Rather than see the evolution of employment policy in terms of factors that are purely interior to it, or in terms of general structural changes, a genealogical approach is attuned to the borrowings, the lateral movements, the displacements and the contingencies which mark the space of government. Earlier chapters suggested that unemployment has been posed as a problem in terms of the way it gets inserted into particular *series*. Chapter 3 discussed a risk-probability series, tracing the movements by which unemployment came to be treated like many of the other risks which pertain to a given population – sickness, injury, accident, etc. Chapter 5 considered another series, noting that in the post-war period unemployment came to be located on a plane with a range of macroeconomic objects, such as inflation and balance of payments questions. In this chapter we noted some of the changes in the government of unemployment once it comes to be addressed in terms of community – just like environmental problems, crime problems, or health questions, it becomes a matter of communities and their responsibilities, a symptom of the fraying of community.

Finally, the chapter has made a contribution to our understanding of social governance in terms of the area of social security. It has stressed how a different principle of security underpins the New Deal – it imagines a society which is secured by the engagement of nearly all its members in some form of paid employment. In Chapter 1 we noted that the emergence of unemployment as a clearly separated and distinct condition from employment corresponded with processes of standardization of work. Employment became an activity bounded in terms of its time, space, and legal and gender definitions. The world of the New Deal is one where work is being destandardized – no longer contained within the space and time of the office or factory, or within the terms of the collective labour contract, less and less the monopoly of the male breadwinner.[61] Paid work is now saturating the social space. If a conspicuous feature of the New Deal is that it targets not just the 'unemployed', but single parents, people with disabilities, the partners of the unemployed, and many other categories of person formally consigned to the spaces of non-employment; if, in other words, it begins to dissolve the line which formerly (and formally) separated the 'unemployed' from the 'non-employed' – it is in part because of this newly fluid character of work. It would take a separate book to analyse the way in which new conceptions of work also serve as conditions of possibility for schemes like the New Deal.

CONCLUSION

In his important and careful attempt to reconstruct key aspects of the social experience of British unemployment over the last 200 years, the historian John Burnett has underlined what he sees as the remarkable degree of continuity marking the history of this phenomenon. 'History is about continuity as well as change', he writes, 'and this study of unemployment illustrates some remarkable consistencies over time in public attitudes and personal responses despite the major economic and social transformations which have occurred during the last two centuries.'[1]

This impression of continuity which tends to attach itself to the history of unemployment is only reinforced by our habit of thinking about unemployment in terms of numbers. Crime rates, poverty statistics, data about health, and, increasingly, information about markets – all regularly feature in the social and political life of nations. However, few of these series quite rival the impact or the cultural salience of the unemployment rate. While serious doubts about its accuracy have arisen in recent years, in part linked to concerns that it has been rather cynically manipulated for political reasons,[2] the unemployment rate remains a key social indicator. Yet it is precisely this social perception that unemployment is, essentially, a number, a quantity, which makes it so familiar. The rate may go up or down, the distribution may change, but the thing remains essentially there.

UNEMPLOYMENT, HISTORY, DIFFERENCE

I want to use this conclusion first of all to reiterate that this study has put forward an alternative perspective, one that analyses the territory of unemployment in terms of difference and multiplicity. Granted, there are certainly powerful themes and issues which span the history of unemployment, whether in terms of the concerns that social commentators, administrators, and political authorities have fastened to the problem, or in the forms of understanding and experience taken by the unemployed themselves. Modern societies have periodically found themselves subject to great economic upheavals and spells of intensive social distress. Each of these periods has seen its share of social commentators who sternly query the work ethic of the unemployed, deplore the leniency of the official support system, and summon for appropriate disciplines to be 'stiffened'. And there have usually been governments who have heeded such calls and responded with a battery of new tests, sanctions, and schemes to 'clamp down' on 'abuse'.

The present study could perhaps be faulted for failing to emphasize these and other continuities. But this is a risk associated with one of its principal objectives, namely, to suggest that the forms of interpretation and administration which have invested and surrounded the phenomenon of worklessness have in fact been remarkably diverse and unpredictable. How is this the case?

Ulrich Beck has identified an aspect of what I have tried to convey. For him, unemployment is typically modern, a characteristic feature of societies in which labour is rigidly standardized in terms of its space, time, and legal framing: employment and unemployment are radically distinct experiences. Yet while the public still talks about unemployment, and while administrative centres still count it, the qualitative reality behind the figures is now very different. Unemployment is not the same thing it was. In place of a society characterized by a 'uniform system of lifelong full-time work', which takes unemployment as its radical alternative, we are seeing the emergence of 'a risk-fraught system of flexible, pluralized, decentralized underemployment, which, however, will possibly no longer raise the problem of unemployment in the sense of being completely without a paid job'.[3]

Beck captures the fact that the word 'unemployment', the figures which express it, can make us inured to the changing social conditions which underlie it. At present there is a gap or a lag between regulatory and administrative concepts, and actual social experiences and predicaments. But while sympathetic to Beck's desire to place the regulation of unemployment in a historical-sociological context, the present study has differed in at least one important respect. The genealogical sensibility informing it is wary of the rather totalizing way in which Beck, and others, periodize history, dividing it in terms of categories like 'the risk society', and ascribing meta-logics to such epochs. Like Beck, I have tried to capture a sense of change, but on a more molecular and somewhat modest scale. The types of changes this study has highlighted are, moreover, confined to a particular dimension of our existence – the governmental. What I have sought to give a sense of are the diverse and changing ways in which unemployment has been posed as a problem by political powers; and how they have sought to act on it.

The striking discontinuities and contingencies I have alluded to can be illustrated in terms of certain histories implicit in this book. One of these is a history of the problematization of the unemployed individual.

We have seen that the manner of posing the problem of the unemployed individual is far from being fixed or predictable. On the contrary, this study has revealed a contingently shifting set of norms, objectives, values, obligations, rights, responsibilities which have been expected of, demanded by, imputed to unemployed people. In many instances the unemployed are seen to be deficient in the competences and attributes a given society deems important. A history of these problematizations is therefore important not just in its own right, but as a 'cut' into the social fabric which can reveal wider cultural values which are finely woven into it.

For much of the nineteenth century, the moral 'character' of the unemployed was an issue for investigators, just as character was of concern to Victorian society more generally. Methods were devised to measure this otherwise intangible attribute. Charitable and other forms of assistance and discipline were criticized and adjusted in the terms of their likely effects on character. By the time of the interwar years, as we saw in Chapter 4, the unemployed are being governed in relation to a changed set of objects and concerns. Although perceptions about it no doubt continue to shape the administration of the unemployed, character is no longer an official administrative concern. Instead, a political-legal notion of 'entitlement', a socio-psychological conception of 'morale', and a finely-calibrated monetarized conception of 'need' all become issues. Their emergence corresponds with the rise of bureaucratic welfare systems. This is not to make the simple-headed assertion that the unemployed were not seen to have needs before this time; but it is to highlight the fact that need gets made into an administratively defined, nationally standardized, and core governmental category at this point.

Today it is a cluster of attributes, such as the adaptiveness, the 'skills', the 'employability' of the unemployed which are particularly prominent in discussions about the unemployed. Again, one should not overemphasize the novelty of such emphases. The notion of 'the unemployable' dates back at least to the late nineteenth century. Similarly, fears that the capacities of the skilled worker would atrophy with prolonged exclusion from work were rife in the 'thirties, while political concerns that shortages of skilled workers in key industrial sectors were hampering economic growth surfaced periodically during the years of 'full employment'. Nevertheless, the manner in which 'skill' is governmentalized at present is quite distinct. 'Skill' is now at the centre of a new complex comprising dedicated methods for assessing and certifying skills. Public policies are being rethought in ways to offer the individual incentives to acquire new skills. At the same time, new flexible ways of certifying skills and learning experiences are helping to reconstitute a number of institutional sites – including the enterprise but also the family, the school, and the community – as places for the regulated transmission of skills. And a mass of trainers and counsellors has emerged with authority over this training system. Anxieties about the skills and the flexibility of the unemployed mirror wider concerns that the future welfare and security of populations in 'the global economy' hinges on their skills and adaptiveness. Hence we have an ironic inversion. At the turn of the century, social experts agreed that for the purposes of good character formation, it was crucial that adult men did not just work, but work regularly. Today, it is precisely the capacity to deal with an irregular and uncertain employment regime which is recommended by many experts on unemployment.[4]

A second history that is suggested by this study is of problematizations of unemployment itself. While historians have drawn our attention to changing ideas of unemployment, something slightly different has been emphasized here: the changing imagined territories and discursive frameworks associated with, and presupposed by, problematizations of unemployment. I have been interested not so much in the details of competing explanations of unemployment, or the extent to which they faithfully represent an external reality, but rather, the common assumptions and the *a priori* embedded in those accounts. How has unemployment been mapped – now as a social phenomenon, now as an economic problem, now as an ethical matter? How have metaphors and images been borrowed from other social sites to render unemployment thinkable?

It is certainly the case that economists and economic concepts have played an important role in supplying discursive resources to render unemployment thinkable. Indeed, we saw that the recognition that it was a condition independent of its bearers only became widespread once unemployment came to be understood in terms of a socio-economic system. With Tariff Reform unemployment is constructed as a matter of international economic and political rivalry, one that is echoed in some ways today in discourses of competitiveness. With Keynes it becomes located at the level of a fully national *macro*-economy.

But we saw also how unemployment has been posed in terms of other economic territories, such as the urban and the regional economy. Besides its deconstruction of unemployment, this study has contributed something to our understanding of the spatiality of the economic.

But it is not simply the case that a more rational, economic understanding comes to displace ill-defined social, moral, and other interpretations. The study has highlighted some of the other territories and forms of reasoning which have been employed to explicate the condition of unemployment. One of these is the 'political imaginary' of insurance, which helped to construct unemployment as an 'external risk'.[5] Another is a psychological territory that is opened up in the 1930s, while today the language of community has once again powerfully inflected discussions of chronic unemployment. This now gets constructed as a form of social malaise, a sign of individuals who fail to take responsibility for themselves, but also a symptom of a society which is lacking a strong sense of mutuality and social responsibility. In each case discursive frameworks are connected with ways of governing. For they highlight the salient mechanisms and processes which are to be targeted – economic variables in an economy, the individual's sense of responsibility, the skills of a local community, and so on.

It is important to recognize that the forms of reasoning which surround the question of unemployment are diverse and multiform. For the appeal of policy developments such as workfare rests precisely with their ability to connect with more than one form of rationalization. Workfare can be endorsed by those who see it as a way to improve the skills of the unemployed, but also by others who regard it in moral terms, as a mechanism for reasserting the value of work as social and personal duty. It is precisely this ambiguity, this potential for slippage, which allows certain policies and programmes to acquire heterogeneous networks of political support.

But it is also important to recognize these multiple objectivations of unemployment and the unemployed for the purposes of 'de-naturalizing' or 'dis-inevitablizing' the present. It is only when we place, say, the current obsession with skills in the context of a wider history of the different ways unemployment has been diagnosed that we weaken the grip which this, or any other figure holds over the present.

QUESTIONS OF AGENCY

A second issue I want to take up here concerns the stance of this work on the question of agency. So far we have not addressed this question at any length so it seems reasonable to do so here. Phil Mizen has recently argued that post-structuralist writers, including certain contributors to

the governmentality literature, fail to undertake 'any systematic examin-
ation of social subjects as active, whether as individuals or in groups,
confronting, frustrating or struggling against welfare's coercive dimensions'. This failure is not, moreover, an oversight, but a 'necessary
outcome of post-structuralism's idealist methodology'.[6] Given that the
present study has not devoted much space to the question of the
resistance of the unemployed, can it be defended against such charges?

First of all, the study was never intended to explore unemployment
'from below', but rather to analyse the changing ways in which
unemployment has been posed as a problem; and how this has shaped,
and been shaped by, attempts to influence the actions of the unemployed. From a governmentality perspective, a focus on mentalities of
rule is not in itself 'idealist'. Ontologies which posit a radical separation
of ideas and materials belong to the past. The position taken in this
study has been that intellectual activity is an eminently technical affair,
and no less dependent upon, and infused with practical devices than,
more conventionally accepted 'material' practices like manufacturing
or consuming. This study has highlighted a whole range of technical
devices which have been utilized in order to make unemployment
thinkable and programmable, whether we are talking of the labour
exchange, the technique of 'living with the unemployed' pioneered by
the social investigators of the inter-war years, or the skills audit of the
local economy. It has also highlighted the way in which theories and
concepts, which have their own determinations, and get developed in
particular institutional settings, condition what it is that can be thought
about unemployment at a given time. As Keynes once observed of
economics, it is a 'technique of thinking adapted to [particular] tasks'.[7]

So this study opted to focus at the level of techniques of posing and
acting on social problems, and not explicitly the resistance of actors.
Nevertheless, it has been cognizant throughout that the norms and
tactics which suffuse the regulation of the unemployed are not simply
dreamt up by eminent statespersons like Beveridge. It is not a disciplinary panopticon that I have sought to describe, a system simply
imposed from above in which the powerless become ensnared and
repressed in perpetuity. The earlier analysis of the political programme
which came to be known as the 'public organisation of the labour
market', as well as of the advent of a state scheme of unemployment
insurance, illustrated why one might view government as a process
involving not so much a head-on collision of social forces bearing only
an external relationship to one another, but rather an activity that
involves subtle movements of appropriation, infiltration, capture, and
subversion. It was argued that the technique of unemployment insurance came, to some extent, 'from below'. Trade unions were seen as the

architects of their own insurance schemes, which were to organize their own trades, to regulate the supply of labour, and collectively to secure the livelihoods of their members. These technologies were selectively appropriated by the state, eventually to regulate labour on a national scale. As the state moved into the field of unemployment insurance it effectively (re)defined the meaning of unemployment, and attached certain social norms to its regulation. For example, 'industrial' causes came to be carefully separated as legitimate grounds for a claim to benefits, from other causes such as industrial disputes and illness. But it was also observed that once established, this state scheme is vulnerable to the organized tactics, as well as the more spontaneous and inventive ways that workers will redefine themselves to be officially regarded as 'unemployed' and eligible for benefit payments. These movements of co-optation, these interweavings of official tactics and counter-tactics continue to animate the government of unemployment today. The Labour government's interest in 'intermediate labour markets' and in partnerships with community-based third-sector organizations – as noted in Chapter 6 – suggests that the world beyond the state continues to be both a vital source of governmental innovation and creativity, and constantly prone to political capture.

There is one final point I want to make regarding the understanding of agency. It has been implied in many places within this study, if not always explicitly stated. It is that a governmentality perspective does not take the existence of actors for granted, or assume the stability of their identities. Rather, it follows the advice of Bruno Latour: that in our analyses we should 'follow the actors' and take seriously the way they define one another intersubjectively – or not, as the case may be.[8] Hence this book has been wary of imposing its own suprahistorical grid of agency on to the social and historical analysis of unemployment. It has tried to avoid making The State, Capital, Labour, The Unemployed privileged categories of explanation. Instead, I have assumed that it is necessary to investigate empirically and in the context of a given issue the manner in which objects and subjects – both human and non-human – are discovered, invented, deployed, instrumentalized, assigned particular roles (which they may or may not resist), ascribed particular functions, enjoined to undertake governmental responsibilities. I have worked with a conceptual space in which objects are simultaneously the targets of strategies, and agents within those strategies.

One finding to come out of this is that, while it is always empirical individuals who suffer the hardship, indignity and desperation of worklessness – whatever its form – the manner in which 'the unemployed' are implicated in the government of unemployment is not constant.

Not all strategies of regulation govern through individuals in the same way, according them the same levels of significance, rights, or responsibilities. Keynesian economic management engages unemployment in a way that does not seem to make the morals or the behaviour of unemployed individuals into an issue for regulation. The same is not true of discourses about the underclass, or programmes like the New Deal. These explicitly draw attention to the attitudes, the skills, or the values of the unemployed, and make them into variables for government and self-government. But this is not an all-or-nothing question. It is more the case that different technologies work through, and instrumentalize, the individual with differing intensities. Social insurance is a less personalized form of governing than charitable relief, but it is not un-personalized.

This study did not analyse proposals for replacing the social security system with a programme of citizens' or guaranteed annual income.[9] But one might note at this point that the radical promise of such schemes is to de-subjectify and de-individualize the government of unemployment and other sectors of the social. We saw how unemployment insurance and other forms of income support construct their subjects as 'the unemployed' and thereby serve to differentiate the unemployed from the wider population. If a basic income were the right of all citizens, regardless of their social or occupational condition, the salience of 'the unemployed' as a distinct, and largely negative, identity would surely be diminished. This would not solve all the social, economic, psychological, and other problems associated with unemployment. But it would perhaps mitigate the tendency to subjectify the problem, to 'blame the victim'.

THE FATE OF THE SOCIAL

Lastly I want to ask what conclusions might be drawn from the study that are of relevance to the wider literature which has sought to rethink our past and our present in terms of the social.[10] If it achieves nothing else, this inquiry has at least clarified some of the ways in which unemployment, like poverty, crime, childhood, health, sexuality, and a host of other key aspects of our existence, came to be problematized and acted on from a social point of view. This can be summarized as follows. In the nineteenth century and before, the condition of the unemployed was understood either as an issue of overpopulation (Malthus), or ascribed to factors exogenous to the market system – perhaps a severe winter, or a distant war that disrupted the normal patterns of trade. It was, of course, also attributed to the moral failings of the poor. Within a political culture dominated by the axioms of liberal political economy it was not possible to conceptualize worklessness as a systemic and impersonal phenomenon.

But a number of developments towards the end of the century changed matters, so that by the 1890s, at least, a socio-economic condition of 'unemployment' could be identified. The fact that the British economy entered into a long recession beginning in the 1870s is only one factor determining this event. To explain how it is that unemployment could be discussed as a socio-economic condition at this time requires that we consider other factors as well. As we saw, these included the rise of social survey-based research, which quantified the sheer scale of poverty and irregular employment in the major cities; changes in political and social thought, which repudiated the atomistic assumptions of liberal political economy in favour of a more holistic and interdependent conception of society; and the political activity of the labour movement and of poor people who began to make political demands in the name of the unemployed, to emphasize their distinct identity. An important consequence of this was that unemployment came to be officially recognized as an outcome of the functioning of a larger socio-economic system, or, as William Beveridge put it, a 'problem of industry'. Henceforth, unemployment could be understood as a normal, albeit regrettable and deleterious, consequence of industrial life. Just like the various other dimensions of the social (suicide, crime, poverty, etc.) that were revealed through the statistical work of social experts and emerging social ministries, unemployment was seen to have its own regularity, its cycles, its social and geographical distribution.

Not only was unemployment now being conceptualized at a social level. The first six decades of this century also saw the development of a host of techniques for *acting* on it at the level of population and national economy. With the advent of unemployment insurance to socialize the wage, a labour exchange system to oversee and distribute the labour force more rationally, regional policy to distribute industrial activity geographically, and, by the end of the Second World War, a political technology of national economic management influenced by Keynes' formalization of macroeconomics, more and more aspects of the problem of unemployment could be tackled at a national-aggregate, rather than an individual or local level. This study has emphasized throughout that these technologies play an active and creative role with regard to definitions and understandings of unemployment.

However, unemployment was not just another concern to become governmentalized. As we saw in Chapter 1, it had a special place within the tactics and strategies of social government. If Beveridge identified unemployment (or 'idleness') as one of the 'five giants' requiring collective action following the Second World War (the others were squalor, ignorance, sickness, and want), the reasoning for this was already apparent to him in his first book on unemployment (1909). By regulating the labour market, it would be possible to secure the patriarchal family, and to ensure that this essentially 'private' social mechanism would be supported as it undertook various social responsibilities.

With the rise of neo-liberalism in the 1980s it was not difficult to believe that the government of unemployment was set to be de-socialized. On the one hand, the force of monetarist arguments helped to redefine inflation as the main concern of government, displacing unemployment as a political concern. On the other, governmental solutions to unemployment began to be framed in terms of the market. Social forms of government, such as employment standards and social security, were now defined as 'barriers' and 'obstacles' inhibiting enterprise; high levels of employment were to be achieved by removing such impediments, or greatly reducing their presence. Keynesianism was defined as part of the problem, not the answer to the jobs crisis. Whereas the depression of the 1930s had been the occasion for a strengthening of arguments and innovations in favour of social government (most notably the Keynesian critique of classical economics), the economic instabilities of the 1970s and early 1980s saw social technologies like social security and active demand management become discredited.

It is true that these and other neo-liberal themes continue to influence the government of unemployment today. For instance, prospects for a revived Keynesian approach to unemployment are not promising at a national level (though the resurrection of Keynesian thinking within international fora cannot be discounted).[11]

However, it would be misleading to conclude that governments no longer care about unemployment, or that they are distancing themselves from the issue. The Labour Party was elected in 1997 on a platform which made the fight against unemployment and social exclusion one of its political priorities. This has been reflected in the attention and resources it has accorded to the New Deal in office. But at the same time, unemployment is no longer being governed according to the same logic and techniques as before. What, then, can the case of unemployment tell us about the trajectories of social government?

First, it is possible to identify a mutation in political reasoning around unemployment. We saw that Labour has called for a renewal of society's sense of obligation and responsibility to support the unemployed. Yet this appeal does not, for the most part, rest upon a *sociological* conception of society. Unemployment is no longer perceived as a risk inherent in the structure of capitalist societies – a 'necessary margin of idleness' required for the functioning of modern labour markets as Beveridge saw it – and therefore a burden which the nation, and not just the victims should shoulder. Instead, the case for unemployment policy has recently been voiced in the name of community, decency, civility; it is made in terms of the social responsibilities we all – especially the unemployed – owe to one another as members of communities. Moreover, we saw that there is more to this appeal than mere rhetoric. It has as one of its correlates the emergence of a different paradigm of voluntary action, at a distance from the state, which we saw as figured by organizations like Business in the Community.

A sense of community is not the only rationalization that exists for collective action around unemployment. Intellectuals close to the Labour party have also stressed the economic costs to society of inequality, in a manner not that dissimilar from the Fabian socialists' problematization of 'efficiency' at the turn of the century.[12] Also, the language of community may prove ephemeral. What we can assume, however, is that the passing of the particular idea of society which was dominant for much of this century – society as an organic, interdependent system – does not in itself mean that unemployment necessarily ceases to be seen from a societal point of view.

A second trajectory concerns the forms of individuality presupposed and encouraged by current forms of government compared with welfare government. Schemes like the New Deal constitute the unemployed person as an active choice-maker who must strategize about the different 'options' available to him or her. The recipient of benefits is addressed as a 'jobseeker', a status which has attached to it new norms concerning the individual's responsibility to look for work and manage their own unemployment. Then there is another trend in employment policy we did not cover but which is consistent with this tendency, namely official encouragement for self-employment as an 'option' for the unemployed. In each case the individual is encouraged to be enterprising, to shape their own destiny. The implication of Chapter 6, and the discussion of the logic of community, is that it would be wrong to see this as simply a reflection of the *neo*-liberal agenda. For the principle of personal responsibility has diverse ethical supports. That is why it seems appropriate to fit these different appeals to the individual under the rubric of 'advanced liberal'.[13] They are liberal because like the other forms of governance we have reviewed, they govern by eliciting the activity, and assuming the freedoms of the governed; advanced, because they assert that whatever its original intentions, welfare governance does not encourage personal responsibility, but the reverse – dependency.

A third trajectory also pertains to the broad concept of advanced liberalism – the pluralization of social technologies. Typical of a whole range of technologies of welfare government, Keynesianism and social insurance both governed in terms of a holistic, totalized, and bounded conception of the socio-economic system. It was an entity which could be macromanaged by the state acting in the name of a unified people/ society. Government through the multiple, overlapping, and voluntary affiliations of community – rather than a singular conception of society – has been proposed as one sense in which there has been a pluralization of social technologies. We have seen that the New Deal seeks to mobilize community.

However, there are other aspects of the current problematic of unemployment which one could also analyse in terms of a pluralization of social technologies. One which this study did not take up, but which certainly merits further investigation, is the idea of lifelong learning. We noted how social insurance offered a diagram for social government, given the way it constructed societal problems as impersonal risks, but also furnished government with a particular mechanism of solidarity. Lifelong learning is much more than a policy for reforming the education system, or an educational philosophy. Like social insurance it is also a diagram of governmental relations. At least as it is understood by governments at the moment,[14] lifelong learning imagines a society which is the correlate of the active subject. It projects a society whose members are constantly adapting to the challenges of an information-intensive world, investing in their skills, acquiring new competences. But the crucial point is that the task of adaptation is not monopolized by the public sector or even the education system. For it cannot be engineered from a single political-administrative centre. Rather, the society of lifelong learning discourse is a 'learning society' where a multitude of sites – families, schools, firms, communities, etc. – have been configured as mechanisms for skilling and self-investment. As Donzelot has observed, society is 'mobilized' as an alternative governmental strategy to the welfare state.[15]

Finally, it would be an oversight to confine these concluding remarks on the future of social government and unemployment to measures which formally address the unemployed. What of tactics which govern the workless and the marginalized without characterizing them formally as 'unemployed'? Besides the mutations internal to social government sketched above, the present is also marked by a revival of penal and criminological approaches to the government of population. As Stan Cohen, among many criminologists, has noted, 'the crime problem has come to dominate the contemporary political rhetoric of Western democracies'.[16] In Britain and other anglophonic countries, one can speak of a 'new punitiveness' which seeks to engage certain 'problem' sections of the population in terms of the logic of the 'crackdown', in terms of a host of disciplinary measures like the boot camp, 'tougher' sentencing regimes, curfews for young people, and 'zero tolerance'.[17] It would take detailed empirical work to establish how, and to what extent, a new penal complex is actually redefining people who would previously have been governed as 'the unemployed', and regulating them as threats to law and public safety. In showing that the discovery of unemployment at the start of the century corresponded with the rise of new modes of governing poverty in terms of social security and social citizenship, this book has shown that unemployment is a contingent and not a necessary aspect of modern societies. Other ways of governing indigence and destitution have existed in the past. It is therefore not inconceivable that the social territory that was governed in terms of unemployment could be altered considerably by the palpable turn towards penality. If that were the case, unemployment could have a shorter history than is often supposed.

NOTES

INTRODUCTION

1 J. A. Hobson, 'The meaning and measure of "unemployment"', *The Contemporary Review*, 67, March 1895.

2 See Christian Topalov, *Naissance du chômeur: 1880–1910*, Paris: Albin Michel, 1994; Robert Salais (with Nicolas Bavarez and Bénédicte Reynaud), *L'invention du chômage: histoire et transformations d'une catégorie en France des années 1890 aux années 1980*, Paris: Paris Universitaires de France, 1986; Malcolm Mansfield, Robert Salais, and Noelle Whiteside, *Aux sources du chômage: une comparison interdisciplinaire entre France et la Grande Bretagne*, Paris: Belin, 1994.

3 Michel Foucault, 'On governmentality', in Graham Burchell, Colin Gordon, and Peter Miller (eds.), *The Foucault Effect*, Hemel Hempstead: Harvester Wheatsheaf, 1991. This volume, and Andrew Barry, Thomas Osborne, and Nikolas Rose (eds.), *Foucault and Political Reason*, London: UCL Press, 1996, represent the best surveys of this approach.

4 Foucault explains that the different concepts he has used to analyse power should not be thought of as a historical series – sovereignty, discipline, government. Instead, they can be related in terms of a triangle 'which has as its primary target the population and as its essential mechanism the apparatuses of security'; 'On governmentality', 102.

5 Nikolas Rose and Peter Miller, 'Political power beyond the state: problematics of government', *British Journal of Sociology*, 43(2), 1992, 174.

6 For example, Donald Winch, *Economics and Policy: An Historical Study*, London: Hodder & Stoughton, 1969; Peter Hall (ed.), *The Political Power of Economic Ideas*, Princeton NJ: Princeton University Press, 1989.

7 The classic work remains José Harris, *Unemployment and Politics: A Study in English Social Policy 1886–1914*, Oxford: Clarendon Press, 1972; but see also Noelle Whiteside, *Bad Times: Unemployment in British Social and Political History*, London: Faber and Faber, 1991.

8 Mitchell Dean, *Critical and Effective Histories*, London: Routledge, 1994, 174.

9 Graham Burchell, 'Liberal government and techniques of the self', in Barry et al. (eds.), *Foucault and Political Reason*, 23.

10 The concept of regulating 'at a distance' is adapted by the governmentality literature from the work of Bruno Latour and Michel Callon. For example, see the discussion of 'action at a distance' in Latour's *Science in Action: How to Follow Scientists and Engineers Through Society*, Milton Keynes, Open University Press, 1987.

11 I am grateful to Gavin Kendall for this way of posing the relationship of governmentality research to the use of history; ' "Governing at a distance": Anglo-Australian relations 1840–1870', presentation to the History of the Present, Toronto Group, August 1997.

12 'Introduction' to Jacques Donzelot, *The Policing of Families: Welfare versus the State*, London: Hutchison, 1979; cf. Nikolas Rose, 'The death of the social? Refiguring the territory of government', *Economy and Society*, 25(3), 1996, 329.

13 Giovanna Procacci, 'Sociology and its poor', *Politics and Society*, 17(2), 1989; Rose, 'The death of the social?'; Pat O'Malley, 'Criminology and the new liberalism', *The 1996 John Edwards Memorial Lecture*, at www.library.utoronto.ca/www/libraries_crim/centre/lecture.htm.

14 O'Malley, 'Criminology and the new liberalism', 2.

15 But see Peter Miller and Nikolas Rose, 'Governing economic life', *Economy and Society*, 19(1), 1990; and Denis Meuret, 'A political genealogy of political economy', *Economy and Society*, 17(2), 1988. For an earlier study of economic questions, which anticipates some of the developments in the governmenality literature, see Keith Tribe, *Land, Labour and Economic Discourse*, London: RKP, 1978.

16 For example, see R. Burrows and B. Loader (eds.), *Towards a Post-Fordist Welfare State?* London: Routledge, 1994.

17 On the contribution of genealogy to methods of historical and social analysis see Foucault, 'Questions of method', in Burchell et al. (eds.), *The Foucault Effect*; and Mitchell Dean, 'A genealogy of the government of poverty', *Economy and Society*, 21(3), 1992.

1 THE DISCOVERY OF UNEMPLOYMENT

1 W. H. Beveridge, *Unemployment: A Problem of Industry*, London: Longman, 1909, 1.

2 For example, J. Garraty, *Unemployment in History: Economic Thought and Public Policy*, New York: Harper & Row, 1978, Chapter 6; J. Harris, *Unemployment and Politics*; J. Burnett, *Idle Hands: The Experience of Unemployment, 1790–1990*, London: Routledge, 1994, Chapter 5.

3 Daniel Defoe, *Giving Alms no Charity, and Employing the Poor a Grievance to the Nation*, London, 1704; cf. Garraty, *Unemployment*, 51.

4 See, for example, Harris, *Unemployment and Politics*; L. Schweber, 'Progressive reformers, unemployment, and the transformation of social inquiry in Britain and the United States, 1880s–1920s', in Dietrich Rueschemeyer and Theda Skocpol (eds.), *States, Social Knowledge, and the Origins of Modern Social Policies*, Princeton NJ: Princeton University Press, 1996.

5 For example, B. Gilbert, *The Evolution of National Insurance in Great Britain*, London: Michael Joseph, 1966.

6 K. Kumar, 'From work to employment and unemployment: the English experience', in R. E. Pahl (ed.), *On Work: Historical, Comparative and Theoretical Approaches*, Oxford: Basil Blackwell, 1988.

7 Ibid. 163. For a consideration of the 'social origins' of unemployment in Massachusetts, see A. Keyssar, *Out of Work: The First Century of Unemployment in Massachusetts*, Cambridge, Cambridge University Press, 1986. Like Kumar, Keyssar identifies the rapid spread of 'dependence of workers on cash wages and industrial employment' (p. 43) as a crucial factor in precipitating the emergence of a political problem of unemployment.

8 It should be noted that at the level of statistics, at least, the estimated numbers of persons involved in manufacture were already equal to those in agriculture by about 1811; by 1881 there were three times as many people employed in the former compared with the latter. See P. Deane and W. A. Cole, *British Economic Growth 1688–1959*, Cambridge: Cambridge University Press, 1962, Table 31; cf. P. Joyce, 'Work', in F. M. L. Thompson (ed.), *Cambridge Social History of Britain 1750–1950*, Cambridge: Cambridge University Press, 1990, 133.

9 See J. Keane, *Democracy and Civil Society*, London: Verso, 1988, 71, who argues that it is only with the historical emergence of employment societies that 'the fact of paid work … emerges on a large scale and as an activity separate from the state and from the household and other institutions of civil society'.

10 Sidney Webb, Preface to B. Hutchins and A. Harrison, *A History of Factory Legislation*, 3rd edn., London: P. S. King & Son, 1926, vii. This book, along with J. Ward, *The Factory Movement 1830–1855*, London: Macmillan, 1962, provides a good account of the history of factory legislation.

11 U. Henriques, *Before the Welfare State: Social Administration in Early Industrial Britain*, London: Longman, 1979, Chapters 4 and 5.

12 For a discussion of liberalism's relation to illiberal forms of governance, see M. Valverde, 'Liberalism and despotic governance', *Economy & Society*, 25(3), 1996.

13 Henriques, *Before the Welfare State*, 69.

14 Ibid. 75.

15 Webb, Preface to *A History of Factory Legislation*, vii.

16 See, e.g., A. Briggs, 'Comers and goers', in H. Dyos and M. Wolff (eds.), *The Victorian City: Images and Reality*, vol. 1, London: Routledge, 1973; Kumar, 'Work, employment and unemployment'; P. Joyce, 'Work'.

17 Sidney Webb and Beatrice Webb, *Industrial Democracy*, London: Longman, 1926 [1897].

18 Ibid. 250–1.

19 *Flint Glass Makers' Magazine*, opening editorial, No. 1, Sept. 1850; cf. Webb and Webb, *Industrial Democracy*, 163.

20 Address of General Secretary at Delegate Meeting of Associated Shipwrights Society, 1885; cf. Webb and Webb, *Industrial Democracy*, 164.

21 D. Powell, *British Politics and the Labour Question, 1868–1990*, London: Macmillan, 1992, 16.

22 J. R. Brooke, 'Unemployment', *Women's Trade Union Review*, No. 74, October 1909, 14.

23 To be more precise, women workers were concentrated in trades defined as 'unskilled'. Yet feminist research has demonstrated that the definition of

'skill' is not neutral, but itself gendered and a site of power relations. For a feminist analysis of contemporary debates about 'skills' and flexible work, see J. Jenson, 'The talents of women, the skills of men: flexible specialization and women', in S. Wood (ed.), *The Transformation of Work: Skill, Flexibility and the Labour Process*, London: Routledge, 1989.

24 It was estimated in 1886 that fewer than 37 000 women were members of trade unions (although female membership rose sharply just before the First World War). Elizabeth Roberts ascribes this to a number of factors including an absence of unions in occupations in which women concentrated (e.g., domestic service), the perception that unions were male-dominated affairs, and a lack of time for union affairs on the part of many married women; *Women's Work 1840–1940*, London: Macmillan Education Ltd, 1988, 59.

25 Brooke, 'Unemployment', 15.

26 Ibid. 15–16. My emphasis.

27 Foucault, 'Two lectures', in Colin Gordon (ed.), *Power/Knowledge: Selected Interviews and Other Writings 1972–1977*, New York: Pantheon, 1980, 99.

28 The following summary of the social question draws especially on D. Garland, *Punishment and Welfare: A History of Penal Strategies*, London: Gower, 1985, 47–59; see also G. Stedman Jones, *Outcast London*, Harmondsworth: Penguin, 1984; N. Rose, *The Psychological Complex; Psychology, Politics and Society in England, 1869–1939*, London: Routledge, 1985; Harris, *Unemployment and Politics*; G. Ritter, *Social Welfare in Britain and Germany*, Leamington Spa: Berg, 1983.

29 For example, A. Mearns, *The Bitter Cry of Outcast London*, London: London Congregational Union, 1883; C. Booth, *Life and Labour of the People*, London: Williams & Norgate, 1902; H. of C. 321/1896, *Select Committee on Distress from Want of Employment: Report of Minutes of Evidence*.

30 Cf. G. Procacci, 'Social economy and the government of poverty', in G. Burchell, C. Gordon, and P. Miller (eds.), *The Foucault Effect: Studies in Governmentality*, Hemel Hempstead: Harvester Wheatsheaf, 1991.

31 On this 'new unionism', see H. Pelling, *A History of British Trade Unionism*, 3rd edn., London: Macmillan, 1976, Chapter 6.

32 J. Stevenson, *Popular disturbances in England 1700–1870*, London: Longman, 1979, 232–3.

33 E. Hobsbawm and G. Rudé, *Captain Swing*, Harmondsworth: Penguin, 1973; cf. Stevenson, *Popular disturbances*, 236–44.

34 On the relationship of emerging socialist doctrines and parties like the Social Democratic Federation to unemployed agitation, see R. Flanagan, *'Parish-Fed Bastards': A History of the Politics of the Unemployed in Britain, 1884–1939*, Westport CT: Greenwood, 1991.

35 While it acquired a greater urgency in the latter part of the nineteenth century, the question of how to identify the genuinely unemployed was not entirely new. As one Parliamentary Committee investigating rural distress in 1824 put it: 'The great object to be aimed at is, if possible, to separate the maintenance of the unemployed man from the wages of the employed labourer: to divide two classes which have been confounded'; *Report of the*

Select Committee on Labourers' Wages, 1824 (392), VI, 6; cf. Burnett, *Idle Hands*, 31.

36 Alsager Hill, *Our Unemployed: An Attempt to Point Out the Best Means of Providing Occupations for Distressed Labourers*, London: 1868, 10, 15. Emphasis in original.

37 The Reverend Canon Barnett, 'The unemployed', *The Fortnightly Review*, 54, December 1893, 743.

38 J. Ditch, 'The Undeserving Poor: Unemployed People, Then and Now', in M. Loney et al. (eds.), *The State or the Market*, 2nd edn., London: Sage, 1991.

39 Barnett, 'The unemployed', 743.

40 J. Treble, *Urban Poverty in Britain, 1830–1914*, New York: St. Martin's Press, 1979, Chapter 4.

41 Harris, *Unemployment*, Chapters 2 and 4; Pat Thane, *Foundations of the Welfare State*, London: Longman, 1983, 70–2.

42 Cd. 4795/1909, *Royal Commission on the Poor Laws*, Appx. Vol. XIX, *Report by Mr Cyril Jackson and Rev. J. C. Pringle on The Effects of Employment or Assistance Given to the 'Unemployed' since 1886 as a Means of Relieving Distress outside the Poor Law*, 65–6.

43 Thane, *Foundations of the Welfare State*, 71; Treble, *Urban Poverty*, 144–8.

44 Cd. 4795/1909, *Royal Commission on the Poor Laws*, 7.

45 I owe this insight to N. Rose, *The Psychological Complex*, Chapter 2.

46 See Gareth Stedman Jones, *Outcast London*, 262–70.

47 Ibid. 287–8.

48 Charles Booth sets out his understanding of poverty in the first volume of his monumental series *Life and Labour of the People*, London: Williams & Norgate, 1902; for a careful reconstruction of Booth's theory, see E. P. Hennock, 'Poverty and social theory in England: the experience of the 1880s', *Social History*, 1, 1976.

49 Besides Booth, another prominent student of dock labour was Eleanor Rathbone who surveyed Liverpool. On casual labour in port transport see N. Whiteside, 'Welfare insurance and casual labour: a study of administrative intervention in industrial employment 1906–26', *Economic History Review*, 2(31), 1979; and G. Phillips and N. Whiteside, *Casual Labour*, Oxford: Clarendon Press, 1985. Jones, *Outcast London*, Part I, provides a comprehensive account of the economy of casual labour in London. The phenomenon is by no means limited to the docks, but is found wherever the demand for unskilled labour is from one day to the next unpredictable, or seasonal.

50 Sidney Webb and Beatrice Webb (eds.), *The Public Organisation of the Labour Market: Being Part Two of the Minority Report of the Poor Law Commission*, London: Longman, 1909, 191.

51 Ibid. 192.

52 *COS Exceptional Distress Report*, vi; quoted by Cd. 4795/1909, *Royal Commission on the Poor Laws*, 6.

53 Miss M. Marshall (Secretary to the Whitechapel Committee of the Charity Organization Society) giving evidence, Cd. 5066/1910, *Royal Commission on the Poor Laws*, Appx. Vol. VIII (Minutes of Evidence), 210n.

54 The Majority Report of the Royal Commission on the Poor Laws notes that 'in relief or distress work, the best method of discriminating between "deserving" and "undeserving" is to take records of past employments, and it has seemed to some that provision should be made for workers generally providing themselves with a kind of industrial *dossier*, where the duration and value of their jobs would appear to their credit. But it is impossible for the casual labourer who is employed by the hour, day, or job, and passes from employer to employer in the course of a week, to build up such a "character"'; Cd. 4499/1909, *Royal Commission on the Poor Laws*, 337 (emphasis in original). For an argument about the importance of the idea of 'character' in Victorian society, see S. Collini, 'The idea of "character" in Victorian political thought', *Transactions of the Royal Historical Society*, Series V, 35, 1985. 'Character' is more than an idea, however. It needs to be understood like the soul, which is for Foucault 'the present correlative of a certain technology of power over the body'; *Discipline and Punish*, London: Allen Lane, 1977, 29.

55 Webb and Webb, *Public Organization*, 244.

56 Cd. 4795/1909, *Royal Commission on the Poor Laws*, 44.

57 Its proceedings were published as a pamphlet; see Women's Industrial Council, *National Conference on the Unemployment of Women Dependent on their Own Earnings*, London, 1907; a copy of which exists in the Beveridge Collection (B, IV, 14).

58 See the evidence of Margaret Smith at the Women's Industrial Council, *National Conference*, 10–13.

59 Miss Irwin, Scottish Council for Women's Trade, in Women's Industrial Council, *National Conference*, 14.

60 S. Webb and B. Webb (eds.), *The Public Organisation of the Labour Market: Being Part Two of the Minority Report of the Poor Law Commission*, London: Longman, 1909: 279, 211. This principle was in fact applied in Glasgow with the Local Government Board's 'special roll' scheme; widows with young children were placed 'on the roll' and paid a weekly allowance which made them subject to public inspection.

61 On the links between casual labour, boy labour, and hooliganism, see H. Hendrick, *Images of Youth, Age, Class and the Youth Male Problem, 1880–1952*, Oxford: Oxford University Press, 1990. For a bureaucratic system for regulating this problem, see the evidence of Ogilvie Gordon, Honorary Corresponding Secretary of the National Council of Women, *Royal Commission on the Poor Laws*, Appx. Vol. IX (Minutes of Evidence) (Cd. 5068), London: HMSO, 1910, 365 ff.

62 In his evidence to the Royal Commission in 1905, J. Ramsay Macdonald, speaking as the Honorary Secretary of the Women's Industrial Council, points out that 'a woman can unfortunately always find employment in vicious ways, and that difficulty in earning enough money honestly must add very strongly to the temptation to earn it in immoral ways'; Cd. 5066/1910, *Royal Commission on the Poor Laws*, 230.

63 Beveridge, 'Metropolitan labour exchanges of the Central (Unemployed) Body', *Toynbee Record*, July–September 1907, 136. My emphasis.

64 The resettlement of the unemployed and the unfit into rural labour colonies was a common response to the unemployed problem throughout Europe. By the 1890s there were camps in Great Britain, France, Switzerland, Belgium, the Netherlands, and the USA. They varied from ostensive penal colonies to utopian experiments in founding new communities which would reclaim land and souls; Garraty, *Unemployment in History*, 120.

65 See R. Plant and A. Vincent, *Philosophy, Politics, and Citizenship; The Life and Thought of the British Idealists*, Oxford: Blackwell, 1984, Chapters 5 and 7.

66 Board of Trade, *Agencies and Methods for Dealing with the Unemployed* (C. 7182), London: HMSO, 1893, 6.

67 José Harris, *Unemployment and Politics*, 12.

68 Hobson, 'The meaning and measure of "unemployment"', *The Contemporary Review*, 67, March 1895, 419–20.

69 Hobson, *The Problem of the Unemployed*, London: Methuen and Co., 1896, 47; cf. M. S. Lawlor, 'Keynes, Cambridge, and the new Keynesian economics', in W. Darity (ed.), *Labor Economics: Problems in Analyzing Labour Markets*, Boston: Luwer Academic publishers, 1992, 22.

70 Hobson, *The Problem of the Unemployed*, viii; cf. D. Winch, *Economics and Policy*, London: Fontana, 1972, 52–3.

71 Beveridge, *Unemployment*, 3.

72 Hobson's anticipation of Keynes has been noted by several historians of economic thought; see Winch, *Economics*, 57–8; Garraty, *Unemployment*, 125–8. It has been noted, for instance, that Hobson uses the 'Keynesian' terms 'aggregate supply' and 'aggregate demand'; see Lawlor, 'Keynes, Cambridge'.

73 Beveridge, *Unemployment*, 4.

74 One exception was A. G. Pigou, one of the few professional economists to tackle the question of unemployment before the First World War. Pigou linked unemployment with a rigid wage system which failed to adjust to economic downturns; see Garraty, *Unemployment*, 142–3.

75 I. Katznelson, 'Knowledge about what? Policy intellectuals and the new liberalism', in Rueschemeyer and Skocpol (eds.), *States, Social Knowledge*, 33; see also Lawlor, 'Keynes, Cambridge', who argues that Marshall's was an ambiguous legacy since it not only 'spawned Pigou's (1933) amazingly out-of-touch treatment, *The Theory of Unemployment*, but also [Maurice] Dobb's subtle and historically informed view of labour markets in his Cambridge Handbook *Wages*'.

76 Lawlor, 'Keynes, Cambridge', 14.

77 H. Nowotny, 'Knowledge for certainty', in B. Wittrock and P. Wagner (eds.), *Discourses on Society: The Shaping of the Social Science Disciplines*, Dordrecht: Kluwer, 1991.

2 INVENTING UNEMPLOYMENT: THE BIRTH OF THE LABOUR EXCHANGE

1 E. P. Hennock, 'The measurement of urban poverty: from the metropolis to the nation, 1880–1920', *Economic History Review*, 2nd series, 40(2), 1987;

Alain Desroisières, 'The part in relation to the whole: how to generalise? The prehistory of representative sampling', in M. Bulmer, K. Bales, and K. Sklar (eds.), *The Social Survey in Historical Perspective 1880–1940*, Cambridge: Cambridge University Press, 1991.

2 The argument that social legislation was used by parties before the First World War to win the working-class vote needs to be carefully qualified. Pat Thane, 'The working class and state "welfare" in Britain, 1880–1914', *The Historical Journal*, 27(4), argues that working-class support for state-organized welfare was highly circumscribed: there was enthusiasm for measures like public housing, whereas schemes which involved official intrusion were regarded with skepticism. For the argument that the entry of social policy into 'high politics' had more to do with what politicians *assumed* would be appealing to working-class voters, see J. Harris, 'The transition to High Politics in English social policy, 1880–1914', in J. Stevenson, *High and Low Politics*, Oxford: Clarendon Press, 1993. See also A. Orloff and T. Skocpol, 'Why not equal protection? Explaining the politics of public social spending in Britain, 1900–1911, and the United States, 1880s–1920', *American Sociological Review*, 49, 1984, 726–50.

3 R. Flanagan, *'Parish-Fed Bastards': A History of the Politics of the Unemployed in Britain, 1884–1938*, Westport CT: Greenwood, 1991, Chapter 3.

4 J. Ramsay Macdonald, 'The new unemployed Bill of the Labour Party', ILP pamphlet, 1907, 6; cf. Harris, *Unemployment and Politics*, 242.

5 Keir Hardie, Labour Leader, 25 August 1905; cf. Flanagan, *Parish-Fed Bastards*, 64.

6 Flanagan, *Parish-Fed Bastards*, 64–73.

7 Ibid. 4.

8 Harris, *Unemployment and Politics*, 242.

9 Flanagan, *Parish-Fed Bastards*, 78.

10 R. J. Scally, *The Origins of the Lloyd George Coalition: The Politics of Social-Imperialism, 1900–1918*, Princeton NJ: Princeton University Press, 1975, 4.

11 For an excellent analysis of Tariff Reform as an economic strategy, see A. Gamble, *Britain in Decline: Economic Policy, Political Strategy and the British State*, Basingstoke: Macmillan, 1994.

12 Donald Winch, *Economics and Policy: An Historical Study*, London: Hodder & Stoughton, 1969, 65; A. Sykes, *Tariff Reform in British Politics, 1903–1913*, Oxford: Clarendon Press, 1979, 55–9.

13 J. Tomlinson, *Public Policy and the Economy since 1900*, Oxford: Clarendon Press, 1990, 19.

14 F. Capie, *Depression and Protectionism: Britain Between the Wars*, London: George Allen & Unwin, 1983, 40–4.

15 M. Pugh, *The Making of Modern British Politics, 1867–1939*, 2nd edn., Oxford: Blackwell, 1993, 106–8.

16 For example, see D. Feldman, 'The importance of being English: Jewish immigration and the decay of liberal England', in D. Feldman and G. S. Jones (eds.), *Metropolis London*, London: Routledge, 1989.

17 Winch, *Economics and Policy*, 67.

18 Sidney Webb and Beatrice Webb (eds.), *The Public Organisation of the Labour Market: Being Part Two of the Minority Report of the Poor Law Commission*, London: Longman, 1909, 228–9; cf. Peter Squires, *Anti-Social Policy*, Hemel Hempstead: Harvester Wheatsheaf, 1990, 111.

19 W. H. Beveridge, *Unemployment: A Problem of Industry*, London: Longman, 207.

20 This remark comes from the founding statement of the New Liberals, a group started by J. A. Hobson, Alfred Marshall, and L. T. Hobhouse in 1896; see H. V. Emy, *Liberals, radicals and social politics, 1892–1914*, London: Cambridge University Press, 1973, 105; cf., Garland, *Punishment and welfare*, 57. On new liberalism see, inter alia, P. Clarke, *Liberals and social democrats*, Cambridge: Cambridge University Press, 1978; S. Collini, *Liberalism and sociology: L. T. Hobhouse and political argument in England, 1880–1914*, Cambridge: Cambridge University Press, 1979.

21 Beveridge, *Unemployment*, 4.

22 Ibid. 237.

23 Ibid. 201.

24 For a more detailed discussion of the way in which the policy of de-casualization is actually about the construction of 'unemployment' in its modern form – i.e., as 'full-time' joblessness rather than casualism – see M. Mansfield, 'Labour exchanges and the labour reserve in turn of the century social reform', *Journal of Social Policy*, 21(4), 1992.

25 Beveridge, *Unemployment*, 223.

26 Patrick Colquhoun, *A Treatise on Indigence*, London: J. Mawman, 1806, 7; cf. M. Dean, *The Constitution of Poverty: Toward a Genealogy of Liberal Governance*, London: Routledge, 1991, 145.

27 Webb and Webb, *Public Organisation*, 242.

28 Harris, *Unemployment and Politics*, 295.

29 Letter from Churchill to Asquith, 14 March 1908, quoted in E. P. Hennock, *British Social Reform and German Precedents: The Case of Social Insurance, 1880–1914*, Oxford: Clarendon, 1987, 161.

30 Pat Thane, *Foundations of the Welfare State*, London: Heinemann, 1982, 81.

31 Ibid. 90.

32 W. Churchill, *Liberalism and the Social Problem*, 2nd edn., London: Hodder. 1909.

33 See, for example, R. Davidson, 'Llewellyn Smith, the Labour Department and government growth 1886–1909', in G. Sutherland (ed.), *Studies in the Growth of Nineteenth-Century Government*, London: Routledge and Kegan Paul, 1972.

34 See G. Phillips and N. Whiteside, *Casual Labour*, Oxford: Clarendon Press, 1985.

35 The notion of the 'diagram' is developed by François Ewald, *L'état providence*, Paris: Bernard Grasset, 1986, 50–1. As Foucault suggests, diagrams are different from Weberian 'ideal types' because they are not the compositions of social scientists, but real generalizations made from real programmes; see his 'Questions of method', in G. Burchell et al. (eds.), *The Foucault Effect*, 80.

36 C. F. Rey, General Manager, Board of Trade Labour Exchanges, 'The National System of Labour Exchanges', in National Conference on the Prevention of Destitution, *Papers and Proceedings, 1st Meeting*, London: P. S. King and Son, 1911.

37 On these struggles of the unemployed see Flanagan, *Parish-Fed Bastards*, Chapter 1; P. Bagguley, *From Protest to Acquiescence? Political Movements of the Unemployed*, Basingstoke: Macmillan, 1991.

38 Beveridge, 'The birth of the labour exchanges', *MinLabour*, 14(1), 1960, 2–3.

39 P. Squires, *Anti-Social Policy*, Hemel Hempstead: Harvester Wheatsheaf, 1990.

40 A. Desrosières, 'The part in relation to the whole'.

41 W. R. Garside, *The Measurement of Unemployment: Methods and Sources in Great Britain 1850–1979*, Oxford: Basil Blackwell, 1980, Chapter 4.

42 Cd. 4499/1909, *Royal Commission on the Poor Laws, Final Report*, 405.

43 Beveridge, quoted in Cd. 4499/1909, 99.

44 Charles Booth, *Life and Labour of the People in London: First Series. Poverty*, vol.1, New York, 1969 [1902], 25–6.

45 Webb and Webb, *Public Organisation*, Chapter 5.

46 The argument that comprehensive information about unemployment can only be obtained if the unemployed are offered some incentive to register themselves as such was made by senior officials at the Board of Trade before the Royal Commission on the Poor Laws – see the evidence of A. W. Fox, F. H. McLeod, and W. H. Dawson, Cd. 5068/1910, *Royal Commission on the Poor Laws*, Appx. Vol. IX (Minutes of Evidence), 448.

47 Beveridge, *Unemployment*, 209.

48 Webb and Webb, *Public Organisation*, 246; emphasis in original.

49 Evans, *The Fabrication of Virtue: English Prison Architecture 1750–1840*, Cambridge: Cambridge University Press, 1982.

50 Ibid.; Peter Miller, 'Psychotherapy of work and unemployment', in Peter Miller and Nikolas Rose (eds.), *The Power of Psychiatry*, Cambridge: Polity, 1986.

3 GOVERNING UNEMPLOYMENT AS A 'RISK'

1 John Williams and Karel Williams, *A Beveridge Reader*, London: RKP, 1985, 73.

2 On the Pensions Act, see Pat Thane, *Foundations of the Welfare State*, London: Longman, 1983, 81–4.

3 See Bentley Gilbert, *The Evolution of National Insurance in Great Britain*, London: Michael Joseph, 1966, Chapter 6.

4 E. P. Hennock, *British Social Reform and German Precedents*, Oxford: Clarendon Press, 1987.

5 William Beveridge and Hubert Llewellyn-Smith were key figures within the Labour Department. On the role played by this body in the construction of the 1911 scheme see, inter alia, José Harris, *Unemployment and Politics: A Study in English Social Policy, 1886–1914*, Oxford: Clarendon Press, 1972,

Chapter 5; Gilbert, *The Evolution of National Insurance*, Chapter 5; and for an account from an 'institutionalist' perspective, Libby Schweber, 'Progressive reformers, unemployment, and the transformation of social inquiry in Britain and the United States, 1880s–1920s', in Dietrich Rueschemeyer and Theda Skocpol (eds.), *States, Social Knowledge, and the Origins of Modern Social Policies*, Princeton NJ: Princeton University Press, 1996.

6 P. Gosden, *The Friendly Societies in England, 1815–1875*, Manchester: Manchester University Press, 1961; S. Yeo, 'Working-class association, private capital, welfare and the state in the late-nineteenth and twentieth centuries', in N. Parry, M. Rustin, and C. Satyamurti (eds.), *Social Work, Welfare and the State*, London: Sage, 1979.

7 Board of Trade, *Agencies and Methods for Dealing with the Unemployed*, C. 7182, 1893–4, lxxxii, 417.

8 As a technique of governance, tramping belonged very much to a world in which labour was still in constant motion, a world of 'wandering tribes' and 'migrating classes'. Raphael Samuel has vividly described this culture in terms of the 'comers and goers' (see his 'Comers and goers', in H. Dyos and M. Wolff (eds.), *The Victorian City: Images and Reality*, vol. 1, London: Routledge and Kegan Paul, 1973). Under the tramping system, the itinerant received a 'blank' which certified that he (for the tramping artisans were overwhelmingly men) was a bona fide member of his society. This enabled him to travel widely between designated 'lodge houses' and offices of his union or society. These provided information about jobs locally, as well as lodging and food. Eric Hobsbawm argues that tramping became less effective and less popular the more that labour markets and depressions became national in scope; 'The tramping artisan', in *Labouring Men: Studies in the History of Labour*, London: Weidenfeld, 1964. We might see this settling of labour as a line of emergence of a sedentary culture.

9 Harris, *Unemployment and Politics*, 297–8.

10 Ibid. 302.

11 For example, Cyril Jackson saw it as an excellent means of 'encouraging the thrift of the working classes'; see his *Trade Unions and Unemployment*, London: Longman Green and Co., 1910, 35.

12 See Noelle Whiteside, 'Welfare legislation and the unions during the First World War', *The Historical Journal*, 23(4), 1980, 859.

13 The principle of 'flat-rate' payments, which became a characteristic feature of the British approach to social security, has been contrasted with a 'status maintenance' principle operating in countries such as Germany. The British system has been based on the principle of providing all eligible unemployed persons with the same basic, but comparatively meagre benefit payment. Under the 'status maintenance' system, social security contributions vary between occupations, and benefit payments are proportional to contributions. Status differentials between occupations are therefore preserved within unemployment; M. Wilson, 'The German welfare state: a conservative regime in crisis', in A. Cochrane and J. Clarke (eds.), *Comparing Welfare States: Britain in International Context*, London: Sage, 1993, 147.

14 Williams and Williams, *A Beveridge Reader*, 74.

15 Edward Fuster in *Bulletin trimestrial pour la lutte contre le chômage*, April–June 1914, 387; cf. Joshua L. Cohen, *Insurance Against Unemployment*, London: P. S. King and Sons, 1921, 221.

16 CAB 37/96/159, 'Unemployment insurance: labour exchanges', by W. S. Churchill, 30 November 1908, 2; cf. Harris, *Unemployment and Politics*, 304.

17 Michel Callon defines enrolment as 'the device by which a set of inter-related roles is defined and attributed to actors who accept them'; 'Some elements of a sociology of translation: domestication of the scallops and the fishermen of St Brieuc Bay', in J. Law (ed.), *Power, Action and Belief: A New Sociology of Knowledge*, London: Routledge, 1986, 209.

18 L. G. C. Money, *A Nation Insured*, 3rd edn., London: The Liberal Publication Department, 1912, 66.

19 This point about the enrolment of the employer is nicely illustrated in debates in the 1920s when the unemployment insurance scheme is being extended across the employment field. Policy-makers argued that the 'outworker' (e.g., women doing dress-making in their homes) could not be insured because there was no formal employer who could verify the truth of their unemployment; Draft Memorandum from Minister of Labour to Unemployment Insurance Statutory Commission, UI 2533/7/1934, in Public Record Office (PRO) PIN 7 #270.

20 Williams and Williams, *A Beveridge Reader*, 74. But see Churchill's speeches on insurance in *Liberalism and the Social Problem*, London: Hodder & Stoughton, 1909. Here he clearly, and at an early stage, envisages a role for social insurance as the pre-eminent technique of welfare.

21 In an important analysis, Noelle Whiteside shows how the triumph of state unemployment insurance came about not so much through a process of ideological conversion on the part of trade unionists, who were, on the whole, keen to preserve their own schemes. It won out because the trade union schemes simply could not cope with the levels of unemployment they encountered during the interwar years; 'Social welfare and industrial relations 1914–1939', in Chris Wrigley (ed.), *A History of British Industrial Relations, Vol. II: 1914–1939*, Brighton: Harvester Press, 1987.

22 Göran Therborn, 'States and classes: welfare states developments, 1881–1981', *Studies in Political Economy*, No. 13, 1984.

23 Ann Shola Orloff and Theda Skocpol, 'Why not equal protection? Explaining the politics of public social spending in Britain, 1900–1911, and the United States, 1880s–1920', *American Sociological Review*, 49, 1984.

24 Wolfgang Mommsen (ed.), *The Emergence of the Welfare State in Britain and Germany*, London: Croom Helm, 1981.

25 François Ewald, 'Insurance and risk', in Graham Burchell, Colin Gordon and Peter Miller (eds.), *The Foucault Effect: Studies in Governmentality*, Hemel Hempstead: Harvester Wheatsheaf, 1991.

26 But see Leslie Pal, 'Relative autonomy revisited: the origins of Canadian Unemployment Insurance', *Canadian Journal of Political Science*, 19(1), 1986, 71–102. Pal discusses what he calls the 'actuarial ideology'. Actuarialism

provided policy-makers with a diagram and a technical and scientific legitimation for reforms to the unemployment relief system. By appealing to the principles of insurance, they could justify a scheme which was to be self-financing and insulated from political interference, which offered a limited liability for the state, and which carefully delimited the claims of the unemployed for assistance.

27 Beveridge, *Unemployment*, 227.

28 Cohen, *Insurance against Unemployment*, 67.

29 Defert, 'Insurance and popular life', in Grahame Burchell, Colin Gordon, and Peter Miller (eds.), *The Foucault Effect*, Hemel Hempstead: Harvester Wheatsheaf, 1991.

30 Claus Offe, *Contradictions of the Welfare State* (edited by John Keane), Cambridge MA: MIT Press, 1984; cf. Anthony Giddens, *Beyond Left and Right: The Future of Radical Politics*, Cambridge: Polity, 1994, 135–6.

31 The advent of a relatively new aspect of unemployment insurance is interesting in this regard – mortgage insurance. The growth of a 'property-owning democracy' means that as well as their labour-power, a significant mass of people own their homes. Hence the need to insure against a failure to meet mortgage payments through unemployment or sickness.

32 'Governing poverty: sources of the social question in nineteenth-century France', in Jan Goldstein (ed.), *Foucault and the Writing of History*, Oxford: Blackwell, 1994, 208–9.

33 Cf. Julian Fulbrook, *Administrative Justice and the Unemployed*, London: Mansell, 1978, 137.

34 However, it was reasoned that by making employees and employers contribute to the insurance fund, the scheme would give them a financial interest in organizing work more efficiently, reducing the incidence of 'frictional' unemployment. Like workmen's compensation, social insurance renders, in a most immediate way, social problems as a cost to the employer. 'In all countries experience has shown that one of the most efficacious ways of inciting employers to reduce the hazards of their industries to a minimum is to make it to the direct pecuniary advantage of each individual employer to cut down the number of accidents in his own particular establishment. Self-interest is the greatest incentive in this matter as in everything else'; H. Villard and P. Tecumseh Sherman, *German Experience in Accident Prevention*, New York: Workmen's Compensation Publicity Bureau, 1914, 15.

35 Winston Churchill, 'Notes on malingering', Memorandum to H. Llewellyn Smith, June 6, 1909; in Beveridge Papers III, 39, British Library of Political and Economic Science.

36 For example, Ulrich Beck, *The Risk Society: Towards a New Modernity*, London: Sage, 1992.

37 Ewald, 'Insurance and risk', 142.

38 Isaac Rubinow, *Social Insurance*, New York: Henry Holt and Co., 1913, 433.

39 Official Report of Parliamentary Debates. Standing Committee B, April 4, 1922. Filed in the Public Record Office PIN 7 #71.

40 In a fascinating account Noelle Whiteside and James Gillespie have shown that the definition of unemployment upheld by the insurance system has

served to distort our understanding of the nature of labour market problems between the wars. For the unemployment insurance system was designed with the assumption that employed and unemployed are clearly distinct conditions. Yet Whiteside and Gillespie show that the extensive casual employment and underemployment of the Victorian era was still prevalent during the 1920s and 1930s. In other words there was a disjunction between social and cultural experiences of unemployment, and official norms and assumptions about it at this time; 'Deconstructing unemployment: developments in Britain in the interwar years', *Economic History Review*, 44(4), 1991.

41 For example, according to Bernard Corry, the primacy of the involuntary concept within the economics literature was 'undoubtedly due to its treatment by Keynes but its usage predates him'; 'Unemployment in the history of economic thought: an overview and some reflections', in Bernard Corry (ed.), *Unemployment and the Economists*, Cheltenham: Edward Elgar, 1996, 12. See also Guy Standing, 'The notion of voluntary unemployment', *International Labour Review* 120(5), 1981; and G. Worswick (ed.), *The Concept and Measurement of Involuntary Unemployment*, London: Allen Unwin, 1976.

42 See *Tables on Rules and Expenditure of Trade Unions in Respect of Unemployment Benefit*, Cd. 5703, 1911.

43 Beveridge, *Unemployment*, 223–6.

44 C. 7182/1893–94, Board of Trade, *Agencies and Methods for Dealing with the Unemployed*, lxxxii, p. i.

45 These statutory conditions are discussed in a number of guides to the operation of the unemployment insurance system. See, for example, H. Emmerson and E. Lascelles, *Guide to the Unemployment Insurance Acts*, 5th edn., London: Longman, Green and Co., 1939.

46 Frank Tillyard, *Unemployment Insurance in Great Britain 1911–49*, Leigh-on-Sea, Essex: Thames Bank Publishing Co., 1949, 19.

47 O. Clark, *The Law of Insurance*, xvi–xvii; cf. Cohen, *Insurance against Unemployment*, 287.

48 Churchill, *Liberalism and the Social Problem*, 313.

49 Pat Thane dates the beginnings of a move away from the 'general mixed workhouse' towards specialized treatment under the Poor Law for different categories of inmate (the old, the infirm, the young, the mad) to the reforms of the 1870s; *Foundations of the Welfare State*, 35–6.

50 Flanagan highlights the adoption of red banners during the Trafalgar Square demonstrations of October 1887. Previously, unemployed demonstrators had borne black banners, symbolizing despair, but also as an appeal to the commiseration of the wealthy. The change of symbols suggests that between 1884 and 1895 'there was a fundamental change in the outlook of the unemployed which manifested itself in their changing from a passive role of beggary and supplication, to an active role of political struggle'. R. Flanagan, *'Parish-Fed Bastards': A History of the Politics of the Unemployed in Britain, 1884–1938*, Westport CT: Greenwood, 1991, 19.

51 Joseph Cohen, *Insurance against Unemployment*, 240.

52 A. I. Ogus, 'Great Britain', in Peter Köhler and Hans Zacher (eds.), *The Evolution of Social Insurance 1881–1981*, New York: St Martins Press, 1982, 205. Ogus provides a highly comprehensive and perceptive overview of the development of social insurance regulations.

53 Sidney Webb and Beatrice Webb, *Industrial Democracy*, London: Longman, 1926 [1897], 165.

54 Llewellyn-Smith, 'Economic security and unemployment insurance', *Economic Journal*, 20, 1910, 522.

55 Ibid. 518. But see Churchill's comments on the matter: 'I do not feel convinced that we are entitled to refuse benefit to a qualified man who loses his employment through drunkenness.'(2) Unemployment insurance was to be a purely contractual arrangement; if a worker had paid and entered the insurance contract, she or he had a basic right to benefit, whatever the cause of dismissal. The individual knew the rules concerning how long they could claim benefits. The regulation of the fund could safely depend upon the individual's conception of self-interest. The uninviting alternative was for the state to get dragged into administrative 'jungles' – a 'system of inquiries, discharge notes, references to employers, foremen, &c'. 'Note on malingering' (to H. Llewellyn-Smith), 6 June 1909, in the Beveridge Papers III, 39 (British Library of Political and Economic Science). For a Foucaultian analysis which highlights the element of self-discipline and self-surveillance in Churchill's 'note', see Squires, *Anti-Social Policy*, 127–34.

56 Llewellyn-Smith, 'Economic security', 526. My emphasis.

57 Ibid. 527.

58 As François Ewald has pointed out: 'Within the disciplinary order, the influence of the norm is primarily local; norms remain attached to specific practices and institutions. With the appearance of insurance, the norm will serve as a means of managing different kinds of actuarial populations, while with the institution of a Social Security system it will become a way to manage the entire population of a given state'; 'Norms, discipline and the law', *Representations*, No. 30, 1990, 141.

59 Ogus, 'Great Britain', 203.

60 Pat O'Malley has written at length on this subject, noting that 'liberalism's governmental relations with resistance are characterized by incorporation of resistant, "indigenous" governances'. 'Indigenous governance', *Economy and Society*, 25(3), 1996, 310.

61 In his famous *Social Insurance and Allied Services* (London: HMSO, Cmnd. 6404/1942, 158–65), Beveridge observes that his 'plan for social security' assumes a political commitment to preventing mass unemployment, and the establishment of a system of national health provision.

62 Patrick Minford, *The Supply-Side Revolution in Britain*, Aldershot: Edward Elgar, 1991, 22.

63 For example, Michel Foucault, 'Two lectures', in Colin Gordon (ed.), *Power/Knowledge*, New York: Pantheon, 1980.

64 Exemplary in this regard is Nikolas Rose, *Governing the Soul: The Shaping of the Private Self*, London: Routledge, 1990.

65 The standard work is P. Gosden, *Self-Help: Voluntary Associations in the Nineteenth Century*, London: Batsford Academic, 1973. For a work which investigates how the survival strategies of the poor often subverted official and charitable forms of assistance, see P. Mandler (ed.), *The Uses of Charity: The Poor on Relief in the Nineteenth-Century Metropolis*, Philadelphia: University of Pennsylvania Press, 1990.

66 Barry Supple, 'Legislation and virtue: an essay on working class self-help and the state in the early nineteenth century', in Neil McKendrick (ed.), *Historical Perspectives: Studies in English Thought and Society*, London: Europe Publications, 1974, 215.

67 Llewellyn-Smith, 'Economic security', 518–19.

68 Winston Churchill, 'Unemployment' (speech delivered in Dundee, February 10, 1908), in *Liberalism and the Social Problem*, 208–9.

69 Rubinow, *Social Insurance*, 5, 3.

70 Ibid. 3; see also Frank Lewis, *State Insurance: A Social and Industrial Need*, London: Archibald Constable and Co., 1909, 52.

71 Canon William L. Blackley, *What is National Insurance?* London: National Providence League, 1885, 1.

72 Ibid. 8.

73 Ibid. 2.

74 Fulbrook, *Administrative Justice.*

75 Cf. Ogus, 'Great Britain', 232.

76 Webb and Webb, *Industrial Democracy*, 165.

77 This issue was discussed at length by the Royal Commission on Labour when it interrogated the Chief Registrar of Friendly Societies, Edward Brabrook; C. 7063-I/1893, *Fourth Report of the Royal Commission on Labour (1893–94)*, (Minutes of Evidence), 80–109.

78 Webb and Webb, *Industrial Democracy*, 156.

79 Edward Brabrook answering questions from the Royal Commission on Labour, C. 7063-I/1893, 1561–3; cf. Webb and Webb, *Industrial Democracy*, 159n.

80 D. Knights and T. Vurdubakis, 'Calculations of risk: towards an understanding of insurance as a moral and political technology', *Accounting, Organizations and Society*, 18(7/8), 732.

81 Beveridge, *Unemployment*, 220.

82 On the history of the NUWM see, inter alia, R. Croucher, *We Refuse to Starve in Silence: A History of the National Unemployed Workers Movement, 1920–46*, London: Lawrence and Wishart, 1987; Paul Bagguley, *From Protest to Acquiescence? Political Movements of the Unemployed*, Basingstoke: Macmillan, 1991; and, by its principal leader, Wal Hannington, *Unemployed Struggles 1919–36*, London: Victor Gollancz, 1938.

83 *An Easy Guide to the New Unemployment Act, London: NUWM*, n.d. See also *Your Rights under the UAB* [Unemployment Assistance Board]. These are available in the pamphlet collection of the British Library of Political and Economic Science. It would be interesting to write a history of claimant activism around unemployment benefits. Bagguley's *From Protest to Acquiescence* provides some interesting insights in this respect, particularly on the

interaction between political activism and state administrative forms. One dimension of current activism consists of a lively struggle to preserve the identity of the claimant, in the face of administrative reforms which seek to replace claimants with 'jobseekers'. See, for instance, the newsletter of Nottingham Claimant's Action, *Up Your Giro!* (http://www.geocities.com/CapitalHill/Lobby/7638/upgiro!html).

84 With their concept 'line of flight', Deleuze and Guattari provide a way to express the unexpected and destabilizing ways in which elements escape – perhaps only momentarily – the gravitational pull of machinic assemblages, where the latter might translate very roughly as provisional orders or regimes around work, health, sexuality, politics, etc. For instance, political systems might train their subjects to be literate, they might find uses for the skills of these subjects within their bureaucracies. But they might also find that these subjects use their skills for non-sanctioned and perhaps seditious purposes. A line of flight has something of the sense of contradiction within Marxist thought, except it is not systematic or dialectical. It is deterritorializing. See G. Deleuze and F Guattari, *A Thousand Plateaus* (trans. B. Massumi), Minneapolis: University of Minnesota Press, 1987.

85 John Hilton, Assistant Secretary to the Minister of Labour, quoted in Cmd. 4185/1932, *Royal Commission on Unemployment Insurance, Final Report*, 69n.

86 W. Gephart, *Insurance and the State*, New York: Macmillan, 1913, 160.

87 Frank Lewis, *State Insurance: A Social and Industrial Need*, London: Archibald Constable & Co, 1909, 33.

88 For example, see Seth Koven and Sonya Michel (eds.), *Mothers of a New World: Maternalist Politics and the Origins of Welfare States*, London: Routledge, 1993.

89 L. G. C. Money, *A Nation Insured*, 1912, 75.

4 GOVERNING *THROUGH* THE LONG–TERM UNEMPLOYED: UNEMPLOYMENT BETWEEN THE WARS

1 But see Noelle Whiteside and James Gillespie, 'Deconstructing unemployment: developments in Britain in the interwar years', *Economic History Review*, 44(4), 1991, which shows how casual employment was widespread in the interwar years. In many cases, unemployment insurance benefits functioned as a wage supplement for part-time and casual workers.

2 S. Glynn, 'The scale and nature of the problem', in S. Glynn and A. Booth (eds.), *The Road to Full Employment*, London: Allen & Unwin, 1987, 7. Glynn provides a useful discussion of some of the problems involved in the interpretation of unemployment statistics, as does W. R. Garside, *British Unemployment 1919–1939*, Cambridge: Cambridge University Press, 1990, 3–7. The following paragraphs are based on these sources, as well as Noelle Whiteside, *Bad Times: Unemployment in British Social and Political History*, London: Faber and Faber, 1991, Chapter 4.

3 C. Feinstein, *National Income, Expenditure and Output of the United Kingdom, 1855–1965*, Cambridge: Cambridge University Press, 1972, Table 58.

4 Whiteside, *Bad Times*, 69.

5 Garside, *British Unemployment*, 11; J. Stevenson and C. Cook, *The Slump: Society and Politics during the Depression*, London: Jonathan Cape, 1977, 13–14; for an overview of Britain's economy between the wars, see S. Glynn and A. Booth, *Modern Britain: An Economic and Social History*, Chapter 4; S. Pollard, *The Development of the British Economy*, 3rd edn., London: Edward Arnold, 1983.

6 Given the predominance of small, family-owned companies, and the extroversion of the economy, patterns of industrial development in Britain have been characterized in terms of 'flawed' Fordism; see B. Jessop, 'Conservative regimes and the transition to postfordism: the cases of Great Britain and West Germany', in M. Gottdeiner and N. Komninos (eds.), *Capitalist Development and Crisis Theory: Accumulation, Regulation and Spatial Restructuring*, London: Macmillan, 1989; similarly, S. Lash and J. Urry, *The End of Organized Capitalism*, Madison, Wisconsin: University of Wisconsin Press, 1987, argue that British capitalism became 'organized' more slowly and less extensively than its major competitors.

7 See, inter alia, B. J. Eichengreen and T. J. Hatton (eds.), *Interwar Unemployment in International Perspective*, Amsterdam: Kluwer Academic Publishers, 1988; W. R. Garside (ed.), *Capitalism in Crisis: International Responses to the Great Depression*, London: Pinter, 1993. France did not experience mass unemployment as a political problem in the same way as Britain. This has been explained by the fact that it had a much larger agricultural workforce, and a greater prevalence of pre-bureaucratic employment relations in firms; see R. Salais, 'Why was unemployment so low in France during the 1930s?', in Eichengreen and Hatton (eds.), *Interwar Unemployment*. But also, recession was managed by migration policy, which displaced work shortages on to non-citizens; see M. Cohen and M. Hanagan, 'Politics, industrialization and citizenship: unemployment policy in England, France and the United States, 1890–1950', in C. Tilly (ed.), *Citizenship, Identity and Social History*, [International Review of Social History Supplement 3] New York: Cambridge University Press, 1996.

8 Whiteside, *Bad Times*, 72.

9 At their height, in 1930, public works employed 56 000 against a background of about 2.5 million registered unemployed; Whiteside, *Bad Times*, 72. For a history of public works see Garside, *British Unemployment*, Chapter 11. For explanations of different policy responses to the depression see Garside (ed.), *Capitalism in Crisis*. J. Tomlinson, *Public Policy and the Economy since 1900*, Oxford: Clarendon Press, 1990, 86–7, summarizes historical explanations for Britain's stunted public works policy.

10 One of the most comprehensive anatomies of the inter-war relief system is provided by E. M. Burns, *British Unemployment Programs 1920–1938*, Washington: Social Science Research Council, 1941; see also A. Deacon, 'Systems of interwar unemployment relief', in S. Glynn and A. Booth (eds.), *The Road to Full Employment*, London: Allen & Unwin, 1987.

11 N. Whiteside, 'Welfare legislation and the unions during the First World War', *Historical Journal*, 23, 1980.

12 Garside, *British Unemployment*, 37.

13 Until 1929 there was in fact a third tier: the Poor Law, which constituted the last resort of the unemployed and / or their families.

14 '[T]here were more than twenty Acts relating to unemployment insurance between 1921 and 1931'; Deacon, 'Systems', 34.

15 Cab 27: 14 (6/10/21) Public Record Office; quoted in A. Deacon, *In Search of the Scrounger: The Administration of Unemployment Insurance in Britain, 1920–31*, London: Bell, 1976, 16.

16 E. W. Bakke, *Insurance or Dole*, New Haven: Yale University Press, 1935, 77.

17 The counterpart of this process of redefinition was that new ways of testing a person's membership in the nation's industrial army had to be fashioned. On the various controversial means tests, 'genuinely seeking work' tests, and 'anomalies regulations', which were hastily assembled in the inter-war period, see Garside, *British Unemployment*, Chapter 2; A. Deacon, 'Concession and coercion: the politics of unemployment insurance in the twenties', in A. Briggs and J. Saville (eds.), *Essays in Labour History 1918–1939*, London: Croom Helm, 1977; Burns, *British Unemployment Programs*; Tomlinson, 'Women as "anomalies": the Anomalies Regulations of 1931, their background and implications', *Public Administration*, 62, Winter 1984. The working of these tests made explicit many of the tacit assumptions surrounding official definitions of 'unemployed'. For instance, their masculinism: means tests were employed in the 1920s suggesting that one had to be a 'breadwinner' as well as a 'wage-earner' to count as 'unemployed' for the purposes of relief.

18 Between 1920 and 1930 the state's contribution to the Unemployment Insurance Fund rose from £3 100 000 to £37 000 000; see Deacon, 'Systems', 9.

19 Tomlinson, *Public Policy and the Economy*, 77.

20 The classic account of this interlude is R. Skidelsky, *Politicians and the Slump*, Harmondsworth: Penguin, 1970.

21 Deacon, 'Systems', 36.

22 Those out of work for over a year rose from 53 000 in 1929 to 300 000 in 1932 to 500 000 in summer 1933; Deacon, 'Systems', 36.

23 Cmd. 4185/1932, *Royal Commission on Unemployment Insurance, Final Report*, 383.

24 Ibid.

25 Garside, *British Unemployment*, 71.

26 Cmd. 4185/1932, *Royal Commission on Unemployment Insurance, Final Report*, 116.

27 Ibid. 74.

28 Ibid. 389.

29 Ibid. 390.

30 Ibid. 393.

31 Ibid. 393, my emphasis. 'Transitional payments' are discussed below.

32 Ibid.105.

33 Ibid. 159.

34 P. Miller, 'Psychotherapy of work and unemployment', in P. Miller and N. Rose (eds.), *The Power of Psychiatry*, Cambridge: Polity, 1986.

35 E. W. Bakke, *Unemployed Man: A Social Study*, New York: E.P. Dutton & Co., 1934, 48–9.
36 Pilgrim Trust, *Men without Work*, London: Cambridge University Press, 1938, xi.
37 H. Beales and R. Lambert (eds.), *Memoirs of the Unemployed*, London: Victor Gollancz, 1934, 8, 16.
38 G. Orwell, *The Road to Wigan Pier*, Harmonsworth: Penguin, 1962.
39 Pilgrim Trust, *Men Without Work*, 3, 45.
40 Bakke, *Unemployed Man*, xiv.
41 Orwell, *The Road to Wigan Pier*, 16.
42 On the slum literature genre, see G. S. Jones, *Outcast London*; and M. Valverde, 'The dialectic of the familiar and the unfamiliar: "the jungle" in early slum travel writing', *Sociology*, 30(3), 1996. I take the term 'dole literature' from Stevenson and Cook, *The Slump*, 75.
43 M. Jahoda, P. Lazarsfeld, and H. Zeisel, *Marienthal: the Sociography of an Unemployed Community* (trans. J. Reginall and T. Elsaesser with the authors), Chicago: Aldine Atherton, 1971 [1933], 1. For a critique see Ross McKibbin, *The Ideologies of Class: Social Relations in Britain, 1880–1950*, Oxford: Clarendon Press, 1990.
44 Beales and Lambert, *Memoirs*, 13.
45 Ibid. 11.
46 Ibid. 35.
47 See P. Miller and N. Rose, 'Production, identity and democracy', *Theory and Society*, 24(3), 1995.
48 Pilgrim Trust, *Men without Work*, 67.
49 Miller, 'Psychotherapy of work'.
50 Beales and Lambert, *Memoirs*, 26.
51 Bakke, *Unemployed Man*, 264.
52 Pilgrim Trust, *Men without Work*, 144.
53 Ibid. 159.
54 Orwell, *Road to Wigan Pier*, 78.
55 The official statistics suggested that long-term unemployment was concentrated on men. According to Beveridge's analysis of unemployment assistance and benefit claimants on 8 June 1936, one in four had been continuously out of work for a year or more, whereas for women the ratio was less than one in ten; 'An analysis of unemployment III', *Economica*, 4, May 1937, 169. Beveridge related this difference first to the fact that long-term unemployment was concentrated in overwhelmingly masculine primary and heavy industrial occupations. However, in the manufacturing industries in which men and women both worked there was still a significantly higher proportion of male long-term unemployment. Here Beveridge speculated that age was a significant factor: as many women withdraw from industry upon marriage a 'much smaller proportion of women in industry are subject to the special difficulties of older people in recovering employment once they have lost it'; ibid. 176.
56 Pilgrim Trust, *Men without Work*, 232.

57 Ibid. 288.
58 Beveridge, 'An analysis of unemployment III', 178.
59 Nikolas Rose, *The Psychological Complex: Psychology, Politics and Society in England 1869–1939*, London: RKP, 1985, 49.
60 Beveridge, 'An analysis of unemployment II', *Economica*, 4, February 1937, 7.
61 Ibid. 11.
62 Pilgrim Trust, *Men without Work*, 27.
63 Ibid. 8; my emphasis.
64 Chapter 5 argues that with Keynes the unemployed subject is completely expelled from the problematization of unemployment. However, the 'supply-side turn' of the 1970s reintroduces a space for problematizations of subjective aspects of the unemployed individual – their skills, their motivation, etc.
65 Bakke, *Insurance or Dole*, 124.
66 *Report of the Unemployment Assistance Board 1935* (Cmd. 5177), London: HMSO, 1936, 17.
67 Beveridge, 'An analysis of unemployment II', 7.
68 International Labour Office, 'The impact of war on long-term unemployment in Great Britain', *International Labour Review*, 45, 1942, 44.
69 See, for example, B. Harris, 'Unemployment insurance and health in interwar Britain', in Eichengreen and Hatton (eds.), *Interwar Unemployment*; N. Whiteside, 'Counting the cost: sickness and disability among working people in the interwar years', *Economic History Review*, 2nd series, 40(2), 1987.
70 For example, S. K. Ruck, 'The increase of crime in England', *Political Quarterly*, 3(2), 1932; cf. Pilgrim Trust, *Men without Work*, 162.
71 Among the major works are A. L. Bowley and M. Hogg's *Has Poverty Diminished? A Sequel to 'Livelihood and Poverty'*, London: P. S. King & Son, 1925, which was a sequel to Bowley's prewar survey of five towns, *Poverty and Livelihood*; Llewellyn-Smith's *The New Survey of London Life and Labour*, London: P. S. King & Son, 1930–, which took Booth's surveys as its referent; and Rowntree's return to York, *Poverty and Progress*, London: Longman, Green & Co., 1941. These surveys, and others which were not comparative, were generally optimistic that progress had been made *vis-à-vis* poverty; see K. Laybourn, *Britain on the Breadline; A Social and Political History of Britain Between the Wars*, Gloucester: Alan Sutton, 1990, 47. There were also detailed surveys of poverty and the overall 'standard of living' in specific places: D. C. Jones (ed.), *The Social Survey of Merseyside*, Liverpool: Liverpool University Press, 1934; A. D. K. Owen's work on Sheffield for the Sheffield Social Survey Committee, 1932–33; Ford's investigation of Southampton, *Work and Wealth in a Modern Port*, London: G. Allen & Unwin Ltd, 1934; and H. Tout's inquiry into *The Standard of Living in Bristol*, Bristol: Arrowsmith, 1938. Further to these, see Harris, 'Unemployment insurance and health in interwar Britain', 155–60.
72 E. P. Hennock, 'Poverty and social theory in England: the experience of the eighteen-eighties', *Social History*, 1, 1976, 74.
73 H. Higgs, 'Workmen's budgets', *Journal of the Royal Statistical Society*, 56, 1893.

74 B. S. Rowntree, *Poverty: A Study of Town Life*, London: Nelson, 1913 [1901], xix; quoted in K. Williams, *From Pauperism to Poverty*, London: RKP, 1981, 347.

75 Williams, *From Pauperism to Poverty*, 350.

76 Ibid. 358.

77 See E. P. Hennock, 'The measurement of urban poverty: from the metropolis to the nation, 1880–1920', *Economic History Review*, 2nd series, XL, 2, 1987; Alain Desroisieres, 'The part in relation to the whole: how to generalise? The prehistory of representative sampling', in M. Bulmer, K. Bales, and K. Sklar (eds.), *The Social Survey in Historical Perspective 1880–1940*, Cambridge: Cambridge University Press, 1991.

78 A similar point was made in Chapter 3. Drawing on the work of Giovanna Procacci it was argued that unemployment insurance is linked to a liberal problematic inasmuch as it takes as its norm the principle of a household that is sustained by a regular wage-income.

79 The evolution of unemployment assistance is described by Garside, *British Unemployment*, Chapter 3; Deacon, 'System'; Burns, *British Unemployment Programs*, Chapter 5 and passim; J. Millet, *The Unemployment Assistance Board*, 1940.

80 E. Briggs and A. Deacon, 'The creation of the Unemployment Assistance Board', *Policy and Politics*, 2(1), 1974.

81 Ibid.; P. Bagguley, *From Protest to Acquiescence? Political Movements of the Unemployed*, Basingstoke: Macmillan, 1991.

82 *Report of the Unemployment Assistance Board 1935* (Cmd. 5177), 11.

83 J. S. Clarke, 'The Assistance Board', in W. Robson (ed.), *Social Security*, London: Geo. Allen & Unwin, 1943, 126.

84 L. Gordon, *The Public Corporation in Great Britain*, London: Oxford University Press, 1938, 2.

85 J. Lee, 'The parallels between industrial administration and public administration', *Journal of Public Administration*, 4(3), 1926.

86 Gordon, *The Public Corporation*, 2.

87 T. O'Brien, *British Experiments in Public Ownership and Control*, London: G. Allen & Unwin, 1937, 17.

88 Cmd. 5177/1936, *Report of the Unemployment Assistance Board 1935*, 6.

89 My understanding of 'need' as providing a point of application for power relations has benefited from Peter Squires, *Anti-Social Policy*, Hemel Hempstead: Harvester Wheatsheaf, 1990.

90 *Report of the Unemployment Assistance Board 1935*, 8.

91 Karl Polanyi, *The Great Transformation*, Boston: Beacon Press, 1957, 77.

92 Whiteside, *Bad Times*, 80–1.

93 See P. Ford, *Incomes, Means Tests and Personal Responsibility*, London: P. S. King and Son, 1939.

94 Burns, *British Unemployment Programs*, 98.

95 On the unemployed club movement, see National Council of Social Service, *Out of Adversity: A Survey of Clubs for Men and Women which Have Grown Out of the Needs of Unemployment*, London: NCSS, 1939; and Pilgrim Trust, *Men without Work*; for a more critical perspective, see R. Flanagan, *Parish-Fed Bastards*.

96 J. Hilton, 'The public service in relation to the problem of unemployment', *Journal of Public Administration*, 15(1), 1937, 8.

5 UNEMPLOYMENT AND ITS SPACES

1 For example, David Dutton, *British Politics Since 1945*, Oxford: Blackwell, 1991; for a Marxist account of this settlement, see Colin Leys, *Politics in Britain*, revised edn., London: Verso, 1989.

2 For example, Peter Hall, 'The movement from Keynesianism to monetarism: institutional analysis and British economic policy in the 1970s', in Sven Steinmo, Kathleen Thelen, and Frank Longstreth (eds.), *Structuring Politics: Historical Institutionalism in Comparative Analysis*, Cambridge: Cambridge University Press, 1992.

3 Bob Jessop, 'The transition to post-Fordism and the Schumpeterian workfare state', in Roger Burrow and Brian Loader (eds.), *Towards a Post-Fordist Welfare State?* London: Routledge, 1994.

4 A classic example of this approach is Doreen Massey, *Spatial Divisions of Labour: Social Structures and the Geography of Production*, London: Methuen, 1984.

5 My attempt to make connections between work in governmentality and poststructuralist geography (where some of the questions of imagined geographies have been posed) has been greatly helped by discussions with Wendy Larner. See her essay on the spatial imaginaries of policies connected with political and economic reform in New Zealand: 'Hitching a ride on the tiger's back: globalisation and spatial imaginaries in New Zealand', *Environment and Planning D: Society and Space*, 16(5), 1998.

6 John Agnew, 'Timeless space and state-centrism: the geographical assumptions of international relations theory', in G. Rosow, N. Inayatullah, and M. Rupert (eds.), *The Global Economy as Political Space*, Boulder, CO: Lynne Reiner, 1994; Peter Taylor, 'Embedded statism and the social sciences: opening up new spaces', *Environment and Planning A*, 28, 1996 (see also discussions of this essay in the same volume). For an attempt to expose the national assumptions of economic theory, see Barry Hindess, 'Neoliberalism and the national economy', in Mitchell Dean and Barry Hindess (eds.), *Governing Australia: Studies in Contemporary Rationalities of Government*, Cambridge: Cambridge University Press, 1998; on the historic, and much overlooked, centrality of the nation to theories and practices of democracy, see David Held, *Democracy and the Global Order*, Cambridge: Polity, 1995.

7 John Agnew, 'Timeless space and state-centrism', 93.

8 One of the best historical accounts of this sociological problematization of the city is contained in Gareth Stedman Jones, *Outcast London*, Harmondsworth: Penguin, 1971; but see also Nikolas Rose, *The Psychological Complex: Psychology, Politics and Society in England 1869–1939*, London: RKP, 1985.

9 Wayne Parsons, *The Political Economy of British Regional Policy*, London: Routledge, 1988, esp. Chapters 1 and 2.

10 John Maynard Keynes, *The General Theory of Employment, Interest and Money*, London: Macmillan, 1971 [1936].

11 Keynes, *General Theory*, 250.

12 Tony Cutler, John Williams, and Karel Williams, *Keynes, Beveridge and Beyond*, London: RKP, 1986.

13 For example, M. Stewart, *Keynes and After*, Harmondsworth: Penguin, 1972; cf. Jim Tomlinson, *Public Policy and the Economy since 1900*, Oxford: Clarendon Press, 1990, 106.

14 Margaret Weir, 'Ideas and politics: the acceptance of Keynesianism in Britain and the United States', in Peter Hall (ed.), *The Political Power of Economic Ideas: Keynesianism across Nations*, Princeton, NJ: Princeton University Press, 1989, 67. See also the other essays in this collection.

15 For example, Grahame Thompson, 'Objectives and instruments of economic management', in G. Thompson and R. Levacic (eds.), *Managing the UK Economy*, Oxford: Basil Blackwell, 1987; Jim Tomlinson, 'Where do economic policy objectives come from? The case of full employment', *Economy and Society*, 12(1); Roger Middleton, *Towards the Managed Economy: Keynes, the Treasury and the Fiscal Policy Debate of the 1930s*, London: Methuen, 1985.

16 See Jim Tomlinson, *Employment Policy: The Crucial Years, 1939–1955*, Oxford: Clarendon Press, 1987, esp. Chapter 6, on the limits of the 'Keynesian Revolution'.

17 The development of macroeconomic policy as a field of political concern and intervention was markedly advanced by the Second World War. It was at this time that many economists and statisticians found employment within the civil service, and when specialist economic intelligence centres – such as the Economic Section – were set up alongside the Treasury. See Jim Tomlinson, *Public Policy and the Economy*, Chapter 6; and for an 'insider's' perspective, Alec Cairncross, *Essays in Economic Management*, London, 1971.

18 For an excellent overview of the history and significance of econometrics, see M. Hasehm Pesaran, 'Econometrics', in John Eatwell, Murray Milgate, and Peter Newman (eds.), *The New Palgrave: A Dictionary of Economics*, London: Macmillan, 1987, vol. 2, 8–22. The following paragraph draws on Pesaran's exposition.

19 E. Malinvaud, *Statistical Methods for Econometrics*, Amsterdam: North-Holland, 1966; cited from Pesaran, 'Econometrics', 8.

20 Pesaran, 'Econometrics', 13, notes a certain irony in the fact that the Keynesian turn in economic policy was accompanied by the advancement of econometrics. For Keynes was critical of the latter on methodological grounds.

21 Sir Bryan Hopkin, 'The development of demand management', in Frances Cairncross (ed.), *Changing Perceptions of Economic Policy*, London: Methuen, 1981, 38.

22 The history of how one compares the economies of nations remains largely unwritten. But for an overview of how the United Nations and the Organization for European Economic Co-operation (later the OECD) played a leading role in making economic statistics internationally comparable, see Jim Tomlinson, 'Inventing "decline": the falling behind of the British economy in the postwar years', in *Economic History Review*, 49(4), 1996, especially 735–9.

23 The classic statement on the relationship between the war and the rise of a welfare-oriented political consensus is Paul Addison, *The Road to 1945: British Politics and the Second World War*, London: Jonathon Cape, 1975. For Addison, the war was the crucible in which a tacit social contract was forged. As early as 1940, the promise of better social provision by the state soon was seen across the political spectrum as the *quid pro quo* for maintaining the public's sustained commitment to the war effort.

24 The famous White Paper in this respect is Cmd. 6527/1944, *Employment Policy*.

25 Larry Elliott and Charlotte Denny, 'A price well worth paying?', *The Guardian*, 20 August 1998, 13. For the basis of the Phillips curve see A. W. Phillips, 'The relation between unemployment and the rate of change of money wages in the United Kingdom 1861–1957, *Economica*, 1958.

26 In the index to Keynes' *General Theory* there is no entry for 'the unemployed'.

27 Robert Castel has argued that in the case of social work and mental medicine recently there is a shift from programmes which target an actual dangerous individual-subject, to programmes which govern in terms of a de-subjectified space of flows of population and factors of risk. Governing through risk instead of through subjects represents a different way of depersonalizing governance from Keynesianism. See Castel, 'From dangerousness to risk', in G. Burchell, C. Gordon, and P. Miller (eds.), *The Foucault Effect: Studies in Governmentality*, Hemel Hempstead: Harvester Wheatsheaf, 1991.

28 Sir Alec Cairncross, *Economic Ideas and Government Policy: Contributions to Contemporary Economic History*, London: Routledge, 1996, 142.

29 For example, Hall, 'From Keynesianism to monetarism'.

30 This point is made by Taylor, 'Embedded statism', 192; and Hindess, 'Neo-liberalism and the national economy', 219.

31 For example, Patrick Minford, *The Supply-Side Revolution in Britain*, Aldershot: Edward Elgar, 1991.

32 The 'supply-side' of the economy needs to be written thus to make the point that it is not a pregiven sector of the economic. Instead, we should see the 'supply-side' as an invention or a discovery, the effect of problematizations, a zone which has since been territorialized by new ways of calculating and steering the economy. Some of its conditions of emergence would doubtless include the backlash against Keynesianism, the economic crises facing OECD nations in the 1970s, and the rivalries of different schools of economists.

33 Hindess, 'Neo-liberalism and the national economy'.

34 Cmnd. 9474/1985, *Employment: The Challenge for the Nation*, 3.

35 For a document which seeks to think the problem of unemployment in the context of an open, global economy, see *The OECD Jobs Study: Facts, Analysis, Strategy*, Paris: OECD, 1994. For influential texts employing the imagery of globalism and economic flows, see Kenichae Ohmae, *The End of the Nation State? The Rise of Regional Economies*, New York: Free Press, 1995; Manuel Castells, *The Rise of the Network Society*, Oxford: Blackwell, 1996; and Scott

Lash and John Urry, *Economies of Signs and Space*, London: Sage, 1994. For a critical reflection on this new characterization of the economic, see Larner, 'Hitching a ride'.

36 See Paul Hirst and Grahame Thompson, *Globalization in Question*, Cambridge: Polity, 1996, where it is argued that the economy is not as global as has been assumed, and that many aspects of economic life continue to be structured inter-nationally.

37 Cm. 3300/1996, Department of Trade and Industry, *Competitiveness: Creating the Enterprise Centre of Europe*.

38 Desmond King uses the term 'informal local government' to refer to '[a] series of authorities ... established independently of local government holding significant powers over the same jurisdictions and discharging policy-making functions which might logically have been assigned to local authorities'. The growth of ILG was a prominent feature of Conservative policy in other areas besides urban policy, including health and education. See King, 'Government beyond Whitehall', in Patrick Dunleavy, Andrew Gamble, Ian Holliday, and Gillian Peele (eds.), *Developments in British Politics 4*, New York: St Martin's Press, 1993.

39 Robert J. Bennett and Andrew McCoshan, *Enterprise and Human Resource Development*, London: Paul Chapman, 1993, 1, 4 (emphasis in original).

40 Christopher Harvie, *The Rise of Regional Europe*, London: Routledge, 1994, 4.

41 Cm. 540,/1988, Department of Employment, *Employment for the 1990s*, 39.

42 For a key statement on the importance of the locality (or in this case the 'region') to new forms of economic organization see Charles Sabel, 'Flexible specialisation and the re-emergence of regional economies', in Ash Amin (ed.), *A Post-Fordist Reader*, Oxford: Blackwell, 1994.

43 Michael Keating, 'The political economy of regionalism', in M. Keating and J. Loughlin (eds.), *The Political Economy of Regionalism*, London: Frank Cass, 1997, 21.

44 See D. Perron, 'Regions and the Single Market', in M. Dunford and G. Kafkalas (eds.), *Cities and Regions in the New Europe: The Global–Local Interplay and Spatial Development Strategies*, London: Belhaven, 1992.

45 E. A. Swyngedouw, 'The Mammon quest: "glocalization", interspatial competition and the monetary order: the construction of new spatial scales', in Dunford and Kafkalas (eds.), *Cities and Regions in the New Europe*; cf. Adam Tickell and Jamie Peck, whose argument informs this paragraph – 'Social regulation after Fordism: regulation theory, neo-liberalism and the global-local nexus', *Economy and Society*, 24(3), 1995, 375.

46 Bob Jessop, 'Post-Fordism and the state', in Amin (ed.), *Post-Fordism: A Reader*; cf. Tickell and Peck, 'Social regulation', 375.

47 For example, see R. Cappellin and P. Batey (eds.), *Regional Networks, Border Regions and European Integration*, London: Pion, 1993.

48 Ohmae, *The End of the Nation-State?*

49 Notable examples include Nicholas Deakin and John Edwards, *The Enterprise Culture and the Inner City*, London: Routledge, 1993; Thomas Osborne and Nikolas Rose, *Governing Cities: Liberalism, Neoliberalism, Advanced liberalism*, Toronto: Urban Studies Programme, Division of Social

Science, York University, [1998]; Colin Hay and Bob Jessop, 'The governance of local economic development and the development of local economic governance', American Political Science Association, Chicago, Sept 1995.

50 John Solomos, 'Institutionalised racism: policies of marginalisation in education and training', in Philip Cohen and Harwant Bains (eds.), *Multi-Racist Britain*, London: Macmillan, 1988.

51 Cmnd. 6845/1977, Department of the Environment, *Policy for the Inner Cities*, 2.

52 See Alan Harding and Peter Garside, 'Urban and economic development', in John Stewart and Gerry Stoker (eds.), *Local Government in the 1990s*, London: Macmillan, 1995, 166–90.

53 Desmond King, 'The Conservatives and training policy 1979–1992: from a tripartite to a neoliberal regime', *Political Studies*, 41(2), 1993.

54 On 'local socialism', see C. Fudge and M. Boddy, *Local Socialism; Labour Councils and New Left Alternatives*, London: Macmillan, 1984.

55 Peter Totterdill, 'Local economic strategies as industrial policy: a critical review of British developments in the 1980s', *Economy and Society*, 18(4), 1989, 478.

56 For example, see GLC, *London Industrial Strategy*, 1985; cf. Totterdill, 'Local economic stategies', 491.

57 On skills audits see G. Haughton, 'In search of a moving target – skills surveys and skills audits', *Local Economy*, 3(1), 1991; and, from a European perspective, Commission of the European Communities, *Employment Action: A Practical Manual*, Luxembourg: Office for Official Publications of the EC, 1992, 5–6, where the problems of 'measuring and developing skills' are discussed.

58 Harding and Garside, 'Urban and economic development', 169.

59 This was consolidated by the Local Government and Housing Act 1989, part of which consolidated local authority's responsibility for engagement in economic development; see Harding and Garside, 'Urban and economic development', 170.

60 John Mawson, 'The re-emergence of the regional agenda in the English regions: new patterns of urban and regional governance', *Local Economy*, 10(4), 1996.

61 For example, Ash Amin argues that much of the thinking at the heart of regional development theory is flawed. It imagines, and seeks to encourage, the region to be a site of endogenous growth. The assumption is that the solution to a depressed region's problems is to come from within. Yet markets are dominated by the 'corporate geographies' of big firms operating on a global scale. The Single European Market project only enforces this tendency. See 'Big forms versus the regions in the Single European Market', in Dunford and Kafkalas, *Cities and Regions in the New Europe*.

62 See Education and Employment Committee, 2nd Report, *The New Deal Vol. II – Minutes of Evidence* (House of Commons Papers 1997–98 HC 263-II); this gathers submissions of evidence made by these 'third sector' organizations, and expert assessments of their work.

63 Department for Education and Employment, *Employment Zones: The Prospectus*, London, 1998, 4.

64 For example, Valerie Symes, *Unemployment in Europe*, London: Routledge, 1996.

65 For example, *The OECD Jobs Study*; Commission of the European Communities, *Growth, Employment, Competitiveness*, Luxembourg: Office for Official Publications of the EC, 1993; see also discussions in the *The Economist* since the mid-1980s.

66 See L. Schweber, 'Progressive reformers, unemployment, and the transformation of social inquiry in Britain and the United States, 1880s–1920s', in D. Rueschemeyer and Theda Skocpol (eds.), *States, Social Knowledge, and the Origins of Modern Social Policies*, Princeton NJ: Princeton University Press, 1996.

67 Grahame Thompson, 'Death of a Keynesian Europe? Prospects for expansion and political constraints', in Jonathan Michie and John Grieve Smithy (eds.), *Creating Industrial Capacity: Towards Full Employment*, Oxford: Oxford University Press, 1996.

68 Loukas Tsoukalis, *The New European Economy Revisited*, Oxford: Oxford University Press, 1997, 164.

69 'EMU's working hypothesis', *The Economist*, 9 November 1996, 134.

70 John Eatwell, 'The international origins of unemployment', in Jonathan Michie and John Grieve Smith (eds.), *Managing the Global Economy*, Oxford University Press, 1995, 284.

71 Thompson, 'Death of a Keynesian Europe?', 182.

72 Jose Viñals and Juan Jimeno, 'Monetary union and European unemployment', *CEPR Discussion Paper No. 1485*, October 1996; cf. *The Economist*, 'EMU's working hypothesis'.

73 For example, see O. Blanchard, R. Dornbusch, and R. Layard (eds.), *Restoring Europe's Prosperity*, Cambridge, MA: MIT Press, 1986; F. Cripps and T. Ward, 'Strategies for Growth and Employment in the European Community' in Jonathan Michie and John Grieve Smith (eds.), *Unemployment in Europe*, London: Academic Press, 1994; cf. Thompson, 'Death of a Keynesian Europe?', 165–6.

74 Eatwell, 'The international origins of unemployment', 280–2; see also Thompson, 'Death of a Keynesian Europe'. Here it is suggested that it is in terms of its 'external' relations with other world powers that the EU could revive Keynesianism at an international level, e.g., by sponsoring a 'Marshall Plan' for Eastern Europe and the ex-USSR.

75 Eatwell, 'The international origins of unemployment', 283.

76 Ibid. 281.

77 Commission of the European Communities, *Growth, Employment, Competitiveness*, Luxembourg: Office for Official Publications of the EC, 1993.

78 OECD, *Employment/Unemployment Study: Interim Report* (London: HMSO, July Regional Trends, 1993); cf. E. Balls and P. Gregg, *Work and Welfare: Tackling the Jobs Deficit*, London: IPPR, 1993, 17.

79 R. Freeman, 'The limits of wage flexibility to curing unemployment', *Oxford Review of Economic Policy*, 11(1), 1995.

80 *The Economist*, 22 October 1994, 14.

81 Bob Jessop, 'Post-Fordism and the State', in Amin (ed.), *Post-Fordism: A Reader*, 264.

82 As Paul Hirst and Grahame Thompson see it, the state must become more adept at 'suturing', that is, holding a new system of governance together by linking international levels and sub-national levels of power, and, vitally, providing mechanisms of democratic accountability; 'Globalization and the future of the nation state', *Economy and Society*, 24(3), 1995.

83 Gary Marks, Fritz Scharpf, Philippe Schmitter, and Wolfgang Streeck, *Governance in the European Union*, London: Sage, 1996.

6 GOVERNING DIVIDED SOCIETIES: THE NEW DEAL

1 Tony Blair, Foreword to Cm. 3205/1998, Department for Social Security, *New Ambitions for our Country: A New Contract for Welfare*, iii.

2 The Employment Service, *New Deal: Operational Vision*, 1997, 3.

3 Rt Hon Gordon Brown, Budget Speech, *Hansard*, 17 March 1998, col. 1104–5.

4 See Dan Finn, 'Labour's New Deal for the unemployed: making it work locally', *Local Economy*, 12(3), 1997, 247–58.

5 For examples, see Guy Standing, 'The road to workfare: alternative to welfare or threat to occupation?', *International Labour Review*, 129(6); Alan Deacon, 'Justifying "workfare": the historical context of the "workfare" debate', in Michael White (ed.), *Unemployment and Public Policy in a Changing Labour Market*, London: Policy Studies Institute, 1994; Phil Mizen, ' "Work-welfare" and the regulation of the poor: the pessimism of post-structuralism', *Capital and Class*, No. 65, 1998.

6 For a critical discussion of the Jobseekers Allowance, see Tony Novak, 'Hounding delinquents: the introduction of the Jobseeker's Allowance', *Critical Social Policy*, 17, 1997, 99–109.

7 Desmond King, 'The establishment of work-welfare programs in the United States and Britain: politics, ideas and institutions', in Sven Steinmo, Kethleen Thelen, and Frank Longstreth (eds.), *Structuring Politics: Historical Institutionalism in Comparative Analysis*, Cambridge: Cambridge University Press, 1992, 217–50.

8 Bob Jessop, 'The transition to post-Fordism and the Schumpeterian work-fare state', in Roger Burrows and Brian Loader (eds.), *Towards a Post-Fordist Welfare State?* London: Routledge, 1994, 24.

9 T. H. Marshall, *Citizenship and Social Class* (published with an essay by Tom Bottomore), London: Pluto Press, 1992, 33.

10 For example, Joseph Rowntree Foundation, *Enquiry into Income and Wealth*, 2 Vols., York: Joseph Rowntree Foundation, 1995; Will Hutton describes a 30–30–40 society in *The State We're In*, London: Jonathan Cape, 1995, Chapters 7 and 8.

11 Alan Howarth, MP (Minister for Employment, Welfare to Work, and Equal Opportunities), 'National consultation points the way for New Deal revolution', Department for Education and Employment, press release 261/97, 26 August 1997.

185

12 J. K. Galbraith, *The Culture of Contentment*, London: Sinclair-Stevenson, 1992; cf. Anthony Giddens, *Beyond Left and Right: The Future of Radical Politics*, Cambridge: Polity, 1994, 141–6.

13 Robert Reich, *The Work of Nations: Preparing for 21st Century Capitalism*, New York: Vintage Books, 1992.

14 The arch-exponent of the underclass thesis, at least within academic circles, is Charles Murray. See the 'warning' he gave to a British audience on this subject: 'The emerging British underclass', in Ruth Lister (ed.), *Charles Murray and the Underclass: The Developing Debate*, London: Institute of Economic Affairs, 1996. But see also in this collection the essay by Frank Field, former Minister for Welfare Reform in the Labour Government. Field's use of the underclass language indicates how it can be taken up by a Christian socialist tradition.

15 For a useful overview of this literature see Hilary Silver, 'Social exclusion and social solidarity: three paradigms', *International Labour Review*, 133, No. 5–6, 1994.

16 Pete Alcock, 'Back to the future: Victorian values for the 21st century', in Lister (ed.), *Charles Murray and the Underclass*, 148.

17 According to Ruth Levitas, 'The concept of social exclusion and the new Durkheimian hegemony', *Critical Social Policy*, 16(1), 1996, this was the meaning originally accorded to the term in Peter Townsend's *Poverty in the United Kingdom: A Survey of Household Resources and Standards of Living*, Harmondsworth: Penguin, 1979.

18 For other accounts of this overlap, which inform my own, see Giovanna Procacci, 'Exclus ou citoyens? Les pauvres devant les sciènces sociales', *Archives européenes sociologiques*, 37(2), 1996; Nikolas Rose, 'The death of the social? Refiguring the territory of government', *Economy and Society*, 25(3), 1996.

19 Lydia Morris, 'Legitimate members of the welfare community', in Mary Langan (ed.), *Welfare: Needs, Rights and Risks*, London: Routledge/Open University Press, 1998, 229.

20 Levitas, 'The concept of social exclusion', 7.

21 For a fuller account of how social exclusion and underclass discourses fragment the poor into multiple groups, but also reunify these ethically and spatially as 'marginal' to the community, see Rose, 'The death of the social?', 344–7.

22 Alain Touraine has observed a similar shift, which he has expressed in somewhat bolder terms, as being from a society of inequality ('up and down') to exclusion ('in or out'). See Isobel Yepez del Castillo, 'A comparative approach to social exclusion: lessons from France and Belgium', *International Labour Review*, 133(5/6), 1994.

23 Gordon Brown, Chancellor of the Exchequer, Budget statement, *Hansard*, 2 July 1997, col. 308.

24 Peter Mandelson and Roger Liddle, *The Blair Revolution: Can New Labour Deliver?* London: Faber & Faber, 1996, 102.

25 Levitas, 'The concept of social exclusion', 13.

26 The emphasis which the Beveridge model of social security places on maintaining work incentives is noted by Gøsta Esping-Andersen in his

well-known comparison of welfare state 'regimes'; see his 'The three political economies of the welfare state', *Canadian Review of Sociology and Anthropology*, 26(1), 1989.

27 *New Ambitions for our Country*, 3, 23.

28 Carole Pateman, 'The patriarchal welfare state', in *The Disorder of Women*, Cambridge: Polity, 1989.

29 OECD, *Employment Outlook 1989*, Paris: OECD, 1989, 9. For elaboration of the 'active society' concept see Mitchell Dean, 'Governing the unemployed self in an active society', *Economy and Society*, 24(4), 1995; William Walters, 'The "active society": new designs for social policy', *Policy and Politics*, 25(3), 1997.

30 Cd. 6404/1942, *Social Insurance and Allied Services* ('The Beveridge Report'), 122.

31 David Blunkett, MP (Secretary of State for Education and Employment), 'A hand up, not a hand out', Department for Education and Employment, press release 261/97, 26 August 1997.

32 See Amitai Etzioni, *The Spirit of Community: Rights, Responsibilities, and the Communitarian Agenda*, New York: Crown, 1993. For an account which stresses the diverse and sometimes contradictory deployments of community within the New Labour project, see Stephen Driver and Luke Martell, 'New Labour's communitarianisms', *Critical Social Policy*, 17, 1997, 27–46.

33 Nikolas Rose, 'The death of the social', 331.

34 For an overview of communitarian economics, see Brian Burkitt and Frances Ashton, 'The birth of the stakeholder society', *Critical Social Policy*, 16, 1996, 3–16.

35 'The death of the social', 334.

36 Alan Howarth (Employment Minister), 'New Deal for generation at risk', Department for Education and Employment, press release 95/97, 13 May 1997.

37 Mandelson and Liddle, *The Blair Revolution*, 101.

38 Department for Education and Employment, 'Blair joins Blunkett in New Deal join-up call', press release 073/98, 11 February 1998.

39 Budget speech, *Hansard*, 2 July 1997, col. 308.

40 See Craig Smith, 'The new corporate philanthropy', *Harvard Business Review*, 72(3), May–June, 1994, 105–16.

41 See its webpage www.arq.co.uk/ethicalbusiness/uksif/ethical.htm.

42 Annual reports and other materials for this Center are available at www.bc.edu/bc_org/avp/acavp/cccr/default.htm.

43 See the Business in the Community webpage www.bitc.org.uk.

44 Sir Peter Davis, Group Chief Executive, Prudential Corporation and Chairman, Business in the Community.

45 Etzioni, *The Spirit of Community*, 3.

46 See HM Treasury, 'The Budget: Equipping Britain for our Long-term Future', *Financial Statement and Budget Report*, July 1997 (HC-85), 32.

47 José Harris, *Unemployment and Politics: A Study in English Social Policy 1886–1914*, Oxford: Clarendon Press, 1972.

48 Gordon Brown (now Chancellor of the Exchequer), 'The politics of potential: a new agenda for Labour', in D. Miliband (ed.), *Reinventing the Left*, Cambridge: Polity, 1994, 114.

49 There is a vast literature in the field of Management on this matter; for important examples, see Rosabeth Moss Kanter, *When Giants Learn to Dance*, London: Routledge, 1992 and P. Senge, *The Fifth Discipline: The Art and Practice of the Learning Organization*, New York: Doubleday, 1990.

50 The Employment Service, *New Deal: Operational Vision*, 3.

51 Dean, 'Governing the unemployed self', 567.

52 There are perhaps certain parallels with the way that employment, under neo-liberalism, is being reconstituted in terms of a proliferation of technologies like stress management and time management.

53 *Operational Vision*, 4.

54 'Ownership' is also stated as an objective of the Employment Zones discussed in the previous chapter. 'At the heart of the Employment Zone concept is a commitment to give individuals a wider choice of paths out of unemployment. Individuals will be given a sense of ownership and choice which will help them improve their own employability'; DfEE, *Employment Zones – The Prospectus*, London: Stationery Office, [1998], 4.

55 Jacques Donzelot, 'The promotion of the social' (trans. Graham Burchell), *Economy and Society*, 17(3), 1988, 421.

56 R. Hay, 'Employers and social policy in Britain: the evolution of welfare legislation, 1905–14', *Social History*, No. 4, 1977.

57 For example, see Gøsta Esping-Andersen, 'After the golden age? Welfare state dilemmas in a global economy', in Esping-Andersen (ed.), *Welfare States in Transition: National Adaptations in Global Economies*, London: Sage, 1996; Ian Gough, 'Social welfare and competitiveness', *New Political Economy*, 1(2), 1996.

58 'Ambitious Brown targets poverty trap. Key extracts from the Chancellor's Budget Speech', *The Guardian*, 18 March 1998, 19.

59 *Hansard*, 2 July 1997, col. 310.

60 HM Treasury, *Financial Statement*, 20.

61 I take this concept of 'destandardization' from Ulrich Beck, *The Risk Society: Towards a New Modernity*, London: Sage, 1992.

CONCLUSION

1 John Burnett, *Idle Hands: The Experience of Unemployment, 1790–1990*, London: Routledge, 1994.

2 See 'Measurement of unemployment in the UK', the report of the Working Party on this issue in *Journal of the Royal Statistical Society* A, 158, Part 3, 1995.

3 Ulrich Beck, *The Risk Society: Towards a New Modernity*, London: Sage, 1992, 143.

4 For example, see the report by M. Carnoy and M. Castells for the OECD, *Sustainable flexibility: a prospective study on work, family and society in the information age*, Paris: OECD, 1997.

5 Anthony Giddens, *Beyond Left and Right: The Future of Radical Politics*, Cambridge: Polity, 1994, 153.

6 Phil Mizen, ' "Work-welfare" and the regulation of the poor: the pessimism of post-structuralism', *Capital and Class*, 65, 1998, 37.

7 Quoted by Alec Cairncross, *Economic Ideas and Government Policy*, London: Routledge, 1996, 261.

8 Bruno Latour, *The Pasteurization of France* (trans. A. Sheridan and J. Law), Cambridge, MA: Harvard University Press, 1988, 35–40.

9 For a discussion of the social philosophy surrounding the basic income idea, see P. Van Parijs (ed.), *Arguing for Basic Income*, London: Verso, 1992.

10 For example, Graham Burchell, Colin Gordon, and Peter Miller (eds.), *The Foucault Effect: Studies in Governmentality*, Hemel Hempstead: Harvester Wheatsheaf, 1991.

11 For example, the Group of Seven industrial nations observed in October 1998 that the present threat to the world economy was not inflation but lack of demand. See L. Elliott and S. Milne, 'Labour's election slogan was "education" but it could have been "work" ', *The Guardian*, 4 January 1999.

12 See Andrew Glyn and David Miliband (eds.), *Paying for Inequality: The Economic Cost of Social Injustice*, London: Institute for Public Policy Research, 1994.

13 See Nikolas Rose, 'Governing "Advanced" liberal democracies', in Andrew Barry, Thomas Osborne, and Nikolas Rose (eds.), *Foucault and Political Reason*, London: UCL Press, 1996. Rose has coined this term to 'identify a more modest yet more durable transformation in rationalities and technologies of government' than that associated with Thatcherism, Reaganism or other neo-liberalisms.

14 OECD, *Lifelong Learning for All*, Paris: OECD, 1996.

15 Jacques Donzelot, 'The mobilization of society', in Burchell et al. (eds.), *The Foucault Effect*.

16 Stan Cohen, 'Crime and Politics: Spot the Difference', *British Journal of Sociology*, 41(1), 1996, 7.

17 Loic Wacquant, 'Penal "Common Sense" comes to Europe', *Le Monde Diplomatique* (English Edition: Monthly Supplement to *The Guardian Weekly*), April 1999.

INDEX